CONTENTS

Contents list continued overleaf

The editions of the five play texts, and all sections not otherwise marked, are by Brian Stone.

All the set reading for these units has been incorporated into the text. You will need to refer to the theatre handbook: The Open University (1977) *Theatres and Staging*, The Open University Press.
Broadcasts associated with these units are:
Television Programme 3, *Medieval Mystery Plays*
Radio Programme 5, *Music in Medieval Drama*
Radio Programme 6, *Theatre in the Round*

INTRODUCTION

1 The subject and the recommended approach

1 We now introduce you to medieval drama in a self-contained study which includes the texts of five plays.

2 From the tenth to the sixteenth century in Europe, various forms of religious and secular drama reached a high level of sophistication in conception and execution. We are concerned with English plays, and with two types only, the cycle play and the morality play. The cycle play was a cosmic drama, embracing the religious history of man from the Creation of the Last Judgement. It comprised many short plays (there might be as many as fifty or as few as twenty-five), all of which were presented in a major religious centre such as a cathedral city at one religious festival, Corpus Christi. Following the promulgation of the doctrine of transubstantiation in 1215, the feast of Corpus Christi was instituted, and eventually confirmed in 1311. No revival or study of medieval religious drama can be complete without performance or study of a whole cycle (Glynne Wickham lists twentieth-century performances of full cycles on pp. 221–6 of *The Medieval Theatre*); that is the only way to get a proper sense of medieval dramatic achievement. But as all the cycles of which texts survive are very long, we shall study four short plays from respectively Wakefield, Chester, Brome and York; to offset this limitation we hope, by concentrating on the York records, to give you a good idea of what the production of a cycle meant to the cathedral city in which it was presented. It is important to understand that the two kinds of play here offered for study are the most important kinds for us, and are only two of many dramatic activities of the Middle Ages, concerning which Glynne Wickham (*The Medieval Theatre*, p. 4) has written:

If we are to approach the drama of the Middle Ages intelligently . . . we must first dismiss all our own contemporary notions of what a theatre should be and of how a play should be written, and then go on to substitute the idea of community games in which the actors are the contestants (mimetic or athletic or both) and the theatre is any place appropriate and convenient both to them as performers and to the rest of the community as spectators. If the contemporary catch-phrase 'total theatre' has any meaning it finds a truer expression in medieval than in modern terms of reference; for song, dance, wrestling, sword-play, contests between animals, disguise, spectacle, jokes, disputation and ritual all figure, separately or compounded, in the drama of the Middle Ages which was devised in celebration of leisure and for a local community. It was a preponderantly social art which could be given a religious, political or sexual dynamic as need and occasion demanded, but which was only rarely concerned with questions of literary theory and genre such as inform our own concepts of comedy, farce, tragedy, melodrama, opera, ballet and so on.

3 This general warning about how to approach medieval drama implicitly explains, at least in part, why we include the subject in this course. It was a community art very different from modern European drama; one in which every member of society could play his part, whether specialized (like that of learned script-writers) or general (like that of a citizen in the audience whose feast—concerning his own religion and his own home city—was being celebrated). Its specific contributions to the dramatic heritage will concern us, especially those to which our own modern theatre returns for inspiration. As elsewhere in the course, study will be based on plays, but since medieval religious drama was so different from our own, a short and highly selective introduction is included. My suggestions for further reading are on p. 149 of this study.

4 The aims of this study may now be briefly stated:

a To give you a good idea of the nature of English medieval cycle plays by providing detailed work on four of them.

b To present the text of, and the work on, one of the four plays in a manner designed to encourage you to produce it yourself.

c To provide you with evidence, and work on that evidence, which proves medieval drama to have been an activity rooted in society as a whole, in which large numbers of clergy and laity, directed by their controlling organizations, the church, the municipal authorities and the guilds, cooperated to plan and mount festivals involving whole city communities.

d To give you work on the greatest of the indisputably English morality plays, *The Castle of Perseverance*.

e At appropriate points, to establish the relevance of medieval to modern drama.

5   The drama with which we are concerned arose directly from the Church's desire to engage people's utmost concern with its teaching—with the events and teaching most important to Christianity, with the lessons to be learnt from knowing and understanding them, and above all with the faith which it was hoped emotional involvement with the events and their interpretation would generate and maintain. I write it 'arose' as if there had been no such drama before. But this is not the place to trace the survival of various kinds of dramatic art from the times of classical antiquity to the beginning of the Middle Ages, and their varying integration with the drama of the medieval Church: you can read about those in one or more of the books suggested for further reading (see p. 149), especially in Rossiter, *English Drama from Earliest Times to the Elizabethans*.

Liturgy and drama

6   In the liturgy (that is, the services of the Church, the chief of which was the Mass), passages from the Bible were narrated with musical accompaniment, and different parts were sung or spoken by different clerics. To put flesh on the bones of that piece of information, read the following extract from the *Concordia Regularis*, drawn up by Bishop Ethelwold of Winchester in the tenth century as a supplement to the Rule of Saint Benedict. It represents him as something of a theatre director, as he advises how the third Nocturn at Matins on Easter morning should be conducted. The biblical event celebrated in this part of the liturgy is the Resurrection itself, emphasis on and celebration of which are central to Christain belief. **Note the dramatic elements, the didactic purpose and method, and the means used to engender emotional response; describe them to yourself as you read.**

While the third lesson is being chanted, let four brethren vest themselves. Let one of these, vested in an alb,[1] enter as though to take part in the service, and let him approach the sepulchre without attracting attention and sit there quietly with a palm in his hand. While the third respond is chanted, let the remaining three follow, and let them all, vested in copes, bearing in their hands thuribles[2] with incense, and stepping delicately as those who seek something, approach the sepulchre. These things are done in imitation of the angel sitting in the monument, and the women with spices coming to anoint the body of Jesus. When therefore he who sits there beholds the three approach

[1] A long, white tunic with tight sleeves.
[2] Vessels for burning incense.

him like folk lost and seeking something, let him begin in a dulcet voice of medium pitch to sing *Quem quaeritis* [Whom seek ye in the sepulchre, O Christian women?]. And when he has sung it to the end, let the three reply in unison *Ihesum Nazarenum* [Jesus of Nazareth, the crucified, O heavenly one]. So he, *Non est hic, surrexit sicut praedixerat. Ite, nuntiate quia surrexit a mortuis* [He is not here; He is risen, as He foretold. Go and announce that He is risen from the dead]. At the word of his bidding let those three turn to the choir and say *Alleluia! resurrexit Dominus!* [Alleluia! The Lord is risen!] This said, let the one, still sitting there and as if recalling them, say the anthem *Venite et videte locum* [Come and see the place]. And saying this, let him rise, and lift the veil, and show them the place bare of the cross, but only the cloths laid there in which the cross was wrapped. And when they have seen this, let them set down the thuribles which they bore in that same sepulchre, and take the cloth, and hold it up in the face of the clergy, and as if to demonstrate that the Lord has risen and is no longer wrapped therein, let them sing the anthem *Surrexit Dominus de sepulchro* [The Lord is risen from the sepulchre], and lay the cloth upon the altar. When the anthem is done, let the prior, sharing in their gladness at the triumph of our King, in that, having vanquished death, He rose again, begin the hymn *Te Deum Laudamus* [We praise Thee, O God]. And this begun, all the bells chime out together [from A. M. Nagler, *A Source Book in Theatrical History*].

7   **What are the 'dramatic elements'?** Experts disagree as to when the enactment of a ritual becomes dramatic in the strict sense. Carrying out a ritual always involves playing a known part, and this is an activity which may loosely be described as 'dramatic'. But physical impersonation of another being does seem to be clearly and precisely a dramatic activity; and we have it here in the 'imitation' of the angel and the 'Christian women' at the tomb, required of his officiating priests by Ethelwold. 'Didactic purpose' is evident in the way the whole action is geared to what we might call physical exposition of the text—explanation is constantly implicit in the enactment of the story. 'Emotional response' is something that can be explained only subjectively. The music and the ceremony, and the constant formal response of the women in unison to the presence and words of that enigmatically powerful angel, generate emotional response all the time, as does the progressive revelation of the meaning and its significance as one action succeeds another. But the final rejoicing act of singing the *Te Deum*, which brings in the whole congregation, generates a climax of emotion and rounds off the whole ritual rhythm of this part of the service.

8   Concerning the text, you will see from the above that though it is based on the Bible account of the visit of the women to the tomb (for example Matthew 28, 3–8 and Mark 16, 2–6), the important words are cast responsorially, i.e. as dialogue, instead of the single speech by the angel, and also that words are added. The word 'trope', which comes from the Latin, *tropus*, meaning 'added melody' (see Glynne Wickham, *The Medieval Theatre,* pp.32–8), came to cover new textual matter as well and is the standard term now used to describe the whole phenomenon under discussion. In the process outlined by Glynne Wickham, musical elaboration of the liturgy came to involve textual elaboration. The basis of free dramatization of the Bible is thus established; what began as a trope with individual parts could and did develop into an episode in a play or into a short play. As you study the plays, it will be useful from time to time to check play content against Bible original, because that will help you to understand the dramaturgic abilities and objectives of the medieval playwrights, and their contribution to the evolving art of drama. You will also see that in their 'free dramatization', playwrights drew on performance traditions which were quite independent of Church activities.

Guidance as to performance

9   As for the development of 'stage directions' as they appear in Ethelwold, since they are so important as expository material, we should not be surprised to find that they still figure prominently in many texts of cycle plays, though not always with such didactic intention. The technical business of stage action and management underlies many stage directions, as these extracts from plays of the *Ludus Coventriae* show.

a   From *The Betrayal,* at the end of which Judas receives 'thirty plates of silver bright':

Here the bishops part in the place [i.e. the main acting area on ground level] and each of them takes their leave by countenance [with gesture], resorting each man to his place with their meinie [attendants] to make ready to take Christ. And then the place there Christ is in shall suddenly unclose round about showing Christ sitting at the table and his disciples each in their degree [R. T. Davies (ed.), *The Corpus Christi Play of the English Middle Ages,* p.264].

b   Two from *The Dream of Pilate's Wife,* the first of which interestingly conveys simultaneous action, with two focuses of interest.

Here enters Satan into the place in the most horrible wise, and while that he plays they shall do on [put on] Jesus clothes, and overest [on top] a white cloth, and lead him about the place, and then to Pilate by the time that his wife has played [Davies, *op.cit.,* p.296].

Here shall the devil go to Pilate's wife, the curtain drawn as she lies in bed. And he shall no din make, but she shall, soon after that he is come in, make a ruely [pitiful] noise, coming and running off the scaffold [a mansion is often called a scaffold], and her skirt and her kirtle in her hand. And she shall come before Pilate like a mad woman [Davies, *op.cit.,* p.298].

10   Not until you come to the age of melodrama, in the first half of the nineteenth century, will you again meet a kind of drama in which the stage directions can be more important than the dialogue, especially at moments of critical action. It is a characteristic of popular drama, in which what is *done* and *seen* is especially important.

3   Staging drama in medieval Europe

11   '. . . The theatre is any place appropriate and convenient . . .' in an age when dramatic art is community art, and there is no such thing as a professional theatre company with its own purpose-designed physical base or home theatre. The latter developed in England in the late sixteenth century, and in its evolution absorbed some of the elements of the various kinds of medieval 'theatre'. Let us summarily describe types of medieval theatrical environment; you will see why it is important to get away from the modern idea of a theatre from the first. **The medieval section of 'Theatres and Staging' (pp. 14–22) is informative on these: turn to it now.** Illustrations, diagrams and plans can be found in all standard theatre histories: chapter 3 in Allardyce Nicoll's book, *The Development of the Theatre,* serves well.

a   The church itself, in which the general frame of locality is set by the high altar for holiest events and the appearance of God, and the western entrance to the crypt as the appropriate underground resort of Satan.

b   The church-like arrangement of an open-air area, such as a market square. The audience can now be above the action in surrounding buildings, as well as on ground level.

c   The purpose-built stationary setting, in which the different focal places for the action—heaven, hell, throne-room, and special places appropriate to particular plays, such as Mount Olivet, Pilate's house, the site of the Crucifixion and so forth— were developed roughly according to their arrangement inside a church as suggested in (a) above.

d   The pageant. Evidently for use when a single play within a cycle had to be shown in different parts of a city. For a discussion of this, see John Purkis's work, paragraphs 25, ff., pp. 65–71).

e   The circular or semicircular setting. A practice apparently developed from several antecedents, and owing something to practical factors. The Roman arena was circular or oval, with the audience all the way round. A circle is formed when a contest takes place. A self-contained area is needed when control must be established within an acting, playing or fighting area. Barriers which can exclude become necessary when payment is exacted for entry, or when an exclusive audience is to be provided for. Richard Southern, in *The Medieval Theatre in the Round* (Appendix 1, pp. 219–36), lists and discusses more than sixty surviving references to a method of mounting religious plays which was based on a circular or roughly circular main acting area at ground level, and was unlocalized. This was supported by raised booth and platform stages on the circumference which were strictly localized (see subsequent discussion of the Fouquet miniature, paragraphs 12 ff., below, and the section on the staging of *The Castle of Perseverance*, paragraphs 4 ff., pp. 73–5) in the sense of representing particular places, of which heaven and hell were chief and most constant in the plays of which we have records. Also see the reference to 'the place there Christ is in' in the instructions for *The Betrayal* quoted in paragraph 9(a), p. 7, which is clearly such a small curtained acting area.

f   The booth or platform stage, which is mentioned in (e) above as accessory to the main acting area in a play or series of plays in a large-scale presentation. It was also, as a single performance place, a piece of equipment basic to the work of any travelling company presenting dramatic or dramatic/musical entertainments. It would usually have scaffolding for a curtain and possibly a roof as well. A company needed municipal permission to set one up, and would choose the most public place consonant with their need for security and continuous performance (not a quiet spot, which could never be guaranteed in a public place unless the players earned it by the attraction of their performance; but at least some sort of uninterruptedness). A backing wall of some kind and reasonable side or interior access would be essential. Many illustrations of such stages exist in late medieval and early Renaissance art. There is good ground for believing that the 'scaffold', or 'mansion' as it might be called, became the basis for the Elizabethan theatre's 'inner stage', and that the main acting area or unlocalized place mentioned in (e) above developed into the broad open stage of such theatres as the Globe or the Swan in Shakespeare's time (see *Theatres and Staging*, pp. 24–5).

12   The 'mansion' or 'scaffold' seems common to most of the types of performance area mentioned. With all the above information in mind, you should now be able to look with informed eyes at Fouquet's famous miniature depicting a performance of *The Martyrdom of Saint Apollonia,* which is on the front cover of this study. Please bear in mind that the miniature is just a manuscript illumination to the Hours of Etienne Chevalier, and that in its composition the illuminator was free to avail himself of all the conventions of medieval art. Just as the designer of a cathedral roof-boss was free to represent such complex scenes as the Sealing of the Sepulchre and the Resurrection of the Innocents (both in Norwich Cathedral transept, and reproduced in M. D. Anderson's excellent *Drama and Imagery in English Medieval Churches*, plates 13c and 11d) on a small roundel, so Fouquet was free to present both plan and elevation of his subject, distorted to fit into the required shape.

13   Look at the cover of this study and comment at least on the following; the foreground barrier, the audience, the mansions, the central action and its possible relation to the mansions, the man with the stick and book.

14   The *foreground barrier* could keep back the press of an outside audience or repel people who wanted to see a free show—assuming that the audience was fee-paying. But the chap up the pole presumably did not pay for his superb point of vantage. If Fouquet was thinking of a circular performing place, then there could be no artistic objection to his flattening the whole thing out, so that everything could be seen two-dimensionally, from the front.

15   The *audience* appear to be on two levels, a lot of them crowded on ground level—though I doubt if they could be *under* the mansions, which I take to be another convenient device of the artist —and some privileged people, mostly women, in two of the mansions. Commentators disagree about these ladies, but in the absence of a clear dramatic function, I think they are spectators.

16   Three of the *mansions* observe a strict convention, which is found all over Europe. Heaven is at audience left, and has those practitioners of celestial harmony, the musicians, next door. At audience right is hell, on two levels: assorted devils above, and hell-mouth itself below. The gaping monster-head was often practical, i.e. it could open and shut according to requirements. The throne mansion is appropriately in the middle, and its occupant is down in the acting area pointing to the suffering saint. This is a good moment to mention that much medieval and Renaissance drama and quasi-dramatic activity (i.e. tournament, pageant, masque) contained two spectacles, one consisting of the play perform-

ance, the other of the royal party or other eminent presence watching.

17 The *central action* is a scene of extraordinary cruelty. The holiness of a saint must be estimated in direct proportion to the extent of the suffering she undergoes in her martyrdom. No Greek decorum here about acts of violence on stage; we should bear this scene, or the York *Crucifixion*, in mind when determining our attitude to the frequent scenes of cruelty in Elizabethan drama, and to the resurgence of the portrayal of cruelty as a refining and didactic technique in some modern plays. The ladders from mansions to main acting area give access both ways, and virtually ensure that action is not confined to ground level.

18 The *man with the stick and the book* is clearly a person of fairly high authority who seems to be exercising the functions of prompter, stage manager and—if a musical analogy may be permitted here—a sort of conductor of the piece. It seems that medieval practice was to engage and pay actors for about three rehearsals, which may not seem much until you remember that most major roles would be played by the same people year after year. They were expected to know their lines, and could be fined for forgetting them, but the presence of a prompter more or less ensured continuity of action. Lastly this man was probably the Expositor or Doctor, whose words of description, explanation and interpretation are often found at the beginning and the end of both the kinds of play we are studying.

THE WAKEFIELD *SECOND SHEPHERDS' PAGEANT*

1 The play and the recommended approach

1 Your first piece of detailed work in the field of medieval drama will be on the play which is known as the Wakefield *Second Shepherds' Pageant*, the standard edition of which is included in *The Wakefield Pageants in the Towneley Cycle*[1], edited by A. C. Cawley. For a briefer consideration, with the play text in modernized spelling and glossed, see the same editor's *Everyman and Mediaeval Miracle Plays*. I give the play here in a new modernized version, complete with music. When you have completed the work on it, I hope some of you will take this text, with the musical and stage directions and your considered and amplified answers to the self-assessment exercises, straight into a college, school or adult drama group and produce it. All this part of Study 4 is designed with that possibility in mind. It would hardly be justifiable to change the play's text and appearance in the way I have without such an express purpose.

The shepherds and the liturgy

2 To begin with, you will want to know how a play like the Wakefield *Second Shepherds' Pageant* arose from the source material, that is, the account of the Nativity in Luke. **You might at this point read the first two chapters of Luke or, if you know the story well enough, concentrate on Luke 2, 8–18, which refers to the shepherds' part in the events. I suggest you keep your Bible open at that place throughout your first reading of the play and consult it constantly so that, while studying, you are always aware of what has its source in the Bible, and what has not.**

3 Now, as to how the *Officium Pastorum* (the Office, or Service, of the Shepherds) came into the liturgy. First, doctrinally speaking, the episode helps to authenticate the divinity of Christ. Secondly, it links the birth of Christ, and its message to humankind, with ordinary people in a universal way. That the birth of Christ was first announced to the poor, and that the poor were entrusted with spreading the good news, both reinforced one of the main messages of the faith and appealed to the biggest group of the potential or actual faithful. So the religious motivation for including this passage of the Bible in the service at Christmas was very strong.

Liturgy texts and instructions

4 Although there are varieties of texts of the *Officium Pastorum* from other centres in Europe, its inclusion in the order of service is associated especially with Rouen Cathedral, the main centre of religion in northern France, and with the provinces influenced by Rouen in the eleventh and twelfth centuries, chief among which was the

[1] So called because the manuscript was owned by the Towneley family of Towneley Hall, near Burnley in Lancashire.

vast new area of Norman hegemony—England. The Rouen liturgies are the most important for the study of all English shepherds' plays. You will see at a glance from the extracts from typical early texts printed below, that this Christmas trope, which appears in north western Europe a century later than the Easter trope, *Quem quaeritis,* is a development inspired by, and partly copied from, the Easter trope:

Easter Trope

Quem quaeritis in sepulchro, o Christicolae?
Whom do you seek in the sepulchre, O Christian women?

Jesum Nazarenum crucifixum.
Jesus Christ who was crucified.

Non est hic.
He is not here.

Ite, nuntiate quia surrexit.
Go, announce that he has risen.

Christmas Trope

Quem quaeritis in praesepe, pastores, dicite?
Whom do you seek in the manger, shepherds, say?
Salvatorem Christum Dominum.
Our Saviour who is Christ the Lord.

Adest hic.
He is here.

Nunc euntes dicite quia natus est.
Now go forth and announce that he is born.

5   Now, please read my translation below of an early 'Officium Pastorum' (probably of the twelfth century) from Rouen, comparing it with the source passage in Luke 2. The original is in Karl Young, *The Drama of the Medieval Church,* ii. 12–13.

In the Nativity of Our Lord, after *Te Deum Laudamus,* [seven] boys in one part of the church should take up position leaning on staves in the likeness of Shepherds; further, one boy high above, wearing amice [clerical cap] and alb [long white tunic with tight sleeves], in the likeness of an Angel announcing the birth of the Lord, should say this verse: Fear not, for behold, I bring you good tidings of great joy, which shall be to all people, for unto you is born this day in the city of David the Saviour of the world, and this shall be the sign to you: You there shall find the babe wrapped in swaddling clothes and laid in a manger.

Let there also be more boys to the right and left similarly clothed, who, at the end of the preliminary antiphon [short piece of introductory plainsong], should begin by singing:

Glory be to God in the highest, and on earth peace to men of good will, alleluia, alleluia.

This again being concluded, let the Shepherds, singing the following antiphon, approach the place in which the Manger has been prepared:

Let us go towards Bethlehem, and see this Word which is made [flesh] which the Lord has made and shown to us.

When they have entered it, two clerks who are in the Manger shall begin to sing:

Whom do you seek in the Manger, Shepherds, say?

The Shepherds shall reply:

The Saviour [who is] Christ the Lord, a babe wrapped in swaddling clothes, according to the word of the Angel.

Those standing in the Manger should then say:

Here with Mary his mother is the little one of whom long ago Isaiah the prophet had said in prophecy: Behold a virgin shall conceive and bear a son, and his name shall be called Emmanuel.

The Shepherds:

There is born to us this day in the city of David a Saviour who is Christ the Lord.
We praise thee O God.

Which being done, the Shepherds also should begin the introit [chant sung while the priest approaches the altar], *The Lord said unto me,* and lead the chorus of the whole Mass. The Mass being concluded . . .

6   Young comments upon this (*The Drama of the Medieval Church,* pp.13–14):

During the singing of the *Te Deum* which immediately precedes this play seven youths costume themselves with amices, albs, tunics, and staffs, to represent shepherds. As they take their place in the church at the beginning of the action, a choir-boy stationed aloft, costumed as an angel, announces the Nativity to them: *Nolite timere,* [do not fear] and is supported by other angels who sing *Gloria in excelsis* [glory in the highest]. The shepherds then proceed to the *praesepe* [manger] —situated, presumably, behind the main altar—singing the appropriate processional *Transeamus usque Bethlehem* [let us go towards Bethlehem]. Here occurs the usual dialogue, only slightly modified, between the shepherds and the two clerics whom we may assume to be costumed for representing the midwives [functional people added to those mentioned in biblical accounts of the Nativity]. In the Mass which follows, the shepherds begin the introit and rule the choir.

7   Young goes on to quote in full later examples of the *Officium Pastorum* from Rouen, one from an ordinary (form for saying Mass) of the fourteenth century, and the other from a gradual (book of antiphons) of the thirteenth. From his summary of the dramatic or quasi-dramatic action in them, which I now give, you will see that, during the Middle Ages, the changes which take place in the way of *Officium Pastorum* figures in the whole service of the Mass are of detail rather than essence, and tend on the whole both to reinforce doctrinal meaning and to develop musical and dramatic elements.

From these two texts together we have ample information concerning the Rouen play, and concerning the participation of the *pastores* in the normal liturgy of the day. The *praesepe*, it appears, was behind the main altar, and contained artificial figures of the Virgin Mary and the Child, behind a curtain. As the five shepherds, suitably costumed, enter the west door of the choir, a boy up under the vaulting, representing an angel, announces the Nativity. After seven other angels have sung *Gloria in excelsis*, the shepherds begin their march to the *praesepe,* singing, as they traverse the choir, first a responsorial poem *Pax in terris* [peace on earth], and then, as they round the altar, the verse *Transeamus*. At the manger they find two priests in dalmatics [wide-sleeved vestments], who represent midwives, and with whom they carry on the familiar dialogue. At the words *Adest hic parvulus* [the little Child is here], the *obstetrices* draw aside the curtain, and point first to the Child, and then, at the words *Ecce virgo* [behold the Virgin], to the Mother. The shepherds kneel· before the figure of the Virgin, singing the verses *Salve, virgo singularis* [hail, incomparable Virgin], and after obeisance to the Child, they return to the chorus, singing the usual sentence *Iam vere scimus* [now in truth we know]. This leads directly into the Mass, during which the *Pastores* rule the choir, and read or sing considerable parts of the liturgical text [Young, *The Drama of the Medieval Church*, ii, 19–20].

Before you go on, check the differences between the details of action noted here, and those in the earlier Rouen 'Officium Pastorum' (paragraph 5, p.10).

Introduction to studying the play

8 Now to introduce the Wakefield *Second Shepherds' Pageant* itself. The unique manuscript on which it appears, as the thirteenth play of thirty, is probably, according to A. C. Cawley (*The Wakefield Pageants in the Towneley Cycle,* p.xii) a 'register', i.e. an official text of the cycle, copied from 'originals' of the individual pageants belonging to the various craft guilds. Internal linguistic evidence suggests that the play was written in the first half of the fifteenth century, but it appears to have been used as the register until well after the Reformation, because there are corrections in sixteenth-century writing, and in particular a deletion in one play of a passage referring to baptism as a sacrament—'a popish doctrine in the eyes of the Reformers' (A. C. Cawley, *op. cit.,* p.xiii).

9 The play is one of six on the manuscript which were almost certainly written by the same man, who is generally referred to as the Wakefield Master. His formal characteristic is a nine-line stanza of typically medieval complexity; here is one, with the spelling modernized (lines 710–8):

Hail, comely and clean! Hail young child!
Hail, maker as I mean, of a maiden so mild!
Thou has wared[1], I ween, the warlock[2] so wild.

[1]cursed   [2]devil

The false guiler[1] of teen[2], now goes he beguiled.
Lo, he merries!
Lo, he laughs, my sweeting!
A well fair meeting!
I have holden my heting[3].
Have a bob of cherries.

But successful dramatic use and control of that most undramatic poetic form would hardly qualify the poet for the description 'Master'. If you are to believe that this title is more than one of broad convenience found in histories of medieval literature, you will need to discover through working on the play his qualities as a playwright, as a sympathetic and penetrating observer of people and society, and as a convincing dramatic presenter of Christian· doctrine.

10 The only further matter I wish to mention before setting you to work on the play is the extraordinary burlesque nativity which occupies most of the playing time. It is an extreme example of an important facet of drama which will crop up repeatedly on this course—the mixture of the serious and the comic. Though such a mixture has always been attacked by pedants and purists of various kinds, it seems to be a reflection of some kind of emotional and intellectual need, and has its roots in primitive man's rites as well as in civilized man's apprehension of the world. The prominence of the burlesque nativity makes this play atypical; but the transition to the real Nativity is managed with such art that the tenderness and significance of the latter are enhanced. Medieval literature is rich in comic content, and although clerics were mostly· critical of the inclusion of 'impure' elements in religious works of art of all kinds, the Church as a body could not have been formally opposed to the comic and the grotesque, as a look at a religious text illuminated in a monastery, or a casual inspection of the decorative sculpture in a well-preserved medieval church, will tell you. Some people think that fifteenth century French farces in which knaves like Mak the sheep-stealer triumphed may have been known to the playwright. But a native tradition, which included Chaucer's work and all that this conveys of the broad European world of the period, must be considered strong enough to have produced good comedy for inclusion in miracle plays, as soon as these could be written fully in the vernacular and could be produced by craft guilds under joint civic and ecclesiastical supervision. I suggest you consider very carefully the effect of the play as a whole, including the comic section.

[1]trickster
[2]suffering
[3]kept my promise

Working through the play

11 I shall now suggest five tasks for you as you read the play. You may prefer to read the play quickly through without pondering, and then return and work in detail on a second reading. Of the five tasks, I suggest you actually write on only two (unless you wish to make additional time, and do them all) and bear the other three in mind. The fifth is the most important; I suggest you do it, together with one of the first four.

i   Note which elements of the Bible account in Luke, and the various liturgical offices described in my preamble, are in the play.

ii   Make producer's notes on the three shepherds, for briefing actors at the first rehearsal after the casting audition, on such things as their characters, interrelations, social standing.

iii   Mark anything relevant to Christian themes before the appearance of the Angel (639).

iv   You will note my direction at the beginning of the play: 'The action is continuous'. Select the most convenient place in which you might produce the play yourself (e.g. your school hall, community building or church) and suggest a staging plan (N.B. do not forget to solve to your own satisfaction the question of different levels, which are clearly indicated in the text at least once —line 650).

v   Write short producer's notes (i.e. inter-pretative commentary and suggestions for action) on the last 170 lines, from 'He's got a long snout' (585) to the end. Do not go over every detail, but make sure you define the main effects you would try to achieve.

2   Acting version of the *Second Shepherds' Pageant*

Dramatis Personae

Coll ⎤
Gib ⎬ Shepherds
Daw ⎦

Mak
Gyll, Mak's wife

Angel
Mary

(Line numbers refer to original text as edited by Cawley in *The Wakefield Pageants in the Towneley Cycle*.)

The action is continuous. Locations: open fields, Mak's cottage, the crooked thorn, the stable in Bethlehem.

Christmas Eve, late evening: open fields. Enter Coll

COLL   Lord, the weather's cold! And I'm half naked.
I snoozed so long that I'm numb and fuddled.
My legs won't hold me up, my fingers are chapped;
Things aren't as I'd like: I'm wrapped
In sorrow.
In storm and tempest,
Now in the east and now in the west,
Woe to the man who gets no rest
Midday, or tomorrow.

But we poor peasants who have to walk the moors,   10
It's almost as if we'd been turned out of doors.
No wonder, as things are, we're poor;
Our ploughland lies as fallow as a bare floor.
You mark my words,
We're so crippled and maimed,
So overtaxed and downtrodden,
They've got us hand-tamed,
These fancy lords.

They rob us of our rest, Our Lady curse them!
And men who are lords' lackeys won't let us plough.   20
They say it's for the best, but we don't.
We peasants are so stamped on, I don't know how

We stay alive.
They hold us under,
They load us with trouble;
It'd be a great wonder
If ever we could thrive.

Such fellows flaunt a lord's sleeve or badge these days,
And woe if you upset them or deny what they say!
However rough they are, you daren't take them on;   30
And yet you can't believe one word they say—
Not even one letter.
They've got the right of requisition;
They brag and boast with it,
And all because they're maintained
By men who are greater.

Along comes this servant, proud as a peacock,
'I must borrow your wagon, your plough also.'
And I've got to give them before he'll go.
And so we live in pain, anger and woe   40
By night and day.
Does he long for it? He'll get it,
And I'll go without it.
I'd better be hanged
Than once say him nay.

It does me good as I walk on my own
To talk of this world and have a good moan.
Now I'll go to my sheep and on the rough grass
Or sitting on a stone, I'll listen to what passes,
And that soon.   50
For I tell you, by God,
If they keep their word
We'll have more company
Before noon.

Retires and sits down. Enter Gib, who does not see him

GIB   *(Crossing himself)*   Benedicite and Dominus, what does it mean?
       We've not often seen the world as bad as this.
       Lord, the weather's cruel and the winds are keen,
       And the frost's so fierce it brings water to my eyes—
       Not a word of a lie.
       Now in dry and now in wet,   60
       Now in snow and now in sleet,
       When my shoes freeze to my feet,
       It's not all that easy.

       As far as I know or have seen things go,
       We poor married men suffer much woe;
       Sorrow after sorrow; it often happens so.
       Silly Copple, our hen, to and fro
       She cackles.
       And when she broods she'll croak
       And groan and cluck.   70
       Then woe to our cock,
       For he's in the shackles.

       We married men don't get our way;
       When we're up against it we always sigh.
       God knows we're hard done by and ill-led:
       We don't answer back, either at board or in bed.
       This very day
       I've found my way
       And learnt my lesson:

Woe to the man that's bound,
For so he must stay.

When Fate gives the order, that's how it'll be.
This wonder makes my heart break when I see it:
Late in their lives—it's a marvel to me—
Some men will have two wives, and some men three
In their keeping.
Some are sad to have any,
But this much I know:
Woe to the man with many!
That's cause of weeping.

To young men in audience

So as for wooing, young men, by God who redeemed you,
Beware of marrying and remember this:
It's no good saying 'If only I'd known!'
Because marriage has brought many a quiet groan
And grief
In many a sharp shower;
For you can catch in one hour
What'll keep things sour
As long as you live.

For I swear by the Bible, my old woman's
As sharp as a thistle, as rough as a briar,
With bristling brows and a bitter look.
When she's wet her whistle, she sings loud and clear
Her Paternoster.
She's as big as a whale,
And has a gallon of gall.
By him who died for us all,
I wish I'd lost her!

COLL   God save the company! You must be deaf!

GIB   (*Startled*)   The devil in your guts for being so long!
        Have you seen Daw anywhere?

COLL   Yes, I heard him blow his horn on the fallow
        Not far away. He's coming. Let's stay quiet.

GIB   Why?

COLL   Because he's coming, I think.

GIB   He'll tell us a pack of lies unless we watch out.

Enter Daw, who does not see the other two. He crosses himself

DAW   Christ's cross guide me, and Saint Nicholas!
        I need their help. Things are getting worse.
        You look at the world and what do you see?
        It's always in terror, it's brittle as glass
        And it fades away.
        It was never like this before—
        Wonder after wonder.
        Now in weal and now in woe,
        And changing all the time.

        Never since Noah's time have such floods been seen,
        Such storms, such fierce winds and rain—
        It's made people stagger and shudder.
        May God turn all to good! I say what I mean,
        It makes me ponder.
        These floods sweep everything away
        And threaten to drown

80

90

100

110

120

130

Both the country and the town;
And that's a wonder.
We that are out at night watching our sheep
See startling sights when other men sleep.

Becomes aware of Coll and Gib

But I'm cheered now; I spy two bad lots,
Two monsters. I'll head off my sheep to safety.
Suspicious, aren't I? Supposing I did that, I'd stub my toes—   140
Easy repentance!

(*To Coll*)   Ah sir, God save you!

(*To Gib*)   And my master!
I badly need a drink and something to eat.

COLL   Christ's curse, you rascal! You're a lazy slave!

GIB   What, the boy's raving! Wait till later. We've had our meal. Bad luck to you.   150
Though the villain came late, yet he's ready to eat—if he had any food.

DAW   (*To audience*)   Labourers like me, who sweat and toil, eat bread that's dry—
and that I hate. We're often wet and weary when the boss is sleeping snug, yet
food and drink are always greatly delayed. You see, when we've been running   160
in mud, both our mistress and our master can lower our rate of hire, as well
as pay us late.

(*To Gib*)   But here's a promise, master: you lay on the food, and I'll perform
accordingly—work as I earn. I'll do a little, sir, and play in between, for
I never yet did a spell in the fields on a full belly. Why should I haggle?   170
I can go and work for someone else. 'Cheap bargain, bad yield.'

COLL   If a chap who was hard up went wooing, you'd be the wrong one for him to
take along.

GIB   Quiet, boy. No more back-talk or I'll shut you up at once, by God. You and
your tricks, we scorn them. Where are our sheep, boy?   180

DAW   Sir, when the bells rang for lauds[1], I left them in the corn. There's good grazing
there, they can't go wrong.

COLL   That's right, By the holy cross, these nights are long. But before we go on, can't
we have a song?

GIB   Just what I was thinking, to cheer us up.

DAW   Good idea.

COLL   I'll sing tenor.

GIB   Top treble for me.

DAW   Then the middle part's mine. You start.

*They sing a pastoral song, towards the end of which Mak enters, wearing a wide-sleeved
cloak over his tunic*

MAK   Now Lord, by thy seven names, who made the moon and more stars than I   190
could count, I do not know what thy will for me is. I'm at odds with myself;
that unsettles my brains. Would to God I were in heaven where the enless
howling of babes is never heard.

COLL   Who's that howling so miserable?

MAK   Would to God you knew how I suffer! Behold a man that walks on the moor,
and has not all his will.

GIB   Mak, where have you been? Tell us the news.

DAW   It's him is it? Then look out for your possessions, fellows!   200

Takes Mak's cloak from him, inspects sleeves for stolen goods

MAK   (*Mock liveried servant, southern accent*)   What! I'm a yeoman, I tell you, and my

[1] Office usually sung at daybreak.

15

name's on the king's list. I'm the messenger of a mighty lord, and so on and so forth. Fie on you! Out of my presence. I must have reverence. What a fine fellow I am!

COLL   Why so stuck up, Mak? That's not right.

GIB   But Mak, are you playing the saint? I bet you yearn to be one!

DAW   I know that crook can put on a show, the devil hang him!   210

MAK   I shall lay a complaint against you, tell them what you're up to with a single word, and have you all flogged.

COLL   But Mak, is that the truth? Spit out that southern drawl and put a true word in it's place.

GIB   Mak, the devil in your eye! I'll give you a clout.

DAW   You know me, Mak? By God, I could do you.

MAK   God save all three of you. I thought it was you. Good company, I reckon.   220

COLL   Ah, so now you remember us?

GIB   Looking around, you crook? Going about so late, what will men think you're up to? You've got a bad reputation for stealing sheep.

MAK   Yet I'm as true as steel, and all men know it. But I've got a severe attack of some illness. My belly's not doing well; it's in a bad state.

DAW   You don't find the devil dead by your gate.

MAK   So I'm sick and in pain. Turn me to a stone if I've eaten a morsel this month and more.   230

COLL   How's your wife doing? By your hood, how is she?

MAK   (*Crosses himself*)   By the rood, she's sprawling by the fire. Yes, and the house full of kids. She drinks well too. No hope of her being good at anything else. But she eats as fast as she can, and every year that comes round, she spawns another baby—and some years, two. So even if I was much better off, I'd be eaten out of house and home. A stinking sweetheart she is, if you go near her. Nobody knows or even dreams of a worse one. You know what I'd give? Every penny I've got, provided it was tomorrow morning to pay for a mass to be sung for her soul.   240   250

GIB   There's no one in this shire more worn out with waking than me. I'd go to sleep, even if it meant less wages.

DAW   I'm cold and naked, and need a fire.

COLL   I'm weary and worn out with walking in the mud.
(*To Gib*)   You stay awake.

He lies down

GIB   No, I'll lie down beside you: I must sleep, truly.

Lies down

    260

DAW   I'm as good as either of you.

Lies down with Mak's cloak over him

But Mak, you come here. You lie down between us.

MAK   Then I shall prevent your whispering together, for sure. From my top to my toe,

Manus tuas commendo, Pontio Pilato![1] Christ's cross me speed!

Gets up

Now's the time for a man who hasn't got what he wants to steal quietly towards the flock, and go nimbly to work without being too bold—in case he has to pay too much for his bargain in the last reckoning.   270

[1] A garbled misquotation of Jesus's last words (Luke 23, 46). Appropriately, this comic villain appeals to Pontius Pilate rather than to God to protect him in his scheming.

Mimes his hanging for sheep-stealing

Time to move fast. Good advice, if there can be any for a chap who'd be rich but hasn't a bean.

Puts a spell on them

Ring a ring around you, a circle like the moon,
Till my tricks confound you, till that it be noon,
Until I've done my will, until I've done it well,
Lie there stone-still and listen to my spell:
Now on high
Over your heads
My hand I lift!
Out go your eyes!
Out goes your sight!

But now I'd better get a move on if that spell's to come right!
Lord, (*to audience*) they're fast asleep! You can all hear them.

Takes back his cloak

I never was a shepherd, but now I'll learn.
The flock may be scared of me, still I'll grab one. Now! Closer!   290

He grabs the ram and wraps it in his cloak

Now to bring us joy out of sorrow,

A fat sheep, I dare say;
A good fleece, I dare lay;
Perhaps, later, I'll repay.
But now, I'll borrow.

Goes off to his cottage

Hey, Gyll, are you in? Get a light!

GYLL   Who's making such a row at this time of night? I'm sitting spinning, and I won't earn a penny by getting up, curse them! That's how things are for a housewife who's always being interrupted in her work. Nothing done,   300
because of these chores.

MAK   Good wife, open the door. Look what I've got!

GYLL   (*Unpins latch*)   You can lift the latch now. Ah, come in, darling!

MAK   Fat lot you care, and me standing outside so long.

GYLL   (*Seeing the ram*)   You'll be hanged by the naked neck for that!

MAK   Quiet! I deserve my food, for when I'm in a fix I can get more than men who   310
toil and sweat all day long. It was my luck to get this, Gyll, I had such grace.

GYLL   It'll be a *dis*grace when you're hanged for it.

MAK   I've often escaped from as bad a jam, Gyllikins.

GYLL   As the proverb says: 'Long goes the pot to the water, but at last it comes home broken.'

MAK   Never say that again! I know the saying well. Quickly come and help me. I wish   320
he was already skinned; I couldn't half eat. I haven't so longed for a mutton dinner this twelvemonth.

GYLL   If they come before he's killed, and hear him bleat. . .

MAK   Then I'd be for it. The thought makes me sweat. Go and bar the door.

GYLL   Yes, Mak. For if they're following behind you. . .

MAK   Then the whole pack of them would give me blue murder.   330

GYLL   I've thought of a good trick, since you can't. We'll hide him here in my cradle till they're gone. Give him to me. Leave me alone. I'll lie down like in childbed, and make a wailing din.

17

MAK   All right, get on with it.

She is tying the ram's legs together

And I shall say you gave birth to a little boy this very night.

GYLL   Now happy the bright day that ever I was born! This is a good trick. A woman's   340
        advice helps in the end. But we don't know who may be on the look-out.
        Hurry back to the others.

MAK   If I don't get there before they wake, it'll blow a cold blast!

Undoes door, and goes back to sleeping shepherds

I'll go and have a kip. The whole lot of them are still asleep. I'll creep silently
up to them, as if I'd never nicked their sheep.

*Lies down, returns his cloak to Daw's body, and pretends to sleep. After a time, Coll
and Gib wake*

COLL   *Resurrex a mortruus!*[1] Give me a hand. *Judas! carnas dominus*[2] I can hardly stand   350
        up! My foot's asleep, by Jesus, and I'm reeling with hunger. I thought we lay
        down somewhere in England.

GIB   Did we then? Lord, but I've slept well! I'm as fresh as an eel, and I feel as
        light as a leaf on a tree.

DAW   (*Waking from a nightmare and throwing the cloak inadvertently over Mak*)   Benedicite!
        I'm shaking. My heart's thumping, I don't know why. What's all this row about?   360
        I'll knit my brows and fight my way to the door. Hey fellows, look alive!
        There were four of us.

Looks round, but Mak is under the cloak

Have you seen Mak anywhere?

COLL   We were up before you. I swear to God, Mak hasn't been away from us.

DAW   (*Finds Mak under cloak*)   I thought he was wrapped in a wolf-skin.

COLL   So are many these days, especially in their souls.

DAW   I dreamed that he'd trapped a fat sheep while we were asleep, without making   370
        a sound.

GIB   Shut up! Your dream has sent you mad! By the rood, it's only a nightmare.

COLL   Now God turn all to good, if it be his will.

They wake Mak

GIB   Get up, Mak, for shame! You're sleeping too long.

MAK   Now Christ's holy name be with us! What's this? By Saint James, I can't walk.
        I'm still me, aren't I? My neck's got a crick in it.   380

They help him up

Thanks a lot. This very night I swear by Saint Stephen I was scared by a
dream: my heart jumped out of my skin. I thought Gyll began to wail and cry,
and just about the first cock-crow was in labour of a young lad to add to our
flock. That doesn't exactly cheer me up: I'd have more flax on my distaff than   390
I had before. Oh my head! A house full of young bellies—the devil knock out
their brains! Woe to the man with many children and little bread to feed them.
I must go home, by your leave, to my Gyll. Do me a favour, just check my
sleeves that I've stolen nothing: I don't want to harm you, or take anything
from you.

Exit Mak

DAW   Yes, off you go, and bad luck with you! Now we must check all our stock at
        first light this morning.   400

COLL   I'll go first and we'll meet later.

GIB   Where?

[1] Garbled Latin—'He rose again from death'.
[2] To do with Judas and Christ's body.

18

DAW	At the crooked thorn.	
	Exeunt	
MAK	(*At his cottage door*)　Open up! Who's at home! How long must I wait?	
GYLL	Who's making that din? The waning moon give you bad luck!	
MAK	Ah Gyll, how's things? It's me, Mak, your husband.	
GYLL	Then we can see the Devil with his own noose round his neck. Sir Guile! He comes with such a racket, you'd think he was being strangled. I can't sit at my work for even a short time.	410
MAK	What a fuss she makes, finding excuses! Playing about all day—nothing but scratching her toes.	
GYLL	Who gets on with the work, and stays awake? Who comes, who goes? Who brews, who bakes? And who makes me hoarse with shouting at him? It's a crying shame. Summer or winter, that household's in misery that hasn't a woman. But how did you get rid of the shepherds, Mak?	420
MAK	The last thing they said when I turned my back was that they'd count all their sheep. I reckon they won't be happy when they find one missing, by God! And whatever happens, they'll suspect me, and make a filthy din crying out against me. So you must do what you promised.	430
GYLL	I will. I'll swaddle it up in my cradle.	
	She does so	
	I'd still help, even if it was a harder trick to play. I'll lie down at once. Cover me up.	
MAK	Yes, I will.	
	He does so	
GYLL	Behind as well. If Coll and his mate come, they'll pinch me hard.	440
MAK	I shan't half give a yell if they find the ram.	
GYLL	Listen for when they call: they'll be coming soon. Make everything ready, then start singing by yourself. Sing a lullaby, because I must groan and cry out by the wall on Mary and Saint John in my pain. Sing 'Lullaby' as soon as you hear them; and if I don't play my part in diddling them, never trust me again.	
	At the crooked thorn. Dawn twilight	
DAW	Ah Coll, good morning to you. What, not asleep?	
COLL	Alas that ever I was born! It's a black mark to us—we've lost a fat ram.	450
DAW	Mary, God forbid!	
GIB	Who'd do that to us? It's an insult.	
COLL	Some crook. I've searched with my dogs all the thickets in Horbury, and with the fifteen lambs I only found the ewe.	
DAW	You mark my words, by Saint Thomas of Kent, either Mak or Gyll's at the bottom of this.	
COLL	Peace, man! I saw when Mak left us. You slander him and you ought to repent at once.	460
GIB	All the same, my life on it that it's him.	
DAW	Let's go to his cottage as fast as we can. I'll never eat bread till I know the truth of it.	
COLL	And I won't touch a drop till I meet him.	
GIB	And I won't rest anywhere till I greet him, dear brother. One thing I swear: till I clap eyes on him I won't put my head down in the same place twice.	470
	Outside Mak's cottage: Mak singing, Gyll groaning	
DAW	Listen to their trilling! Our man's having a croon.	
COLL	I never heard such an out-of-tune bawling. Call him.	
GIB	Mak, open up at once!	
MAK	Who's that, yelling as loud as if it was midday? Who's there, I say?	480

DAW	Good fellows, if only it was day!	
MAK	If you can, good people, speak quietly, for the sake of a sick woman in distress. I'd rather be dead than bring her any more suffering.	
GYLL	Go somewhere else! I can hardly breathe: every step you take makes my head ring.	
COLL	Tell us, Mak, if you will, how are you?	490
MAK	But you're at my place this morning. How are *you*?	

MAK *Letting them in*

You've been out in the mud and you're still wet. I'll make you a fire if you'll sit down. I must get a nurse. You remember my dream? Well, I've got my wages. Look there. (*Indicates cradle*) I've more than enough kids already. But we must drink as we brew; (*mock resigned*) that's only fair. I'd like you to have a bite before you went. I think you're sweating? 500

GIB	No. Food and drink won't improve things.	
MAK	Why, has anything but good happened to you?	
DAW	Yes, the sheep that we tend were stolen from where they were grazing. It's a big loss.	
MAK	Phew! Here, have a drink! If I'd been there, the thieves would have regretted it.	
COLL	Marry, some men think you were there, and that's what bothers us.	510
GIB	Mak, some men think it must be you.	
DAW	Either you or your wife, we say.	
MAK	Now if you suspect Gyll or me, come and ransack our house, (*Daw accepts the invitation*) and then you'll find out who had her. If I took away a sheep, a cow or a heifer—and Gyll my wife hasn't stirred since she was brought to bed—as I'm an honest man, before God I swear it, this (*points to cradle*) is the first meal I shall eat today.	520
COLL	Mak, as I hope for joy, take care. 'He learned early to steal who could not say "No".'	
GYLL	I'm swooning. Out, thieves, from my house! You've come here to rob us.	
MAK	Can't you hear her groaning? Your hearts should melt.	

Coll approaches the cradle, sniffing

GYLL	Get away from my baby, robbers! Not so near!	530
MAK	If you knew what she's gone through, your hearts'd bleed. You do wrong, I tell you, to come here to a woman when she's been in labour—but I'll say no more.	
GYLL	Oh my heart, my belly!	

Mock dying

I pray to God so mild that if ever I tricked you, I may eat this child that lies in the cradle.

MAK	Peace woman, for the sake of Christ's suffering, and don't cry out so. You're damaging your brain, and giving me misery.	540
GIB	I think our ram's been killed. What d'you think, you two?	
DAW	(*Returning from his search*) We're doing no good. We might as well go. But blast it! I can find no meat, hard or soft, salt or fresh, only two empty plates. I swear I can't find any livestock but what's in the cradle, that smells as strong as our lost ram did.	
GYLL	(*Pretending to take this to mean that they're going to eat her baby*) No, no! may God bless me, and give me joy of my child!	550
COLL	We've made a mistake. We've been tricked.	
GIB	Yes, out and out.	
	(*To Mak*) Sir—may Our Lady save him!—is your baby a boy?	
MAK	Any lord could have this child as his heir: when he's awake he grabs your finger—it's a joy to see.	

DAW	Happiness and good fortune to him! But who was ready to be his godparents so soon?
MAK	Good luck to them!...
COLL	(*Aside*) Listen to that lie!
MAK	...May God thank them! Parkin and Gibbon Waller, they were, and gentle John Horne—what a fuss he made, him with his long legs!
GIB	Mak, we'll make friends, for we've nothing against you.
MAK	We! Count me out, you haven't made it up to me. Good riddance, all three of you! I'll be glad when you've gone.
DAW	Fair words we may speak, but no love this time.

They leave

COLL	Did you give the child anything?
GIB	Not a farthing.
DAW	I'll go back. Wait here for me.

Reenters cottage

	Mak, don't be cross if I give your baby a welcome.
MAK	No, you've shamed me, and you haven't played fair.
DAW	The child won't be offended then, the little morning star. Mak, by your leave, let me give your baby a sixpence.
MAK	No! Clear off, he's asleep.
DAW	I think his eyes are open.
MAK	If he wakes he'll cry. For heaven's sake, go away!

Reenter Coll and Gib

DAW	Let me kiss him: uncover him a bit. What the devil's this? He's got a long snout!
COLL	(*Frightened and superstitious*) He's deformed. We should keep our noses out of it.
GIB	'Ill-spun weft makes bad cloth': that's what I say.

Looking closer

	Ah, so that's it. He's like our ram.
DAW	What, Gib, let me see.
COLL	(*Still thinking it's a deformed child*) 'Bad nature'll crawl there if it can't walk upright.'
GIB	A crafty trick! A cunning dodge!—A filthy swindle!
DAW	Yes sirs, that it was.

Drags Gyll out of bed

	Let this hag be burned. Bind her tightly! A false scold hangs at the last, and so shall you. Just look how they've tied his four feet together!

Unties the ram's legs, uses the cord to tie up Gyll

	I never saw a horned baby till this moment.
MAK	Peace I say. Stop your row! I sired him, and this good woman bore him.
COLL	What devil's name will you give him, Mak? Look, before God, Mak's son and heir!
GIB	Enough of that! God rot him, I saw it.

He has examined the ram and found it unharmed

GYLL	He's as pretty a child as ever sat on a mother's knee, a precious lamb, by God, to give his father joy.
DAW	I know him by the ear-mark—a sure sign.
MAK	I tell you sirs! Listen! His nose is broken. A priest told me afterwards that he was bewitched.

560

570

590

600

610

COLL	This is a filthy crime. I'll be avenged. Get out your weapons!	
GYLL	He was bewitched by a goblin, I saw it myself. When the clock struck twelve he changed shape.	620
GIB	You're a fine pair of crooks.	
COLL	They're facing it out. Let's have them put to death.	
MAK	(*Kneeling*) If I steal again, chop off my head. I put myself in your power.	
DAW	Sirs, take my advice. We won't curse or quarrel on account of this crime. We won't fight or sermonize. We'll just toss him in a blanket.	

They toss him, at each heave shouting: 'Are you in labour then?' 'Will it be a boy?' 'Is it a precious lamb then?' etc. Mak screams. They leave him dizzy on the floor and starting to untie Gyll, and go back to the fields with the ram

COLL	Lord, I'm worn out, and ready to burst: I can't go on, and so I'll rest.	630
GIB	He weighed like a hundred-and-forty pound sheep! I could lie down anywhere now and doze off.	
DAW	Let's rest here on this green.	
COLL	I'm still thinking about those thieves.	
DAW	Why go on about it? Do as I say.	

They sleep. An Angel appears and sings Gloria in excelsis

ANGEL	Arise, gentle shepherds! This night is he born	
	Who shall win from the Devil those souls forlorn	640
	Whom Adam's sin lost. For God has sworn	
	To be your friend from this very morn.	
	Now pass	
	To Bethlehem and see	
	The noble child lying	
	In a manger in poverty	
	With ox and ass.	

Exit. The shepherds wake

COLL	This was the strangest voice that ever I heard. It's a marvel indeed to be so scared.	
GIB	He spoke from on high of God's son of heaven. He made the whole wood as if lit up by lightning.	650
DAW	He said something about a baby in Bethlehem, I tell you.	
COLL	That star is our guide. We'll look for him in that direction.	
GIB	What was that song he sang? Didn't you hear how fancy it was, and him singing three shorts to a long?[1]	
DAW	Yes, by Mary, he didn't half trill: not a crotchet[2] wrong, every note perfect.	
COLL	I know how we can make a part-song of it, just as he sang his shorts and longs.	660
GIB	Have a go at it then. But you'll only be barking at the moon.	
DAW	Stop your chatter. Come on then.	
COLL	Right, pay attention and join in. (*Sings*)	

They all sing

GIB	He said we must go to Bethlehem. I'm afraid we've dawdled too long.	
DAW	Be merry and not sad—we sing of gladness. Without trouble we can have everlasting joy as a reward.	
COLL	That's why we shall go there, though we are wet and weary, to see that child and lady. We must remember what we're about.	670

[1] i.e. *modus perfectus*. Perhaps one might translate 'just perfect'.
[2] In modern terms a semiquaver.

Starts to sing the Gloria in excelsis *again*

GIB   Not again! We find by the prophecies of David and Isaiah and others whose names I don't remember—they prophesied through their learning—that he should come down from heaven and lie in the womb of a virgin, and save all our kind from misery. Isaiah said so. *Ecce virgo concipiet.*[1]   680

DAW   We can be happy now, waiting to see that lovely one who is almighty. Lord, I should be everlastingly glad to do homage on my knee and speak to that Child. But the Angel said that he was laid in a manger, poorly and meanly wrapped, and meek and mild.   690

COLL   Patriarchs who once lived, and prophets of old, longed to see this child that is born. They are long dead; they missed him. But we shall see him, I think, before dawn, God's gift. When I see him before me, I shall know for sure that it's as true as steel what the prophets have spoken: that he would first show himself to poor people like us; first find us, then declare his birth through his messenger.   700

GIB   Come, let us go now. The place is near.

DAW   I'm ready and willing; let's go together to that bright one.
Lord, if thy will it be—
Though we are simple all three—
Grant us the joy
Of comforting thy little one.

The Virgin and Child are revealed

COLL   Hail, comely and clean! Hail, young Child!   710
Hail, Creator, born of a maiden so mild!
That bringer of woe, the Devil fierce and wild,
The evil trickster is beguiled.

Goes nearer

Lo, he merries!
Lo, he laughs, my sweeting!
Welcome! Happy meeting!
Have a bob of cherries[2].

GIB   Hail sovereign saviour, because thou hast sought us!
Hail, noble blossom, who all things hast wrought!   720
Hail, full of good will, who made all from naught!
Hail, I kneel low! This bird[3] I have brought
To my babe.
Hail, little tiny mop!
Of our faith thou art head.
I would drink from thy cup,
Little day-star.

DAW   Hail, darling dear, full of God's grace!
I pray thee be near when I have need.
Hail, sweet is thy face! My heart's like to bleed   730
To see thee lie here so poorly dressed,
With no pennies.
Hail! Put forth thy fist.
I bring thee but a ball[4],
Have it and play withal,
And go to the tennis.

MARY   The father of heaven, God omnipotent,
Who made all in seven days, his son has sent.

[1]'Behold, a virgin shall conceive.'
[2]Cherries were a symbol of midwinter fertility.
[3]Bird—symbol of the Holy Ghost.
[4]The ball symbolizes the orb, i.e. the world and all that is in it, and God's universal lordship over it.

He named me and alighted in me before he went.
Truly I conceived through his might, as he meant.
And now he is born.
May he keep you from woe!
I shall pray him so.
Tell it forth as ye go,
And remember this morn.

COLL   Farewell, lady, so fair to behold
With thy child on thy knee.

GIB   But he lies full cold.
Lord, I am content now. Thou seest, we depart.

DAW   Truly, already the good news seems to be told
Very oft.

COLL   What grace we have found!

GIB   Come forth: we are redeemed now.

DAW   To sing thanksgiving we are bound.
Raise your voices aloft.

They sing

Here ends the Second Shepherds' Pageant

3   Discussion of the *Second Shepherds' Pageant*

12 This discussion is based on the five tasks suggested in paragraph 11, p. 12. Please note that these five sections are not meant to be exhaustive. Except for the first task, your notes for which should be precise, any response must be selective, and is likely to be to some extent impressionistic. The concrete particulars which would force closer definition, such as an actual group of actors and an actual stage and social milieu for the presentation under discussion, are lacking.

i   Elements from the Bible

13 a The strict biblical content begins at line 639. The Angel's speech is a verse paraphrase of Luke 2, 10–12.

b Coll's fear is a reflection of verse 9—'and they were sore afraid'.

c The sense of verse 16—'And they came with haste'—is beautifully perverted by the need the playwright evidently felt to make two points, one dramatic and one doctrinal. The dramatic point is to lift the tone as far as possible above that of the preceding comedy; so the shepherds sing the Angel's song. The doctrinal point is to emphasize the Nativity as a fulfilment of prophecy.

d Mary's instruction to the shepherds to 'Tell it forth as ye go' covers (and also personalizes

interestingly) the point of verse 17—'they made known abroad'.

Elements from the 'Officium Pastorum' not included above

14 e The Angel appearing 'high above' (though you might agree that that is implied in verse 9 of Luke 2).

f The accompanying angels and priests who function as choir have no exact parallels in the play, which has very few stage directions in the manuscript version. As a practical matter, if a producer is to obtain a good effect of supernatural majesty at and after line 639, he will be hard put to it if he contents himself with a single angel.

g As for the sung offices, some of which are mentioned by Young in his summary of the Rouen material (see paragraph 6, p. 10), *Pax in terris* is not expressed, but *Gloria in excelsis* is (639). So are *Transeamus* (652–3), *Adest hic parvulus* (710) and *Salve, virgo singularis* (first half of 710). And *Iam vere scimus* is implicit in the ending of the play.

h The prophecy of Isaiah is included (680).

i The 'We praise thee O God' from the early Rouen *Officium Pastorum* provides the last speech of the play, and the song sung by the shepherds ought accordingly to be a *Te Deum Laudamus*.

ii Producer's notes on the three shepherds

15 I think my main concern as producer would be to help the actors taking these parts to realize them both as individuals and members of a group. One literary critic takes the view that the playwright is not much concerned to differentiate between the shepherds in their individual contributions to the dialogue, but allots speeches in the order '1 Pastor', 2 Pastor', 3 Pastor' fairly regularly. This critic acknowledges a difference of age and status between '3 Pastor', who is Daw in our version, and the others, but that is about all. I believe an acting group working under a producer will discover some differences among the three upon which to build, quite apart from Daw's youth and inferior status. But this inferior social status is offset by a superior dramatic status. Thus, though Daw is employed by Gib (44), once Mak's plot is fully under way, Daw takes all the initiatives associated with superior status and intelligence. He initiates the stock check after Mak's departure (400), the meeting at the crooked thorn (404), suspicion of Mak and Gyll (458), and the search of Mak's cottage (515–45). He discovers the sheep (585), is the first to mention the crucial Christ-image by calling Mak's baby a 'morning star' (578), suggests that Mak be tossed in a blanket (an ancient device for bringing on labour, by the way: doctors still sometimes advise healthy women to walk down steps bouncingly in order to bring on labour), and is clearly the leader of the party in the devotional and ritual dénouement. In dramatic *origin* he is the Garcio, or Gartius (Boy), a character who crops up in various forms in both miracle plays and moralities. In this play and the Chester *Shepherds' Pageant*, he is the one with the clearest religious illumination, which is instinctive rather than learned (**reread 675–701 for the contrast between him and his elders**). In the Chester play he is outside the fasting brotherhood of the three shepherds, who will not let him have food, like Coll and Gib in this play. But Gartius beats them in turn at wrestling before leading them in religious discovery—an important allegory of Christ's victories in religious debate. (But in *The Castle of Perseverance*, pp. 72 ff., his supernatural affinities bring him a detestable and almost diabolical function in the decay of Mankind.) Daw's activity in the secular part of this play—his worldliness, his membership of the oppressed part of the community, his insight into his own and humanity's predicament, his sense of responsibility (he is the one who was actually guarding the sheep), his intuition (remember his nightmare), his common sense and above all his youth—make him, in the dramatic terms established by the playwright, the best guide to the epiphany of the play's ending. He is the most colourful and the most real of the three shepherds, and the one with whom we can identify most easily. We identify with him in human sympathy because he is the underdog, and in dramatic sympathy because he is the centre of action on the virtuous side, as Mak is on the vicious side.

16 Coll and Gib may be dealt with more briefly. Though they are a pair in the sense of being older than Daw, rather simple and given to quoting proverbs, yet there are differences between them. Coll is bitter (1–55); a practical joker (109); hard on men generally (148, 172) and especially vengeful against Mak (616, 623); a compulsive singer (185, 660) with a good ear (466); and superstitious (586). Gib is more religiously resigned in an orthodox way (55–70), which goes with his conventional antifeminist outburst (65–105). He sleeps well (357); he is the first to wish to make friends with Mak and his 'baby' (553–4, 556). He pushes home the investigation when Daw reveals the 'baby's' long snout (586). But both are hard on Daw at the start, and they unite in distrust of Mak. They are essentially a pair.

iii Matters relevant to the Christian theme before the appearance of the Angel

17 'Everything in life is related to religion'—so this might be a trick question. I think the job of a modern producer is to remember that the original audiences attended this play as one of a cycle, one item in a great annual religious celebration. Accordingly, he must try to find the right focus for playing it today, secure in his sense (derived from studying the text) that the playwright is concerned, whatever else, to communicate accurate doctrine in an appropriate tone.

18 First, the social theme which is so powerfully announced in the early soliloquies of the three shepherds, is significant because of that part of the Christian message contained in the Beatitudes (see Luke 6, 20–1 especially); the two references to Isaiah, the prophet of social justice, reinforce the message. Throughout, the shepherds are variously oppressed, tired and hungry. Then, the choice of *shepherds* to discover the Lamb of God is obviously important. My next point is open to question, but nevertheless I shall make it. I think that the first song should not be too rollickingly bucolic; something in the harmony or the tune should constitute fit preparation for the music to follow, and its functions. Mak is technically the villain—if you like, the evil power who is worsted before the new god is born. The shepherds certainly mistrust him, and seem even slightly to dread him and his power to deceive and rob. The subtle change of moral tone when the shepherds decide to forgive him (remember the devil can never be forgiven, but a bad man shorn of his power to do evil can), and the sense of a passage of action being rounded off, need to be sharply underlined, because they prepare directly for the sudden assault of sight and sound at the appearance of the Angel.

iv A staging plan

19 If I were staging the play in a church, I should prefer to use the altar area for the Nativity, especially if it were raised; that would be in conformity with medieval practice for the *Officium Pastorum*. But I should place the burlesque nativity at the west end, following one medieval tradition that hell is at the farthest point from heaven, and in the part of the church where often there were steps going down into the crypt. This to my mind ideal arrangement would necessitate clearing a broad way down the nave for the out-of-doors action, which means that the audience or congregation would fill the north and south aisles. I should have to safeguard sightlines towards the altar. My Angel would appear in the pulpit or near the eastern end of the clerestory. I think there is a contrary argument for siting the burlesque nativity in the same place as the real one, but there is a danger of real disrespect to the altar (which is sacred at all times), quite different from the implied disrespect of including a burlesque nativity in the play at all. The latter, as you are probably discovering, subtly reinforces the religious meaning.

v Producer's notes on the last 170 lines (585ff.)

20 *585–625* The worst possible mistake is to mask the essential social fact behind this passage: that sheep-stealing is a hanging matter. Gyll and Mak may seem comic, but their terror is genuine and their shifts are desperate: Mak's capitulation (623) ought, in spite of all the furious action and comic business preceding it, to be moving. It will be so only if the changing feelings of the three shepherds, and their subtle interaction as a group right up to the tossing of Mak in the blanket (which is a 'game' as Glynne Wickham uses the term), are properly managed. Gib is the first to be really aware of Mak's crime, pronounces moral judgements on it, but is forgiving almost at once (607), but Coll is more interested in discomfiting Mak (604) and in taking revenge (614 and 621). Daw is the one who resolves the disagreement, which he does by appealing to his elders' sense of humour. Throughout, all three shepherds show concern for the ram itself.

21 *629–39* A blackout on Mak's cottage, a weary walk by the three shepherds in which the

values of the social theme must again be echoed: the mood relaxed, the pace slow, the dialogue dragging and contemplative. It might be a good idea to emphasize the solidarity of the three by the positions in which they fall asleep.

22 *640* A blaze of light, a blaze of sound. I should consider using organ and a hidden choir (but see Trevor Bray's section on the music, paragraphs 26 ff., pp. 27–9). At the end of the Angel's speech, silence and dimness for a long moment before the shepherds awake.

23 *647–709* As so often, the producer must be concerned with *rhythm* in a passage of dialogue and action. The transition here is from awe at the supernatural, to a reestablishment of human values through characters we already know, to a popular, religious, anticipatory joy culminating in prayer. I should stress the significance of Daw as the young leader of the process.

24 *710–36* The revelation of the Virgin and Child seems, from the earliest extant examples of the *Officium Pastorum,* always to have been conducted with maximum effect. For example, in church a curtain was withdrawn. The way you achieve your effect will depend on the resources you command (auditory as well as visual, if you wish) and the style of the whole production. At this moment I think I should favour a slow illumination accompanied by quiet music: when light was full, the Virgin would make a definite movement, perhaps of solicitude for the Child. Then the shepherds would begin their salutations, which I should again plan as a cumulative rhythmic effect. Elements in this would be the movements towards the manger, alternations between standing (distant) and kneeling (close) salutation, and the congregating of shepherds. The ritual salutation catches fire with Coll's 'Lo, he is merry', and there is a common pattern in the three verses. All the same, the characterization already established should be maintained, even, I should say, accentuated.

25 *937–end* The speech of Mary is especially difficult. Qualities of stillness, authority, compassion, and all that the word 'bliss' signified in the Middle Ages, are needed; and every word is doctrinally important. A carefully considered piece of stage action is needed between the end of Mary's speech and Coll's first word of farewell; the slow fade which I should begin just before Coll's speech would not be complete until the end of Gib's speech. By the time Daw speaks, I should have all three shepherds well away from the manger, and possibly I should cut 'come forth' (but Christ did bring *comfort*) because it seems to apply to a production in which a pageant, or an inner part of it, was used for the manger. I should like the shepherds well among the congregation for the last three speeches, and mingling with them for the final music, which might, as I have already suggested, be a *Te Deum*.

4 The music

What sort of music?

26 This is the first time in the course that we have considered the incidental music to a play, so it would be useful, before concentrating on the music in the Wakefield *Second Shepherds' Pageant,* to consider the problems facing a producer when thinking about the sort of music he wants for his production. How can he make a sensible choice from all the material available? What guidelines can help him make this choice? For instance, when producing Shakespeare's *Love's Labour's Lost,* is it a good idea to have incidental music in the style of popular music of the 1920s? (I have heard this done!) If you were planning a new production of Ibsen's *Peer Gynt,* would you feel you had to use Grieg's music? For me, the most important criterion for choosing incidental music is that it should be *suitable* for the play. It should underline the main features of the play by reflecting a mood or elaborating a character, by highlighting a dramatic moment or psychological conflict or development. It might even provide a pointed contrast at a particular moment.

27 Incidental music has taken many forms—occasional songs, dances, background music, music both before and after acts. In fact, it can be used anywhere. In general though, it should remain faithful to the spirit of the play and, if very successful, could even add an element of understanding which might otherwise be lacking. **How do you think that your choice of suitable music for a play—any play—would work out in a practical way?**

28 There are many possibilities here.

a   Firstly, you might feel it would be most interesting to find out the sort of music that was used when your play was first produced. Your production may be sticking as closely as possible to the type of performance current when your play was written. Similarly, the music should be authentic.

b   However, you might find that the music you were hoping to use is no longer extant—in time, the manuscript on which it was written has been lost or destroyed. The instruments used at that time might also have disappeared or at least would be too costly to hire from private owners. Also, the effect of this music on the listener today is quite different from its effect on its con-

temporaries and you may feel that in order to communicate forcefully with your audience, music in a readily accessible style is necessary—a modern 'translation', so to speak.

c   Availability of instruments is of prime importance, and for most producers the music provided for a production would be governed by the instruments that could be found in their school, college or theatre, not forgetting the availability of musicians. Some theatrical groups might be lucky and have a composer in their midst, in which case the producer might like to have his music specially composed. Then the composer would have to face the problem of what style his music should be, how much to include and so on.

d   Another possibility is that your production is influenced by a special viewpoint. The play you are going to produce has been performed countless times before and, through your production, you want to establish a new interpretation of it. In doing this, you could choose music that might well be considered by many as definitely unsuitable, but which would produce the effect you wanted by shock tactics.

e   Finally, there are many plays for which incidental music would be quite unsuitable. Some themes simply do not need any sort of musical accompaniment and obviously the first question you should ask yourself is 'Do I need incidental music at all?'

29 There are many possibilities and they are well worth thinking over before your final choice. The overriding considerations will be availability and cost. If your instrumental resources are slender or non-existent but you have a tape recorder, remember that any sound can be used as raw material and, with sufficient imagination, your incidental music could simply be sounds on tape.

An authentic approach

30 In the following section I want to discuss an authentic approach to providing music for the Wakefield *Second Shepherds' Pageant.* We have taken the deliberate decision to try to recreate the sound of the music as it was heard in the mid-fifteenth century, although we are aware that the language of the play has been modernized for a twentieth-century audience.

31 The role of music was limited in the miracle and mystery plays. Unlike its important treatment in the earlier liturgical dramas, where large portions of the drama were sung by the actors, music was used in the plays basically to increase the spectacular effect. The amount of music varied from one performance to another, depending on how many musicians were available in any town and how much money there was to pay them. Traditionally, musicians were grouped on or beside the platform representing heaven. A choir of angels, who could sing not only plainsong[1] but also in parts, was joined by several instrumentalists, most usually playing wind instruments, trumpets or an organ. If you look at the miniature by Jean Fouquet on the front cover, *The Martyrdom of Saint Apollonia*, you can see the platform representing heaven at the top left, with the choir and instrumentalists. The instruments are three trumpets, probably two cornetts[2] (they're difficult to distinguish), a bagpipe and an organ.

32 Another traditional place for music was in pastoral scenes. It has been suggested that 'the image of a happy shepherd spending his carefree days singing, dancing, and playing on one of a variety of rustic wind instruments seems to have captured the imagination of the time. A shepherd almost never appears on any kind of fifteenth- or sixteenth-century stage, without at least talking about music (Howard Mayer Brown, *Music in the French Secular Theatre, 1400–1500*, p.45). In Nativity plays one of the shepherds would often leave a recorder as his present for the baby Jesus. We can therefore expect the shepherds to be musical. Unfortunately, the original music of the *Second Shepherds' Pageant* has not survived, but by carefully studying all the references to music in the play, Nan Cooke Carpenter ('Music in the *Secunda Pastorem*') has demonstrated convincingly the sort of music used. Additional evidence is provided, both by references to music in the Wakefield *First Shepherds' Pageant*, and also, most important of all, by music from other mysteries of the same period—for example, music from the York cycle of plays is extant.

33 From your reading of the play you will have realized that the shepherds are, indeed, very

musical. They can not only sing in three parts (185–9), but also appreciate the more sophisticated music of the Angel. The shepherds are overcome by the Angel's artistry and pay homage in a short discussion (655–60).

Gib
What was that song he sang? Didn't you hear how fancy it was, and him singing three shorts to a long?

Daw
Yes, by Mary, he didn't half trill: not a crotchet wrong, every note perfect.

Coll
I know how we can make a part-song of it, just as he sang his shorts and longs.

(N.B. The relationship between longs and shorts [the two note-values *longa* and *brevis*] was defined in the thirteenth century, and at that time, the usual division of a long was into three shorts.)

34 The shepherds feel the most extraordinary point is the elaborate shape of the Angel's melody with its fast, running notes, a performance which fills them with awe. The complexity of the Angel's song with its quick notes is also discussed by the shepherds in the Wakefield *First Shepherds' Pageant* —there, a long is divided into twenty-four notes. These discussions of musical technicalities suggest that although the shepherds are aware and can recognize the sophisticated treatment of the Angel, their music is less florid and rhythmically less complex, despite the three parts. It seems probable therefore that the shepherds sang in the English *discant* style. Basically this was a technique of singing in parallel sixth-chords with the melody in the bottom part. There was little embellishment—each note in one part moving with a note in the other two parts. Because the three parts moved in parallel motion it was fairly easy to improvise and the shepherds need not have been professionals to have done this. You can see that where the shepherds first sing, Coll takes the tenor which would have the tune, Gib the top part and Daw the middle part.

35 The five short pieces which have survived from the York Cycle add support to this hypothesis. They are only in two parts but are composed in a style called *gymel* where the two parts proceed in parallel thirds and sixths. The discant style consists simply of the addition of another parallel part. By the time of the Wakefield *Second Shepherds' Pageant*, the English discant style had been flourishing for about a century. The shepherds' music is suitably conservative. In contrast, the Angel's music with its quick notes and rhythms is more up-to-date.

36 Here then, is a checklist of the music needed for the play.

[1] Plainsong is the large body of liturgical chants used by the Roman Catholic Church. It developed over a long period, attaining its finalized form during the ninth century. Plainsong is monophonic, has only a single part, and has a free rhythm.

[2] The cornett is a woodwind instrument, most popular in the medieval and Renaissance periods, which was either straight or slightly curved in shape with an octagonal cross-section. Its gentle, sweet sound blended well with the human voice.

a *189* 'A pastoral song'. Possibly in English discant style, but not necessarily.

b *190–5* Coll's reference to 'howling' is a description of Mak's singing. The bad character of Mak is suggested immediately at his first entrance by his lack of musical ability. This makes a notable contrast with the good, musical shepherds. A well-known plainsong melody, out of tune and half-forgotten, will be appropriate for Mak's guise.

c *473* Mak is trying to sing a lullaby.

d *639* Angel sings *Gloria in excelsis*.

e *667* The shepherds sing *Gloria* in discant style.

f *At the end* *Te Deum Laudamus*, plainsong.

37 You will be able to hear what most of these pieces sound like in Radio Programme 5, *Music in Medieval Drama*. It would be a good idea, especially if you are thinking of working practically on the play, to make a tape recording of the programme.

THE THIRD CHESTER PAGEANT: *NOAH'S FLOOD*

1 Introduction

1 **Before you read the play, I would like you to jot down what you can remember of the story of Noah and the Deluge. If you do not know the story at all, look it up in Genesis 6–9, but only do this if you must.** Even if you think you do not know much about the Old Testament, you will probably be surprised how much you have remembered of this story. The myth of the Flood and Noah's Ark is surprisingly long-lasting in western civilization, and it has lasted without much addition or loss of its main content. **Why might this have happened?** (I realize that there might be a Jungian answer to this: could we just have the obvious one?)

2 Your answer should recognize that this is one of our earliest children's stories in the West, and that Noah's Ark is a traditional children's toy. We all known that the animals went in two by two; with them in the Ark will be Mr and Mrs Noah, plus Shem, Ham and Japhet and their wives. There are also certain proverbial expressions connected with the dove and the olive branch; and the rainbow has remained a symbol of a promise (think of Wordsworth's poem and D. H. Lawrence's novel).

3 This cultural heritage would pose problems if you were asked to dramatize the story. Certain parts of the spectacle, the deluge and the animals, for example, cannot be left out. On the other hand, a well-known story has certain advantages, as we have seen in Greek drama. A mere hint may suffice to indicate the course of the action.

4 The original presenters of this pageant had to deal with the story

a in half an hour

b by using a pageant-wagon (a carnival-float) which was built up to resemble the Ark. They would also use another platform in front of the Ark, or possibly the street. This drawing by C. Walter Hodges (p. 30) gives you an idea of the appearance of the pageant.[1]

5 There are five manuscripts of the Third Chester Pageant, *Noah's Flood,* all late sixteenth- or early seventeenth-century transcriptions. I have compared the Early English Text Society edition of 1893 by Herman Deimling, which is based on a 1607 text, with that included in A. W. Pollard's *English Miracle Plays, Moralities and Interludes,* which is based on a 1592 transcription by George Bellin: and produced a text in which I have tried always to go by the version
a which is the fullest
b makes better sense
c is metrically less imperfect.

In particular, I have gone for the fullest stage directions and translated the majority, which were in Latin. Twice, I have included slightly differing stage directions from two versions at the same point in the text; the Pollard precedes the Deimling. (Since I prepared this text, a new, authoritative, complete Chester cycle has appeared, edited by R. M. Lumiansky and David Mills.)

---

[1] I have deliberately held back here from diverting your attention from the text towards the staging of plays. Please realize that hardly anything is known *for a fact* about the original performances of these plays and that even the few simple points made in this bald summary could be challenged and debated. I shall attempt a reconstruction in paragraphs 11 ff., pp. 61–9.

C. Walter Hodges' drawing showing one possible reconstruction of the staging of Noah's Flood. Note the cart on which the Ark is set.

2 The text of *Noah's Flood*

The Chester Pageant of the Water-Leaders and Drawers in Dee

And first in some high place or in the clouds, if it may be, God speaketh unto Noah standing without the Ark with all his family

GOD   I, God, that all this world hath wrought,
Heaven and earth, and all of naught,
I see my people in deed and thought
Are set foul in sin.

My *ghost shall not linge in man*   *my spirit shall stay in man*
That through flesh-liking is my *fonne*,   *enemy*
But till six score years be comen and gone   *only till*
To look if they will *blynne*.   *cease*

Man that I made I will destroy,
Beast, worm and fowl to fly;
For on earth they do me *nye*,   *harm*
The folk that are thereon.

It harms me so hurtfully,
The malice that doth now multiply,
That sore it grieves me heartily
That ever I made man.

Therefore, Noah, my servant *free*,   *noble*
That righteous man art, as I see,
A ship soon thou shall make thee,
Of trees dry and light.

10

20

Little chambers therein thou make
And binding *slyche* also thou take,   *pitch*
Within and *without thou ne slake*   *outside*   *do not neglect*
To anoint it through all thy might.

Three hundred cubits it shall be long
And fifty broad, to make it strong,
Of height fifty the *mete* thou *fong,*   *dimension*   *take*
Thus measure it about.

One window *work* through thy wit,   *make*
A cubit of length and breadth make it,
Upon the side a door shall sit
For to come in and out.

Eating places thou make also,
Three roofed chambers in a row:
For with water I *think* to *slo*   *intend*   *kill*
Man that I *can* make.   *did*

Destroyed all the world shall be
Save thou, thy wife and children three,
And their wives also with thee
Shall saved be for thy sake.

NOAH   O Lord, I thank thee loud and *still*   *constantly*
That to me art in such will
And spares me and my house to *spill,*   *destroy*
As I now *soothly* find.   *truly*

Thy bidding, Lord, I shall fulfil,
And never more thee grieve nor *grill,*   *annoy*
That such grace hath sent *me till*   *to me*
Amongst all mankind.

Have done, you men and women all!
Hie you lest this water fall   *hurry*
To work this ship, chamber and hall,
As God hath bidden us do.

SHEM   Father, I am all ready *boun;*   *prepared*
An axe I have, by my crown,
As sharp as any in all this town
For to *go thereto.*   *set about it*

HAM   I have a hatchet wonder keen
To bite well, as may be seen;
A better grounden, as I ween,
Is not in all this town.

JAPHET   And I can make well a *pin,*   *nail*
And with this hammer knock it in.
Go we work *bout more din,*   *without more ado*
And I am ready *boun.*   *prepared*

NOAH'S WIFE   And we shall bring timber too,
For we *mone* nothing else do;   *can*
Women be weak to *underfoe*   *undertake*
Any great travail.

SHEM'S WIFE   Here is a good *hack-stock!*   *chopping block*
On this you may hew and knock.
Shall none be idle in this flock,
Ne now may no man fail.   *nor*

HAM'S WIFE   And I will go gather *slyche*   *pitch*
The ship for to caulk and pitch.
Anoint it must be every stitch,   *daubed everywhere*
Board, *tree* and *pin.*   *beam*   *wooden bolt*

30

40

50

60

70

JAPHET'S WIFE	And I will gather chips here
	To make a fire for *you in fere,* *all of you*
	And for to *dight* your dinner *prepare*
	Against your coming in.

Then Noah beginneth to build the Ark, and speaketh Noah:
(*Then they make movements as if working with various tools*)

NOAH	Now in the name of God I will begin
	To make the ship that we shall in,
	That we may be ready for to swim
	At the coming of the flood.

These boards here I pin together
To bear us safe from the weather,
That we may row both hither and thither
And be safe from the flood.

Of this tree will I make the mast,
Tied with cables that will last,
With a sail yard for each blast,
And each thing in their kind.

With topcastle and bowsprit,
With cords and ropes I *hold all meet*   *secure well*
To sail forth at the next *weet.*   *wet, i.e. rain*
This ship is at an end.

Wife, in this vessel we shall be kept,
My children and thou; I *would in ye leapt.*   *want you to go in*

NOAH'S WIFE	In faith, Noah, I had as lief thou slept!
	For all thy *frynish fare* *French, i.e. polite, behaviour*

I will not do *after thy rede.*   *as you advise*

NOAH	Good wife, do now as I thee bid.
NOAH'S WIFE	By Christ! Not ere I see more need,
	Though thou stand all the day and stare.
NOAH	Lord, that women be crabbed ay!
	And none are meek, I dare well say.
	This is well seen by me today
	In witness of you *each one.* *i.e. the audience*

Good wife, let be all this *beare*   *din*
That thou makest in this place here,
For all they *ween* that thou art master,   *think*
And so thou art, by Saint John!

*Then Noah with all his family shall make a sign as though they wrought upon the ship
with divers instruments and after that God shall speak to Noah, saying:*

GOD	Noah, take thou thy *meiny,* *company*
	And in the ship *hie* that you be, *hurry*
	For none so righteous man to me
	Is now on earth living.

Of clean beasts with thee thou take
Seven and seven, *or then thou slake,*   *before you pause*
He and she, make to *make*   *mate*
Belive in that thou bring.   *bring them in quickly*

Of beasts unclean two and two,
Male and female, *bout moe.*   *without more*
Of clean fowls seven also,
The he and she together;

80

90

100

110

120

Of fowls unclean twain and no more,
As I of beasts said before;
That man be saved *through my lore*   *according to my instructions*
Against I send this weather.

Of all meats that *mone* be eaten   *may*   130
Into the ship look there be getten;
For that may be no way forgetten.
And do all this *bydene*   *immediately*

To sustain man and beast therein
Till the water cease and *blin*.   *stop*
The world is filled full of sin
And that is now well seen.

Seven days be yet coming,
You shall have *space* them in to bring.   *time*
After that it is my liking
Mankind for to *annoy*.   *afflict*   140

Forty days and forty nights
Rain shall fall *for their unrights,*   *on account of their evil-doings*
And that I have made through my *mights,*   *powers*
Now think I to destroy.

NOAH   Lord, to thy bidding I am *bain;*   *obedient*
Seeing *no other grace* will gain,   *nothing else*
It will I fulfil *fain,*   *willingly*
For gracious I thee find.

A hundred winter and twenty
This ship making tarried have I,   150
If through amendment thy mercy   *to see if*
Would fall to mankind.

Have done, you men and women all;
Hie you lest this water fall,   *hurry*
That each beast were in stall
And into the ship brought.

Of clean beasts seven shall be,
Of unclean two, this God bade me.
The flood is nigh, you may well see,
Therefore tarry you not.   160

Then Noah shall go into the Ark with all his family, his wife except, and the Ark must be boarded round about, and on the boards all the beasts and fowls painted

(Additional stage directions in a third text: ... *must be painted that these words may agree with the pictures*)

SHEM   Sir, here are lions, leopards in,
Horses, mares, oxen and swine
Goat and calf, sheep and kine
Here sitten thou may see.

HAM   Camels, asses man may find,
Buck and doe, hart and hind
And beasts of all manner kind
Here be, as thinketh me.

JAPHET   Take here cats and dogs too,
Otter, and fox, *fulmarts* also;   *polecats*   170
Hares hopping gaily can go,
Here have *coule* for to eat.   *cabbage*

NOAH'S WIFE   And here are bears, wolves set,
Apes, owls, marmoset,

	Weasels, squirrels and ferret, Here they eaten their meat.	
SHEM'S WIFE	Here are beasts in this house, Here cats make it *crousse,* Here a *ratten,* here a mouse That standeth nigh together.	*lively* *rat*	180
HAM'S WIFE	And here are fowls less and more, Herons, cranes and *bittor,* Swans, peacocks, and them before *Meat for this weather.*	*bitterns* *a store of food for the flood*
JAPHET'S WIFE	Here are cocks, kites, crows, Rooks, ravens, many rows, Cuckoos, curlews, whoever knows, Each one in his kind;	
	Here are doves, ducks, drakes, Redshanks running through the lakes; And each fowl that *leden* makes In this ship men may find.	*sound*	190
NOAH	Wife, come in: why standst thou there? Thou art ever *froward,* I dare well swear. Come in, *on God's half!* Time it were, For fear lest that we drown.	*contrary* *for God's sake*
NOAH'S WIFE	Yea sir, set up your sail And row forth with *evil heal,* For withouten any fail I will not out of this *town.*	*misfortune* *place*	200
	But I have my gossips every one One foot further I will not gone. They shall not drown, by Saint John, *And* I may save their life.	*unless* *if*
	They loven me full well, by Christ! But thou let them into thy *chest,* Else row now *where thee list,* And get thee a new wife.	*container, i.e. Ark* *wherever you like*
NOAH	Shem, son, lo! thy mother is *wrawe:* Forsooth, such another I do not know.	*angry*	210
SHEM	Father, I shall fetch her in, I trow, Withouten any fail.	
	Mother, my father after thee send, And bids thee into yonder ship wend. Look up and see the wind, For we been ready to sail.	
NOAH'S WIFE	Shem, go again to him, I say; I will not come therein today.	
NOAH	Come in, wife in twenty devils' way! Or else stand there without.		220
HAM	Shall we all fetch her in?	
NOAH	Yea, sons, in Christ's blessing and mine. I would you *hied you betime,* For of this flood I am in *doubt.*	*hurried early* *fear*
THE GOOD GOSSIPS	The flood comes *fleeting* in full fast, On every side that spreads full far; For fear of drowning I am aghast; Good gossips, let us draw near,	*rushing*

	And let us drink ere we depart,	
	For oft times we have done so;	230
	For at a draught thou drinks a quart,	
	And so will I do ere I go.	

	Here is a *pottel* full of Malmsey good and strong,	*quart-pot*
	It will rejoice both heart and tongue.	
	Though Noah think us never so long,	
	Here will we drink alike.	

JAPHET Mother, we pray you all together,
For we are here, your own *childer,*   *children*
Come into the ship for fear of the weather,
For his love that *you bought!*   *redeemed you*   240

NOAH'S WIFE That will not I for all your call
But I have my gossips all.   *unless*

SHEM In faith, mother, yet you shall,
Whether thou wilt or not.

Then she shall go

NOAH Welcome, wife, into this boat.

NOAH'S WIFE Have thou that for thy *note!*   *labour*

And having been overpowered she gives him a slap on the face

NOAH Ha ha! *Marry,* this is hot!   *by our lady*
It is good for to be *still.*   *meek*

Ha! Children, methinks my boat removes.
Our tarrying here highly me grieves;   250
Over the land the water spreads;
God do as he will.

Ah, great God, that art so good,
That works not thy will is wood.   *whoever does not do thy will is mad*
Now all this world is on a flood,
As I see well in sight.

This window I will shut *anon,*   *immediately*
And into my chamber I will gone
Till this water, *so great one,*   *high as it is*
Be slacked through thy might.   260

(Then Noah shall shut the window of the Ark, and for a little while they shall sing the psalm 'Save me O God' under the roof; then he shall open the window and look about)

NOAH Now forty days are fully gone
Send a raven I will anon
If *oughtwhere* earth, tree or stone   *anywhere*
Be dry in any place.

And if this fowl come not again
It is a sign, sooth to sayn,
That dry it is on hill or plain,
And God hath done some grace.

Then he shall send forth the raven and taking the dove in his hands shall say:

Ah Lord, wherever this raven be,
Somewhere is dry, well I see.   270
But yet a dove, by my *lewte,*   *faith*
After I will send.

Thou wilt turn again to me,
....
For of all fowls that may fly
Thou art most meek and *hend.*   *gentle*

Then he shall let go the dove, and there shall be within the ship another dove bearing an olive in its beak which somebody shall send from the mast by a rope into the hand of Noah; and after that Noah shall say:

Ah, Lord, blessed be thou *ay,*   *for ever*
That me hast comfort thus today.
By this sight I may well say
This flood begins to cease.

My sweet dove to me brought has   280
A branch of olive from some place.
This betokeneth God has done us some grace
And is a sign of peace.

Ah Lord, honoured must thou be,
All earth dries now, I see,
But yet till thou command me
Hence I will not hie.

All this water is away;
Therefore as soon as I may
Sacrifice I shall do in *fay*   *faith*   290
To thee devoutly.

GOD   Noah, take thy wife anon
And thy children everyone,
Out of the ship thou shalt *gone,*   *go*
And they all with thee.

Beasts and all that can fly
Out anon they shall hie
On earth to grow and multiply:
I will that so it be.

NOAH   Lord I thank thee through thy might;   300
Thy bidding shall be done in *hight,*   *haste*
And as fast as I may *dight*   *prepare*
I will do thee honour

And to thee offer sacrifice.
Therefore *comes in all wise*   *come by all means*
For of these beasts that been his
Offer I will this *store.*   *quantity*

Then going forth from the Ark with all his family, he shall take his animals and birds and shall offer them and make sacrifice

Lord God in majesty,
That such grace hath granted me
Where all was *lorn,* saved to be,   *lost*
Therefore now I am *boun,*   *prepared*
My wife, my childer, my *meiny,*   *company*
With sacrifice to honour thee   310
With beasts, fowls, as thou mayst see,
And full devotion.

GOD   Noah, to me thou art full *able,*   *obedient*
And thy sacrifice acceptable,
For I have found thee true and stable;
On thee now must I *myne;*   *think*

Warry Earth I will no more   *curse*
For man's sins that grieves me sore,
For of youth man *full yore*   *from earliest times*
Has been inclined to sin.   320

You shall now grow and multiply,
And earth again to *edify,*   *settle*

Each beast, and fowl that may fly,
Shall be *feared* of you;   *afraid*

And fish in sea that may fleet
Shall sustain you, I thee *behet*.   *promise*
To eat of them *ye ne let*   *you need not refrain*
That clean been you may know.   *which you know to be clean*

Thereas you have eaten before
Grass and roots since you were bore,   330
Of clean beasts now, less and more,
I give you leave to eat.

Save blood and flesh *both in fere*   *together*
Of *rough* dead carrion that is here,   *wrongly killed*
Eat not of that in no manner,
For that ay you shall *let*.   *forgo*

Manslaughter also you shall flee,
For that is not pleasant unto me;
They that shed blood, he or she,
Oughtwhere amongst mankind,   340

That blood *foully* shed shall be   *sinfully*
And vengeance have, that men shall see.
Therefore beware now all ye
You fall not into that sin.

A *forward,* Noah, with thee I make,   *covenant*
And all thy seed, for thy sake,
Of such vengeance for to *slake,*   *loosen*
For now I have my will.

Here I *behet thee a hest*   *promise you a promise*
That man, woman, fowl ne beast,   350
With water, while this world shall last,
I will no more *spill*.   *kill*

My *bow* between you and me   *rainbow*
In the firmament shall be
By very token that you shall see
That such vengeance shall cease,

That man ne woman shall never more
Be *wasted* with water, *as hath before;*   *destroyed*   *as before*
But *for* sin that grieveth me sore   *because of*
Therefore this vengeance was.   360

Where clouds in the welkin been
That *ilke bow* shall be seen   *same rainbow*
In tokening that my wrath and *tene*   *fury*
Shall never thus *wroken* be.   *avenged*

The string is turned towards you,
And toward me is bent the bow,
That such weather shall never show,   *as a sign that*
And this *behight* I thee.   *swear*

My blessing now I give thee here
To thee, Noah, my servant dear,
For vengeance shall no more appear;
And now farewell, my darling dear.

Here ends the Third Pageant

37

6   What are your initial reactions to this as a work of art?

a   You may feel that it is rather childish—and I will try to answer that in a moment.

b   You may, on the other hand, have liked the simplicity and lucidity of the presentation. The Chester cycle, on the whole, does not have diversions like those in the Wakefield *Second Shepherds' Pageant*. There is one exception in this pageant, though: Mrs Noah and her gossips. **Make a note about their function in the story and in the drama.** We will return to them later.

7   Is the simplicity necessarily a disadvantage? This play was written for performance by the water-carriers and those who drew water from the River Dee: I cannot believe that in any age this profession would attract intellectuals. (The pageant was given to them as being appropriate to their trade: it is even possible that they may have improvised water-machines to create the effect of a deluge, though there is no indication of this in our text.) They and their audience would expect the main points of the story to be clearly and simply told.

8   In the Middle Ages there were several levels of allegorical interpretation of the story of Noah's Ark. If the author had wished he might have dazzled us with such points as these:

a   That Noah is a type of Christ who saves mankind by wood and water (i.e. the Cross and baptism.

b   The teaching of Saint Augustine:

Undoubtedly, the ark is a symbol of the City of God on its pilgrimage in history, a figure of the Church which was saved by the wood on which there hung the 'Mediator' between God and man, himself man, Christ Jesus.

Even the very measurements of length, height and breadth of the ark are meant to point to the reality of the human body into which he came as it was foretold that he would come. It will be recalled that the length of a human body from head to foot is six times the length from one side to the other and ten times the thickness from back to front. Measure a man who is lying on the ground, either prone or supine. He is six times as long from head to foot as he is wide from right to left or left to right, and he is ten times as long as he is high from the ground up. That is why the ark was made 300 cubits in length and fifty in breadth, and thirty in height. As for the door in the side, that, surely symbolises the wound made by the lance in the side of the Crucified, the door by which those who come to him enter in, because it was from there that the sacraments flowed by which believers are initiated. It was ordered that the ark be made of squared timbers—a

symbol of the four-square stability of a holy life, which, like a cube, stands firm however it is turned. So it is with every other detail of the ark's construction. They are all symbols of something in the Church . . . no one is free to think however that there is no deeper meaning in the written words or that all we should look for is the truth of the facts without regard to any allegorical purpose. On the other hand, no one should think that the whole story is merely a fabric of words and by no means facts, or, whether fact or fiction, that it has no prophetic relevance to the Church [*De Civitate Dei*, XV, 26, 26,].

Well, I would agree that it shows magnificent self-restraint, a high sense of relevance, an artistic conscience on the part of our author to keep all this out of the picture. This is the simplicity which has to be earned, not naïveté.

9   Nevertheless, a few points are made which relate to this symbolism and which the learned members of the audience might pick up. Consider the case of Noah's wife:

a   There is no Biblical authority for this character.

b   She is clearly related to the antifeminist tradition in medieval literature and art. (Compare the wife's treatment of her husbands in *The Wife of Bath's Prologue* and this scene from a bench-end.)[1]

Domestic scene from a bench-end in Westminster Abbey.

c   In the play she is forced into the Art and then cooperates—or so we assume from her silence after line 246. (It is true that she also cooperates in the first scene, but there she serves a choric function.)

d   Notice the references to *Christ*. Some are merely oaths, **but what do you make of lines 222 and 240? Are these just anachronisms? What is the point of the Noah's wife episode?**

[1] You may know that the Wife of Bath visited miracle plays (see her prologue, line 558). And Chaucer's *Miller's Tale* is a kind of parody of a Noah play, with references to medieval acting.

10   You get my sympathy if you say comic relief. I do not think this is an adequate answer in this instance, though. Dramatically, she introduces the opposition to Noah and his crazy project which is implicit in the story; the drinking-song and the slap in the face add reality to what could be a pious legend. We in the twentieth century appreciate this. The fifteenth-century clerk in the audience would have seen something quite different, however. She is the type of the recalcitrant sinner who must be forced to come into the Church. (**Now reread the references to Christ— do you see that they are not just anachronisms?**) When she is in the Ark we may assume that she submits herself to Noah's authority.

11   In the cycles, Noah's Flood is seen as the closing scene of the dispute between God and man which opened with Cain's murder of Abel. (In the Chester cycle this is the play immediately preceding.) It ends with the reconciliation between God and man and the promise conveyed by the rainbow:

Where clouds in the welkin been
That ilke bow shall be seen
In tokening that my wrath and tene
Shall never thus wroken be.

The string is turned towards you
And toward me is bent the bow,
That such weather may never show
And this behight I thee.

With Noah the human race is given a fresh start:

'the second age' begins.

12   These serious points are conveyed well in this pageant. It is, I think, the stylization of the verse, the patterning of the quatrains, which add dignity to the simplicities in the presentation. The dramatist is able to rekindle the imaginative involvement of the child in the adult minds of his audience. This may be a Wordsworthian point to make, but that which enters the mind in early childhood is never forgotten: and those watching the spectacle are drawn deeper into the action than they realize. They will be indulgent towards the lack of illusionist tricks and subterfuges, and open to the deeper truths which the myth presents in symbolic form.

13   When you have studied Brecht I would like you to reread this pageant; you will then see why it is relevant to modern European drama. As Professor Glynne Wickham has said:

The characters . . . succeed in revealing themselves as effectively as do characters of our own drama . . . Noah's wife, young Isaac, and Sir Pilate of the Chester Cycle, for example, are no less recognizably human in terms of what they say than Mrs Tanqueray, Young Woodley or Lord Windermere. The latter group are of course punctilious in the accuracy of their observations on time, date or distance, where the former are scandalously lax; but they pay a heavy price for it. Where Mrs Noah can leave her village, board the Ark, drift on the ocean and land on Mount Ararat, Ibsen's Nora, Shaw's Candida and Pinero's Mrs Tanqueray are virtual prisoners in their drawing-rooms [*Early English Stages* 1, 132].

THE BROME *ABRAHAM AND ISAAC*

1   Introduction

1   The work that I propose on the Brome *Abraham and Isaac* is brief and concentrated, but if you become especially interested in it, you could profitably base a comparative study of medieval dramatic method, didactic drama and aesthetic taste on the subject. The reason is that there are six *Abraham and Isaac* plays, one in each of the four surviving cycles, this one, and the Northampton *Abraham*. R. T. Davies, in his *The Corpus Christi Play of the English Middle Ages,* prints all of them (pp.101-8 and 377-440). His critical comment (*op.cit.* pp.62-8) is brief but good; if you wish to know more about the *Abraham and Isaac* plays and their background you should read pp.145-53 of Rosemary Woolf's *The English Mystery Plays*. As far as dramatic criticism is concerned, both these writers seem to be chiefly concerned with estab-

lishing sound general judgement of the six plays: my concern will be to persuade you to make a full response to, and a sound detailed judgement of, one play, by doing a single exercise.

2   **First, if you do not already know the Bible account on which the play is based, read Genesis 22, 1–19.**

3   Now, as to the *typology* (i.e. the respects in which Old Testament material prefigures New Testament material). Just as God, who willingly for the sake of man offered his son as a sacrifice, so Abraham, willingly for the sake of God, prepared to sacrifice his son to God. The grief of God and Abraham, and their compassion for their sons as sacrificial victims, are essential qualities to portray and understand. And just as

Jesus died willingly for the redemption of man at the instigation of his father, so Isaac was willing to die for his father at the instigation of God. Both Jesus and Isaac are not only willing, but understand the purpose of the sacrifice. The 'ram caught in a thicket by his horns' (Genesis 22, 13), which is sacrificed instead of Isaac, also directly represents Jesus, who was sacrificed in place of mankind. There is more general allegory in the Abraham story in that Isaac is a type of the obedient child, and Abraham is a type of the man obedient to God (strictly speaking, that is in the *tropological* sense, i.e. relating to morals in the whole religious perspective). These remarks on typology, which could be much expanded using the method dear to medieval theologians, help to explain why there are six *Abraham and Isaac* plays, and go some way towards explaining why, of all the medieval plays, they tend to have the strongest dramatic line and to be among the most moving. They deal by analogy with the central matter of the Christian faith, the Passion, and the ritual implicit in them is that of the Mass, which moves from sadness to final joy. The name Isaac is derived from the Hebrew word for 'laugh'. **Now please read the play.**

2 The text of *Abraham and Isaac*

ABRAHAM   Father of Heaven omnipotent,
With all my heart to thee I call;
Thou hast give me both land and *rent,*   *income from land*
And my *lifelod* thou has me sent;   *livelihood*
I thank thee highly ever more *of* all.   *for*

First of the earth thou madest Adam,
And Eve also to be his wife;
All other creatures of them two came;
And now thou hast grant to me, Abraham,
Here in this land to lead my life.   10

In my age thou hast granted me this,
That this young child with me shall *won*;   *dwell*
I love no thing so much, *iwis,*   *certainly*
Except thine own self, dear Father of bliss,
As Isaac here, my own sweet son.

I have diverse children *mo*   *more*
The which I love not half so well;
This fair sweet child he cheers me so,
In every place where that I go,
That no *disease* here may I feel.   *harm*   20

And therefore, Father of Heaven, I thee pray
For his health and also for his grace.
Now Lord, keep him both night and day
That never *disease* nor no *fray*   *harm*   *terror*
Come to my child in no place.

Now come on Isaac, my own sweet child,
Go we home and take our rest.

ISAAC   Abraham, mine own father so mild,
To follow you I am full *presst*   *ready*
Both early and late.   30

ABRAHAM   Come on, sweet child, I love thee best
Of all the children that ever I begat.

GOD   Mine angel, fast *hie* thee thy way,   *hurry*
And on to *middle-earth* anon thou go;   *i.e. the world between heaven and hell*
Abraham's heart now will I *assay*   *make trial of*
Whether that he be steadfast or no.

Say I commanded him for to take
Isaac, his young son that he love so well,

And with his blood sacrifice he make,
If any of my friendship he will feel.   40

Show him the way unto the hill
Where that his sacrifice shall be;
I shall assay now his good will
Whether he loveth better his child or me.
All men shall take example him *be   by*
My commandments how they shall fulfil.

ABRAHAM   Now Father of Heaven that formed all thing,
My prayers I make to thee again,
For this day my tender offering
Here must I give to thee certain.   50
Ah, Lord God, almighty king,
What manner beast will make thee most fain?   what sort of beast will please you most
If I had thereof *very* knowing,   *true*
It should be done with all my *main   strength*
Full soon anon.
To do thy pleasing on an hill
Verily it is my will,
Dear Father, God alone.

ANGEL   Abraham, Abraham, *well thou rest!   be at ease*
Our Lord commandeth thee for to take   60
Isaac, thy young son that thou lovest best,
And with his blood sacrifice that thou make.

Into the *Land of Vision* thou go   *Moriah, see Genesis 22, 14*
And offer thy child unto thy Lord.
I shall thee lead. And show also
Unto God's *hest*, Abraham, accord   *command*
And follow me upon this green.

ABRAHAM   Welcome to me be my Lord's *sand,   messenger*
And his hest I will not withstand.
Yet Isaac, my young son *in land,   on earth*   70
A full dear child to me have been.

I had *liefer*, if God had been pleased,   *rather*
For to a *forebore* all the good that I have.   *done without*
Than Isaac my son should a be *diseased,   harmed*
So God in heaven my soul may save!

I loved never thing so much *in erde,   on earth*
And now I must the child go kill.
Ah, Lord God! My conscience is strongly stirred,
And yet my dear Lord, I am sore afeared
To *groche anything* against your will.   *complain at all*   80

I love my child as my life,
But yet I love my God much more,
For though my heart would *make any strife,   protest*
Yet will I not spare for child nor wife,
But do after my Lord's *lore.   command*

Though I love my son never so well,
Yet smite off his head soon I shall.
Ah, Father of heaven, to thee I kneel,
An hard death my son shall feel
For to honour thee, Lord, withal.   90

ANGEL   Abraham, Abraham, this is well said,
And all these commandments look that thou *save;   observe*
But in thy heart be nothing dismayed.

ABRAHAM   Nay, nay forsooth, I *hold me well paid   count myself well rewarded*

To please my God with the best that I have;
For though my heart be *heavily set*   *grief stricken*
To see the blood of my own dear son,
Yet for all this I will not *let,*   *desist, i.e. from pleasing God*
But Isaac my son I will go *fet,*   *fetch*
And come as fast as ever we *con.*   *know how*   100

Now Isaac, my own son dear,
Where art thou, child? Speak to me.

ISAAC   My fair sweet father, I am here,
And make my prayers to the Trinity.

ABRAHAM   Rise up, my child, and fast come hither,
My gentle bairn that art so *wysse,*   *well-behaved*
For we two, child, must go together
And unto my Lord make sacrifice.

ISAAC   I am full ready, my father, lo!
Even at your hands I stand right here,   110
And whatsoever ye bid me do,
It shall be done with glad cheer,
Full well and *fine.*   *thoroughly*

ABRAHAM   Ah, Isaac, my own son so dear,
God's blessing I give thee, and mine.

Hold this *faggot* upon thy back,   *N.B. typological of the Cross*
And here myself fire shall bring.

ISAAC   Father, all this here will I *pack;*   *load on my shoulder*
I am full fain to do your bidding.

ABRAHAM   Ah, Lord of Heaven, my hands I wring,   120
This child's words *to-wound* my heart.   *greatly wound*

Now, Isaac son, go we our way
Unto yon mount with all our *main.*   *strength*

ISAAC   Go we, dear father, as fast as I may,
To follow you I am full fain,
Although I be *slender.*   *weak*

ABRAHAM   Ah Lord, my heart breaketh in twain,
This child's words, they be so tender!

Ah Isaac, son, anon lay *it* down!   *i.e. the faggot*
No longer upon thy back it hold,   130
For I must make me ready *boun*   *prepared*
To honour my Lord God as I should.

ISAAC   Lo, my dear father, where it is!
To cheer you alway I draw me near;
But father, I marvel sore of this,
Why that ye make this heavy cheer.

And also father, evermore dread I,
Where is your *quick* beast that ye should kill?   *living*
Both fire and wood we have ready,
But quick beast have we none on this hill.   140

A quick beast, I *wot* well, must be dead   *know*
Your sacrifice for to make.

ABRAHAM   Dread thee nought, my child, I thee *red,*   *counsel*
Our Lord will send me unto this *sted*   *place*
Some manner of beast for to take
Through his sweet *sand.*   *messenger*

ISAAC   Yea, father, but my heart beginneth to quake
To see that sharp sword in your hand.

| | Why bear ye your sword drawn so?
Of your countenance I have much wonder. | | 150 |

ABRAHAM   Ah Father of heaven, so I am woe!
          This child here breaketh my heart asunder.

ISAAC   Tell me, my dear father, ere that ye cease,
          Bear ye your sword drawn for me?

ABRAHAM   Ah Isaac, sweet son, peace, peace!
          For *iwis* thou break my heart in three.   *certainly*

ISAAC   Now truly somewhat, Father, *ye think*   *it seems*
          That ye mourn thus more and more.

ABRAHAM   Ah Lord of heaven, *thy grace let sink,*   *let your grace descend*   160
          For my heart was never half so sore!

ISAAC   I pray you, Father, that ye will let me it *wit*   *know*
          Whether shall I have any harm or no?

ABRAHAM   *Iwis*, sweet son, I may not tell thee yet,   *certainly*
          My heart is now so full of woe.

ISAAC   Dear father, I pray you, hideth not from me,
          But some of your thought that ye tell on.

ABRAHAM   Ah Isaac, Isaac, I must kill thee.

ISAAC   Kill me, father? Alas, what have I done?

          If I have trespassed against you ought,
          With a *yard* ye may make me full *mild*;   *stick   obedient*   170
          And with your sharp sword kill me nought,
          For iwis, father, I am but a child.

ABRAHAM   I am full sorry, son, thy blood for to spill,
          But truly, my child, I may not *chese*.   *choose*

ISAAC   Now I would to God my mother were here on this hill!
          She would kneel for me on both her knees
          To save my life.
          And *sithen that* my mother is not here,   *since*
          I pray you, father, *change your cheer,*   *change your mind*
          And kill me not with your knife.   180

ABRAHAM   Forsooth son, *but* if I thee kill   *unless*
          I should grieve God right sore, I *dread*;   *fear*
          It is his commandment and also his will
          That I should do this same deed.

          He commanded me, son, for certain
          To make my sacrifice with thy blood.

ISAAC   And is it God's will that I should be slain?

ABRAHAM   Yea truly, Isaac, my son so good,
          And therefore my hands I wring.

ISAAC   Now father, against my Lord's will   190
          I will never *groche, loud nor still*;   *complain in any way*
          He might a sent me a better destiny
          If it had a been his pleasure.

ABRAHAM   Forsooth son, *but if* I did this deed   *unless*
          Grievously displeased our Lord will be.

ISAAC   Nay nay, father. God forbid
          That ever ye should grieve him *for me*.   *on my account*

          Ye have other children, one or two,
          The which ye should love well by *kind*;   *nature*
          I pray you father, make ye no woe,   200
          For be I once dead and from you go,

I shall be soon out of your mind.

Therefore do our Lord's bidding,
And when I am dead, then pray for me;
But, good father, tell ye my mother nothing.
Say that I am in another country dwelling.

ABRAHAM   Ah Isaac, Isaac! Blessed may thou be!
My heart beginneth strongly to *rysse*   *rebel*
To see the blood of thy blessed body.

ISAAC   Father, since it may be no other wise,   210
Let it pass over as well as I.   *get it over, as I (mean to)*

But father, ere I go unto my death,
I pray you bless me with your hand.

ABRAHAM   Now Isaac, with all my breath,
My blessing I give you upon this land,
And God's also thereto, iwis.
Ah Isaac, Isaac, son! Up thou stand
Thy fair sweet mouth that I may kiss.

ISAAC   Now farewell, my own father so fine,
And greet well my mother *in erde.*   *on earth, i.e. there*   220
But I pray you, father, to hide my *eyne*   *eyes*
That I see not the stroke of your sharp sword,
That my flesh shall defile.

ABRAHAM   Son, thy words make me to weep full sore;
Now, my dear son Isaac, speak no more.

ISAAC   Ah my own dear father, wherefore?
We shall speak together here but a while.

And *sithen* that I must needs be dead,   *since*
Yet my dear father, to you I pray,
Smite but few strokes at my head   230
And make an end as soon as ye may,
And tarry not too long.

ABRAHAM   Thy meek words, child, make me *afray,*   *afraid*
So welawey may be my song   *i.e. I shall mourn unless God's will alone is done*
Except all only God's will.
Ah Isaac, my own sweet child,

Yet kiss me again upon this hill!
In all this world is none so mild.

ISAAC   Now truly, father, all this tarrying
It doth my heart but harm;   240
I pray you father, make an ending.

ABRAHAM   Come up, sweet son, unto my arm;

I must bind thy hands too
Although thou be never so mild.

ISAAC   Ah mercy, father! Why should ye do so?

ABRAHAM   That thou shouldst not *let* me, my child.   *resist*

ISAAC   Nay, father, I will not let you;
Do on for me your will,   *do what you will with me*
And on the purpose that ye have set you
For God's love keep it forth still.   250

I am full sorry this day to die,
But yet I *keep* not my God to grieve;   *care*
Do *on your list* for me *hardily,*   *as you please*   *confidently*
My fair sweet father, I give you leave.

	But father, I pray you evermore,	
	Tell ye my mother *no dell*;	*nothing*
	If she *wost* it she would weep full sore,	*knew*
	For iwis, father, she loved me full well.	
	God's blessing have may she!	
	Now farewell, my mother so sweet,	260
	We two be like no more to meet.	

ABRAHAM Ah Isaac, Isaac, son! Thou makest me to *greet,*   *weep*
And with thy words thou *distemperest* me.   *upset*

ISAAC Iwis, sweet father, I am sorry to grieve you,
I cry you mercy of that I have done,
And of all trespass that ever I did *meve* you;   *cause*
Now dear father, forgive me that I have done.
God of Heaven be with me!

ABRAHAM Ah dear child, leave off thy moans;
In all thy life thou grieved me never once.   270
Now blessed be thou, *body and bones,*   *i.e. altogether*
That thou were bred and born to me.

Thou hast be to me child full good;
But iwis child, though I mourn never so fast,
Yet must I needs here at the last
In this place shed all thy blood.

Therefore dear son, here shall thou lie;
On to my work I must *me stead.*   *apply myself*
Iwis I *had as lief* myself to die   *would be as pleased*
If God will be pleased with my death,   280
And mine own body for to offer.

ISAAC Ah mercy, father, mourn ye no more;
Your weeping make my heart sore
As my own death that I shall suffer.

Your kerchief, father, about my eyes ye wind!

ABRAHAM So I shall, my sweetest child *in erde.*   *on earth*

ISAAC Now yet good father, have this in mind,
And smite me not often with your sharp sword,
But hastily that it be *sped.*   *over quickly*

Here Abraham laid a cloth over Isaac's face, thus saying:

ABRAHAM Now farewell my child so full of grace!   290

ISAAC Ah father, father, turn downward my face,
For of your sharp sword I am ever a-dread.

ABRAHAM To do this deed I am full sorry,
But Lord, thine *hest* I will not withstand.   *command*

ISAAC Ah, Father of Heaven, to thee I cry!
Lord, receive me into thy hand!

ABRAHAM Lo, now is the time come, certain,
That my sword in his neck shall bite.
Ah Lord, my heart *raiseth thereagain,*   *rebels against it*
I *may* not find it in my heart to smite.   *can*   300
My heart will not now thereto,
Yet fain I would *work* my Lord's will;   *do*
But this young innocent lieth so still,
I may not find it in my heart him to kill.
O Father of Heaven, what shall I do?

ISAAC Ah mercy, father, why tarry ye so,
And let me lie thus long on this heath?

<table>
<tr><td></td><td>Now I would to God the stroke were do.</td><td>done</td><td></td></tr>
<tr><td></td><td>Father, I pray you heartily, short me of my woe,</td><td>relieve</td><td></td></tr>
<tr><td></td><td>And let me not look thus after my death.</td><td>wait anxiously for</td><td>310</td></tr>
</table>

ABRAHAM Now heart, why wouldst thou not break in three?
Yet shall thou not make me to my God unmild.   disobedient
I will no longer let for thee   hold back for your sake
For that my God aggrieved would be.
Now hold the stroke, my own dear child.   take

Here Abraham drew his stroke and the Angel took the sword in his hand suddenly

ANGEL I am an angel, thou mayst be blithe,   happy (to know)
That from heaven to thee is sent;
The Lord thank thee an hundred sythe   times
For the keeping of his commandment.

He knoweth thy will and also thy heart,   320
That thou dreadest him above all thing,
And some of thy heaviness for to depart,   take away
A fair ram yonder I gan bring;   did

He standeth tied, lo! among the briars.
Now Abraham, amend thy mood,
For Isaac, thy young son that here is
This day shall not shed his blood.

Go make thy sacrifice with yon ram,
For unto heaven I go now home.
Now farewell, blessed Abraham.   330
The way is full gain that I mote gone.   straight must go
Take up thy son so free.   noble

ABRAHAM Ah Lord, I thank thee of thy great grace!
Now am I yethed in diverse wise.   comforted ways
Arise up, Isaac, my dear son, arise!
Arise up sweet child, and come to me.

ISAAC Ah mercy, father, why smite ye not?
Ah, smite on father, once with your knife!

ABRAHAM Peace, my sweet son, and take no thought,
For our Lord of heaven hath grant thy life   340
By his angel now,

That thou shalt not die this day, son, truly.

ISAAC Ah father, full glad then were I,
Iwis, father, I say iwis
If this tale were true!

ABRAHAM An hundred times, my son fair of hue,
For joy thy mouth now will I kiss.

ISAAC Ah my dear father Abraham,
Will not God be wroth that we do thus?

ABRAHAM No no, harly, my sweet son,   certainly   350
For he hath sent us yon same ram
Hither down to us.

Yon beast shall die here in thy stead
In the worship of our Lord alone;
Go fetch him hither, my child indeed.

ISAAC Father, I will go hent him by the head,   seize
And bring yon beast with me anon.

Ah sheep, sheep! Blessed may thou be
That ever thou were sent down hither!
Thou shall this day die for me   360

In the worship of the Holy Trinity.
Now come fast and go we together
To my father in *hye*;   *haste*
Though thou be never so gentle and good,
Yet had I *liefer* thou sheddst thy blood,   *rather*
Iwis, sheep, than I.

Lo father, I have brought here full *smart*   *quickly*
This gentle sheep, and him to you I give.
But Lord God, I thank thee with all my heart,
For I am glad that I shall live   370
And kiss once my dear mother.

ABRAHAM   Now be right merry, my sweet child,
For this quick beast that is so mild
Here shall I present before all other.

ISAAC   And I will fast begin to blow,
This fire shall burn a full good speed.
But father, while I stoop down low,
Ye will not kill me with your sword, I trow?

ABRAHAM   No, *harly,* sweet son, have no dread,   *certainly*
My mourning is past.   380

ISAAC   Yea, but I would that sword were in a *gleed,*   *fire*
For iwis, father, it make me full ill aghast.

Here Abraham made his offering, kneeling and saying thus:

ABRAHAM   Now Lord God of Heaven in Trinity,
Almighty God omnipotent,
Mine offering I make in the worship of thee,
And with this *quick* beast I thee present.   *living*
Lord, receive thou mine intent,
As thou art God and ground of our *gree.*   *grace.*

GOD   Abraham, Abraham, well may thou *speed,*   *prosper*
And Isaac, thy young son thee by!   390
Truly Abraham, for this deed
I shall multiply *your botherys seed*   *the seed of both of you*
As thick as stars be in the sky,
Both more and less;   *big and small, i.e. all*
And as thick as gravel in the sea,
So thick multiplied your seed shall be;
This grant I you for your *goodness.*   *benefit*

Of you shall come fruit great
And ever be in bliss without end,
For ye dread me as God alone   400
And keep my commandments every one.
My blessing I give, wheresoever ye *wend.*   *go*

ABRAHAM   Lo! Isaac my son, how think ye
By this work that we have wrought?
Full glad and blithe we may be
Against the will of God that we *grucched* not   *complained*
Upon this fair heath.

ISAAC   Ah father, I thank our Lord *every dell*   *every whit*
That my wit served me so well
For to dread God more than my death.   410

ABRAHAM   Why, dearworthy son, were thou adread?
Hardily, child, tell me *thy lore.*   *boldly*   *what you think*

ISAAC   Yea, by my faith, father, now *have I red,*   *I believe*
I was never so afraid before
As I have been at yon hill.

But by my faith, father, I swear
I will nevermore come there
But it be against my will.

ABRAHAM Yea, come on with me, my own sweet son,
And homeward fast now let us gon.   420

ISAAC By my faith, father, thereto I *un,* *agree*
I had never so good will to go home
And to speak with my dear mother.

ABRAHAM Ah, Lord of heaven, I thank thee,
For now may I lead home with me
Isaac, my young son so *free,* *noble*
The gentlest child above all other.

Now go we forth, my blessed son.

ISAAC I grant, father, and let us gon,
For by my troth, were I at home
I would never go out *under that form,* *in that manner*   430
This may I well avow.
I pray God give us grace *evermo* *evermore*
And all *tho that we be holding to.* *those that we are associated with*

DOCTOR Lo, sovereigns and sires, now have we showed
This solemn story to great and small:
It is good learning to *learned and lewd,* *scholarly and lay people*
And the wisest of us all
Withouten any barring, *bar none*
For this story sheweth you here   440
How we should keep to our *power* *best ability*
God's commandments without *groching.* *complaining*

Trow ye sires, *and* God sent an angel *believe   if*
And commanded you your children to slain,
By your troth is there any of you
That either would *groche or strive thereagain?* *complain or fight against it*

How think ye now, sires, thereby?
I trow there be three or a four or *mo;* *more*
And these women that weep so sorrowfully
When that their children die them *fro,* *from*
As nature will and kind, *as nature requires*
It is but folly, I may well avow,
To groche against God or to grieve you,
For you shall never see him *mischiefed,* well I know, *discomfited*
By land nor water, have this in mind.

And groche not against our Lord God
In *weal* or woe, *whether* that he you send, *wealth   whichever*
Though ye be never so hard *bestead,* *beset*
For when he will, he may it amend.

His commandments truly if ye keep with good heart,   460
As this story hath now showed *you before,* *to you already*
And faithfully serve him while ye be *quart,* *in good health*
That ye may please God both even and morn,
Now Jesu, that weareth the crown of thorn,
Bring us all to heaven-bliss!

Finis

4   For the single exercise that I propose on the Brome *Abraham and Isaac*, which is an investigation of its dramatic pathos—an ingredient you have already met in Greek and other plays, and which appears to me one of the most widely-found qualities of great theatre—I must provide some qualifying material in the form of two judgements of the play by critics whom I have already mentioned. The first is R. T. Davies:

That Isaac is a child, in the Brome play, makes more pathetic the varied devices by which this play plucks at the heart and exploits the sentimental potentialities of the situation more than any other does. This movement of the heart has both a moral and a typological justification: children should be obedient as Isaac, whatever their painful difficulties, and the obedient suffering of Christ on behalf of man was no less tragically human for being that of God the Son. But the play is singularly plangent and the invention of verisimilar dialogue and realistic psychology outstandingly ample and confident [*The Corpus Christi Play of the English Middle Ages*, p.65].

The second is Rosemary Woolf:

The Brome play is a little more ample [i.e. than the Ludus Conventriae *Abraham*], Isaac's compassion for his parents being yet more intensified, and his willingness to die being yet more movingly expressed. The amplifications are felicitous, but the general effect of the accumulation comes close to excess [*The English Mystery Plays*, p.151].

A little further on, in discussing the possible relation of two of the *Abraham* texts, Miss Woolf remarks: '...the Brome author may have embellished the Chester text with sentimental variations on the basic pattern...' (Note this second use of the word 'sentimental' in criticism of the play.) Miss Woolf's further stricture on the play is one I shall take up in the discussion notes after you have read the play: it concerns the epilogue spoken by the Doctor:

Unlike a typological exposition, this moral is disconcertingly constrictive, and from the purely literary point of view even more infelicitous than the fairly common moral that the play demonstrates—how children should be obedient to their parents. [*The English Mystery Plays*, p.153].

5   In your investigation into the qualities of dramatic pathos, the following suggestions, which I frame as questions, may help:

a   What examples of 'verisimilar dialogue' and 'realistic psychology outstandingly ample and confident' (see Davies, paragraph 4 above) do you find in
i   Abraham

ii   Isaac?
and what is their dramatic function?

b   Do you find that 'the general effect of the accumulation comes close to excess' (see Woolf, paragraph 4 above)? What is the exact effect of the accumulation on you? How would you as producer try to give it practical expression?

c   Forgetting for the moment Rosemary Woolf's stricture on the role of the Doctor (a doctor of theology, of course), assess the effect and purpose of the Epilogue. It is worth mentioning at this point that of all the *Abraham* plays, only the Chester play contains an explanation of the typology: the last eight lines of this play, spoken by 'Expositor', are:

By Abraham I may understand
The father of heaven that can *fand*   *undertake*
With his son's blood to break that *band*   *imprisonment*
The Devil had brought us to.

By Isaac understand I may
Jesu that was obedient ay
His father's will to work alway,
His death to *underfong*.   *receive*

That epilogue effectively distances the human into the divine.

Discussion

6   Briefly, I agree with Davies about the 'movement of the heart', which I find satisfying and harmonious throughout. That does not mean that, as a producer, I should expect successfully to communicate the movement to an audience. But I should apply what, for me, is a golden rule: I should look for the fundamental structure of the whole action of the play, which in this case is a single longish scene, and relate the detail of the speech and the action to its rhythms. I identify two main movements. The first is the long downward movement to the climax (which is the moment when Abraham raises his sword to kill Isaac). The second is a sudden upward movement which begins with the appearance of the Angel, and broadens into relief, joy and thanksgiving. (I deliberately disregard the epilogue for the time being.) The first of these movements proceeds by conflict of two kinds: one is the conflict between natural human feeling and the desire to serve God, which takes place within both characters; and the other is a reluctant conflict between the two characters as they struggle to accommodate themselves and each other within the dreadful frame of divine necessity. Both these conflicts are resolved by the Angel's seizing of

Abraham's sword. (You might try supplying the missing stage directions for lines 314–31.)

7 The 'verisimilar dialogue' and the 'realistic psychology' are the means of progress in these conflicts, and nearly every step is an accumulation of pathos, as Rosemary Woolf suggests. The job of a producer is to see that the progress is harmonious; not necessarily exactly gradual, but *variously and intelligibly cumulative.* To get the right intensifying effect he will not, for example, in the passage during which Isaac learns what his fate is to be (110–70), make too much of the first pathetic ironies. I should be inclined to establish an initial mood by having Isaac somersault exuberantly at line 113, and be very brisk with the loading of faggots and the uphill journey. I should delay the child's first uneasiness until 147, and should not let it last through his first attempts to comfort his father (157–66). There is a kind of blandness in the simplicity of Isaac's words and reactions to the news that his father intends to kill him, rather like that of some of the peasant utterances in Pasolini's film of *The Decameron,* in which many of the parts were taken not by actors, but by ordinary Italian people. I should let that blandness come through, because it is a long time before Isaac becomes completely terrified (292) in spite of his intellectual acceptance. The awful thing for Isaac is that Abraham says he must kill him some time before revealing that it is God's command (see lines 167–83). Abraham is so upset at his own predicament that he forgets the one thing that will keep him human in his son's eyes. Then allowing for the typological interpretation of binding (244), laying down (277) and blindfolding (290) Isaac, which must in the action of the play carry the kind of ritual force appropriate to the torturing of Jesus at the crucifixion, the climax of pathos must be reached only at Isaac's last speech (306–10), which should be a cry of agony something like Jesus's *'Eli, Eli, lama sabachthani?'* (Matthew 27, 46). I do not find the comparative distancing of *'consummatum est'* (John 19, 30) in Isaac's words or demeanour. At the moment before his imagined death, the child

Isaac has come a long way from the typically medieval knightly acceptance of his fate that he earlier expressed:

He [i.e. God] might a sent me a better destiny
If it had a been his pleasure.
(192–3)

In the second movement, there must be relief for the audience, but of the right kind: it is supplied by Isaac's delighted blessing of the 'gentle sheep' (358–68) which is to suffer sacrifice instead of him. But a device that binds the two parts realistically is Isaac's continued fear of his father's sword. I should make much of that big, glittering weapon, and make Isaac apprehensive of it throughout.

8 I disagree with Rosemary Woolf's opinion, because I find the Doctor's epilogue effective. It is unusual in emphasizing not the central matters of the crucifixion and the redemption of man, but two aspects of the typological meaning of the play which might particularly affect the emotions and conduct of the audience. The Doctor is practising one of the first rules of teaching, which is to relate the subject-matter to the life of his students—to challenge them to identify themselves with the protagonist Abraham. His audience would have particular experience of infant mortality through the plague or other sickness, and the lessons he brings home to them (not to give way to immoderate grief, and to bow to the will of God) had just been marvellously though painfully exemplified in the foregoing pageant.

9 Finally, if you find that a pathos which can be resolved by the flick of a god's finger can never be tragic, especially when a few hours' suffering on the cross or a few years' suffering on earth can be rewarded by an eternity of bliss, you may be fairly certain that there were people like you among the original audiences, and that they were, nevertheless, like me, interested and moved by an art which successfully expressed human suffering and joy.

THE YORK CORPUS CHRISTI PLAY

1 Please read the play carefully first of all. Then make notes on:

a What actions are presented in this pageant?

b What would the actors need to do to give the necessary illusion of reality, while avoiding hurting the actor playing Christ?

c What is the verse form? Comment on the way in which the soldiers' speeches and Christ's speeches exploit this form.

Christ Nailed to the Cross – a picture from c. 1450 by the Master of the Karlsruher Passion.

1 The text of the York *Crucifixion*

The Thirty-Fifth Pageant: The Pinners and Painters

Four soldiers with Jesus

SOLDIER 1	Sir Knights, take heed hither *in hye,*	*at once*
	This deed *ondergh* we may not *draw.*	*without trouble do*
	Ye wot yourself as well as I	
	How lords and leaders of our law	
	Has given *doom* that this dolt shall die.	*judgement*
SOLDIER 2	Sir, all their counsel well we know	
	Since we are comen to Calvary;	
	Let *ilke* man help now as *him awe.*	*each he ought*
SOLDIER 3	We are all ready, lo,	
	That *forward* to fulfil.	*agreement*
SOLDIER 4	Let hear how we shall do,	
	And go we *tyte theretill.*	*speedily thereto*
SOLDIER 1	It may not help here for to *hone*	*delay*
	If we shall any *worship win.*	*honour gain*
SOLDIER 2	He must be dead *nedelyngis* by noon.	*necessarily*
SOLDIER 3	Then is good time that we begin.	
SOLDIER 4	Let *ding* him down; then he is done,	*knock*
	He shall not *dere* us with his din.	*hurt*
SOLDIER 1	He shall be *set* and *learned* soon,	*beaten taught*
	With *care* to him and all his kin.	*sorrow*
SOLDIER 2	The foulest death of all	
	Shall he die for his deeds.	

10

20

| SOLDIER 3 | That means *cross* him we shall. | *crucify* |
| SOLDIER 4 | Behold *so right he redes.* | *he (i.e. the Third Soldier) gives correct advice* |

SOLDIER 1   Then to this work us must take heed,
So that our working be not wrong.

SOLDIER 2   None other *note* to *neven* is need,   *business name*
But let us haste him for to hang.

SOLDIER 3   And I have *gone for* gear, good speed,   *brought*
Both hammers and nails large and long.   30

SOLDIER 4   Then may we boldly do this deed.
Come on, let kill this traitor strong.

SOLDIER 1   *Fair might ye fall in fere*   *you may do well in company*
That has wrought on this wise.

SOLDIER 2   Us needs *nought for to lere*   *nothing to learn*
Such *faitoures* to chastise.   *pretenders*

SOLDIER 3   Since ilke thing is right arrayed,
The wiselier now work may we.

SOLDIER 4   The cross on ground is goodly *graied,*   *prepared*
And bored even as it ought to be.   40

SOLDIER 1   Look that the lad *on length* be laid   *along*
And made me *thane unto this tree*.   *fixed firm to this cross*

SOLDIER 2   For all his *fare* he shall be *flayed;*   *boasting terrified*
That *on assay* soon shall ye see.   *when it is tried*

SOLDIER 3   Come forth, thou cursed knave,
Thy comfort soon shall *kell*.   *cool*

SOLDIER 4   Thine *hire* here shall thou have.   *payment*

SOLDIER 1   Walk on; now work we well.

JESUS   Almighty God, my father *free,*   *noble*
Let these matters be made in mind.   50
Thou bade that I should *buxom* be,   *obedient*
For Adam plight for to be *pined*.   *tortured*
Here to death I oblige me
From that sin to save mankind,
And sovereignly beseech I thee
That they for me may favour find.
From the fiend them defend
So that their souls be safe
In *wealth* withouten end;   *well-being*
I *keep* nought else to crave.   *care*   60

SOLDIER 1   Wee! *Hark,* sir knights, for *Mahound's* blood!   *listen Mahomet's*
Of Adam-kind is all his thought.

SOLDIER 2   The *warlock waxes* worse than *wood;*   *madman grows mad*
This *doleful* death he dreadeth not.   *painful*

SOLDIER 3   Thou should *have mind with main and mood*   *think as hard as you can*
Of wicked works that thou has wrought.

SOLDIER 4   *I hope that he had been as good*   *I think he should have been good enough to stop saying such*
Have ceased of saws that he up sought.   *things as he thought up*

SOLDIER 1   Those *saws shall rue him sore*   *sayings he shall bitterly regret*
For all his *sauntering* soon.   *babbling*   70

SOLDIER 2   Ill speed them that him spare
Till he to death be done.

SOLDIER 3   Have done *belyve*, boy and make thee *boun,*   *quickly   ready*
            And bend thy back unto this *tree.*   *i.e. cross*

SOLDIER 4   Behold, himself has laid him down
            In length and breadth as he should be.

SOLDIER 1   This traitor here *teynted* of treason,   *convicted*
            Go fast and fit him then, ye three.
            And since he claimeth kingdom with crown,
            Even as a king here *have* shall he.   *i.e. have it*   80

SOLDIER 2   Now *certes,* I shall not *fine*   *certainly   stop*
            Ere his right hand *be fast.*   *is secured*

SOLDIER 3   The left hand then is mine,
            Let see who *bears him* best.   *acquits himself*

SOLDIER 4   His limbs *on length* then shall I lead.   *to their full length*
            And even unto the *bore* them bring.   *bore-hole*

SOLDIER 1   Unto his head I shall take heed,
            And with mine hand help him to hang.

SOLDIER 2   Now since we four shall do this deed,
            And *meddle with* this *unthrifty* thing,   *are involved in   unprofitable*   90
            Let no man *spare for special speed*   *try less than his hardest*
            Till that we have made ending.

SOLDIER 3   This *forward* may not fail,   *agreement*
            Now are we right arrayed.

SOLDIER 4   This boy *here in our bail*   *held confined by us*
            Shall *bide* full bitter *brayde.*   *undergo   sudden injury*

SOLDIER 1   Sir knights, say, now *work we ought?*   *are we doing anything, i.e. useful?*

SOLDIER 2   Yes, certes, I *hope* I hold this hand.   *think*

SOLDIER 3   And to the *bore* I have it brought   *bore-hole*
            Full *busomly* withouten *band.*   *unresistingly   bonds*   100

SOLDIER 4   Strike on then hard, *for him thee bought.*   *by him that redeemed you*

SOLDIER 1   Yes, here is a *stub* will stiffly stand,   *thick nail*
            Through bones and sinews *it shall be sought.*   *i.e. if you want to find it*
            This work is well, I will *warande.*   *guarantee*

SOLDIER 2   Say sir, how do we there?
            This *bargain may not blin.*   *job will never end*

SOLDIER 3   *It fails a foot and more,*   *it is a foot or more short*
            The sinews are so *gone in.*   *shrunk*

SOLDIER 4   I *hope* that mark amiss be bored.   *think*

SOLDIER 2   Then must he bide in bitter *bale.*   *pain*   110

SOLDIER 3   In faith, it was *over-scantly scored;*   *inaccurately marked*
            That makes it *foully* for to *fail.*   *badly   match*

SOLDIER 1   Why carp ye so? *Fast* on a cord   *fasten*
            And tug him to by top and tail.

SOLDIER 3   Yea, thou commands *lightly* as a lord,   *as readily*
            Come help to haul, *with ill hail.*   *curse you*

SOLDIER 1   Now certes that shall I do,
            Full snelly as a snail.   *as quickly*

SOLDIER 3   And I shall *tacche* him too   *fasten*
            Full *nemely* with a nail.   *nimbly*   120

            This work will hold, that dare I *heete,*   *swear*
            For now are *feste faste* both his hands.   *fastened securely*

SOLDIER 4	Go we all four then to his feet,	
	So shall our *space* be *speedily* spent.	*time* *well*
SOLDIER 2	Let see *what bourd his bale might bete;*	*what joke might reduce his suffering*
	Thereto my back now would I bend.	
SOLDIER 4	Ow! This work is all *unmeet,*	*badly done*
	This boring must all be *amende.*	*done again*
SOLDIER 1	Ah, peace man, *for Mahound,*	*for Mahomet's sake*
	Let no man *wot* that wonder!	*know*
	A rope shall *rugge* him down	*roughly pull*
	If all his sinews go asunder.	*even if*
SOLDIER 2	That cord full *kindly* can I *knit*	*properly tie on*
	The comfort of this *carl* to *kell.*	*churl cool*
SOLDIER 1	*Fest* on then fast that all be fit,	*fasten*
	It is *no force how fell he feel.*	*no matter how bad he feels*
SOLDIER 2	Lug on ye both a little yet.	
SOLDIER 3	I shall not cease, *as I have seele.*	*as I hope for (eternal) bliss*
SOLDIER 4	And I shall *fond* him for to hit.	*try*
SOLDIER 2	Oh haul!	
SOLDIER 4	Ho now, I hold it well.	
SOLDIER 1	Have done, drive in that nail	
	So that no fault be found.	
SOLDIER 4	This working would not fail	
	If four bulls here were bound.	*i.e. if four bulls were doing the work*
SOLDIER 1	These cords have evil increased his pains,	
	Ere he were *till* the borings brought.	*to*
SOLDIER 2	Yea, asunder are both sinews and veins	
	On *ilke* side, *so have we sought.*	*each as we have wanted*
SOLDIER 3	Now all his *gauds* nothing him gains,	*tricks*
	His *sauntering* shall *with bale be bought.*	*babbling, i.e. preaching be paid for with suffering*
SOLDIER 4	I will go say to our sovereigns	
	Of all these works *how we have wrought.*	*how (well) we have done*
SOLDIER 1	Nay sirs, another thing	
	Falls first to you and me:	
	I bade we should him hang	
	On high that men might see.	
SOLDIER 2	We *wot* well *so their words wore,*	*know that was what they said*
	But sir, that deed will do us *dere.*	*harm*
SOLDIER 1	It *may not mend* for to *moot* more,	*will not help argue*
	This *harlot* must be hanged here.	*rascal*
SOLDIER 2	The mortice is made *fit therefore.*	*ready for it*
SOLDIER 3	*Fest on* your fingers then *in fere.*	*take hold with together*
SOLDIER 4	I ween it will never come *thore:*	*there*
	We four raise it not right *to yere.*	*this year*
SOLDIER 1	Say man, why carps thou so?	
	Thy lifting was but light.	
SOLDIER 2	He means there must be *mo*	*more*
	To heave him up on height.	

130

140

150

160

SOLDIER 3	Now certes, I *hope* it shall not need *consider*	
	To call to us more company.	170
	Methinks we four should do this deed	
	And bear him to yon hill on high.	
SOLDIER 1	It must be done *withouten dread*; *doubtless*	
	No more! But look ye be ready;	
	And this part shall I lift and *lead*; *carry*	
	On length he shall no longer lie. *horizontal*	
	Therefore now makes you *boun*! *ready*	
	Let bear him to yon hill.	
SOLDIER 4	Then will I bear here down	
	And *tend* his toes *untill*. *attend unto*	180
SOLDIER 2	We two shall see *till either side*, *i.e. to each side of the cross*	
	For else this work will *wry* all wrong. *go*	
SOLDIER 3	We are ready! In God, sirs, abide,	
	And let me first his feet up *fong*. *take*	
SOLDIER 2	Why *tent* ye so to *tales this tide?* *attend talk at this time*	
SOLDIER 1	Lift up!	
SOLDIER 4	Let see!	
SOLDIER 2	Oh! Lift along.	
SOLDIER 3	From all his harm he should him *hide* *protect himself*	
	And he were God. *if*	
SOLDIER 4	The devil him hang!	
SOLDIER 1	For great harm have I *hent*: *taken*	
	My shoulder is asunder.	190
SOLDIER 2	And certes I am near *shent* *worn out*	
	So long have I borne under.	
SOLDIER 3	This cross and I in two must *twin* *sunder*	
	Else break my back asunder soon.	
SOLDIER 4	Lay down again and leave your din,	
	This deed for us will never be done.	
SOLDIER 1	*Assay* sirs, let see if any *gin* *try device*	
	May help him up withouten *hone*; *delay*	
	For here should *wight* men worship win, *strong*	
	And not *with gauds all day to gone*. *play about all day*	200
SOLDIER 2	*More wighter* men than we *stronger*	
	Full few I *hope* ye find. *think*	
SOLDIER 3	This *bargain will not be*, *job will not be done*	
	For certes *me wants wind*. *I am out of breath*	
SOLDIER 4	So *wille of* work never we *wore*; *at a loss with were*	
	I *hope* this *carl* some *cautels* cast. *think fellow spells*	
SOLDIER 2	My burden *set me wonder sore*, *grieved me remarkably*	
	Unto the hill I might not last.	
SOLDIER 1	Lift up, and soon he shall be *thore*, *there*	
	Therefore *fest on* your fingers fast. *grasp with*	210
SOLDIER 3	Oh, lift!	
SOLDIER 1	Wee, loo!	
SOLDIER 4	A little more.	
SOLDIER 2	Hold then!	

SOLDIER 1	How now!	
SOLDIER 2	The worst is past.	
SOLDIER 3	He weighs a wicked weight.	
SOLDIER 2	So may we all four say	
	Ere he was heaved on height	
	And raised *in his array.*	*into his proper position*

SOLDIER 4   He *made us stand as any stones,*   *brought us to a standstill*
    So *boustous* was he for to bear,   *huge*

SOLDIER 1   Now raise him *nemely for the nonce*   *nimbly   at once*
    And set him by this mortice here;   220
    And let him fall in all at once—
    For certes that pain shall have no peer.

SOLDIER 3   Heave up!

SOLDIER 4   Let down, so all his bones
    Are asunder now on sides *seere.*   *several, i.e. everywhere*

SOLDIER 1   This falling was more *fell*   *cruel*
    Than all the harms he had;
    Now may a man well *tell*   *pick out*
    The least *lith* of this lad.   *joint*

SOLDIER 3   Methinketh this cross will not abide
    Ne stand still in this mortice yet.   230

SOLDIER 4   At the first time *it* was over-wide,   *i.e. the mortice*
    That makes it *wave,* thou may well *wit.*   *wobble   know*

SOLDIER 1   It shall be *set* on *ilke* side   *wedged   each*
    So that it shall no further *flit.*   *move*
    Good wedges shall we take this *tide*   *time*
    And *fest* the foot, then is all fit.   *secure*

SOLDIER 2   Here are wedges *arrayed*   *designed*
    For that, both great and small.

SOLDIER 3   Where are our hammers laid
    That we should work *withal?*   *with*   240

SOLDIER 4   We have them here even at our hand.

SOLDIER 2   Give me this wedge, I shall it in drive.

SOLDIER 4   Here is another yet *ordande.*   *supplied*

SOLDIER 3   Do *take* it me hither *belyve.*   *give   quickly*

SOLDIER 1   Lay on then fast.

SOLDIER 3   Yes, I *warrande.*   *warrant*
    I *thryng them same,* so may I thrive.   *drive them all in*
    Now will this cross full stably stand:
    All if he rave they will not *rive.*   *even if   break apart*

SOLDIER 1   Say sir, how likes thou now
    This work that we have wrought?   250

SOLDIER 4   We pray you says us how
    Ye feel, or faint ye *ought?*   *to any extent*

JESUS   All men that walks by way or street,
    Takes tent ye shall no travail tyne: *take care that you do not miss my suffering*
    Behold mine head, mine hands and my feet,
    And fully feel now *ere ye fine*   *before you finish (looking)*
    If any *mourning* may be *meet*   *sorrow   equal to*
    Or *mischief* measured unto mine.   *misfortune*

My Father, that all *bales may bete*,   *harms can cure*   260
Forgive these men that does me *pine*.   *suffering*
What they work wot they not,
Therefore my Father I crave
Let never their sins be *sought*,   *looked at*
But see their souls to save.

SOLDIER 1   Wee! Hark! He *jangles* like a jay.   *chatters*

SOLDIER 2   Methinks he patters like a *pie*.   *magpie*

SOLDIER 3   He has been doing all this day,
And made great *moving of* mercy.   *appeals for*

SOLDIER 4   Is this the same that *gan us say*   *told us*   270
That he was God's son almighty?

SOLDIER 1   Therefore he feels full *fell affray*,   *cruel onslaught*
And *deemed* this day for to die.   *was condemned*

SOLDIER 2   Yah! *qui destruis templum!*   *thou that destroyest the Temple (Matthew 27, 40)*

SOLDIER 3   His *saws* were so, certain.   *sayings*

SOLDIER 4   And sirs, he said to some
He might raise it again.

SOLDIER 1   *To muster that he had no might,*   *he had no power to do that*
For all the cautels *that he could cast,*   *spells*
All if he were in word so wight,   *even   strong*
For all his force now is he fest.   *despite   made fast*   280
As Pilate *deemed* is done and *dight*,   *commanded   performed*
Therefore I *rede* that we go rest.   *advise*

SOLDIER 2   This *race* must be *rehearsed* right   *action   reported*
Through the world both east and west.

SOLDIER 3   Yah! Let him hang here still
And make *mowes on* the moon.   *faces at*

SOLDIER 4   Then may we *wend at will*.   *go when we please*

SOLDIER 1   Nay good sirs, not so soon.

For certes us needs another *note*.   *business*   290
This *kirtle* would I of you crave.   *tunic*

SOLDIER 2   Nay nay sir, we will look by lot
Which of us four falls it to have.

SOLDIER 3   I rede we draw cut for this coat—
Lo, *see how soon all sides to save!*   *to take all of us into account*

SOLDIER 4   The short cut shall win, that well ye *wot*,   *know*
Whether it fall to knight or knave.

SOLDIER 1   Fellows, *ye thar not flyte,*   *do not argue about it*
For this mantle is mine.

SOLDIER 2   Go we then hence *tyte,*   *speedily*
This travail here we tyne.   *our work here is profitless*

Finis

2 Comments on the York *Crucifixion*

2 Here are my suggested answers to the questions in paragraph 1, p. 51.

a The main points are:
Christ lies down on the cross voluntarily.
One arm is nailed to a hole already bored.
It is then found that the holes do not match the body.
Cords are used to stretch the body.
An attempt is made to lift the cross.
A second attempt is successful.
The cross is carried to 'the hill' and dropped into the 'mortice' (socket).
It is necessary to wedge the cross in its socket.
There is a dispute over the garment.

b The cords are used to fasten the actor; these have got to be *secure*, but not too tight. The pinners (nail makers) would presumably be able to use fearsome-looking nails to some effect. The two attempts give the actors a trial heave, and a second chance to lift the heavy cross and body. The wedging is necessary for safety.

c The play is written in twelve-line stanzas; each stanza contains eight 4-stress lines followed by four 3-stress lines. The verse is alliterative. The soldiers' staccato utterances are played off against Christ's two long speeches. Notice that Christ does not address the soldiers, but God and the audience, and the uninterrupted verse-stanza, the words of which are paraphrases of the liturgy, marks off his speeches as if they are on a different plane.

3 Many critics have commented on the 'cruelty' of this play, and I expect you will probably react strongly in one way or another. **I should like you to note down your first impressions at this point, and be prepared to discuss them with fellow students or your tutor.**

4 For those studying completely on their own, a mock discussion follows. In it, I try to represent points of view which might be taken about the play.

Christianus
A Roman crucifixion in AD 30 may well have been crueller. The York playwright has tried to make the gospel accounts come alive. It's all there in the Bible.

Pius
But do you really see this play as a means to increase devotion among the faithful? All this jeering at Our Lord won't do at all. If I were putting on the York cycle today I should leave out this play.

Spectator
That's an interesting point of view. There used to be a legal obstacle to showing this play: the Lord Chamberlain's regulations didn't allow the Crucifixion to be presented on the stage. Now that we've had our own 'Theatre of Cruelty' you can't call this play cruel.

Modernus
I think there's something psychologically odd about this cruelty. At certain periods the physical details of Christ's suffering are dwelt on *ad nauseum*. In fact, the religious imagination seems to love stigmata, wounds and blood. It's plain sadistic. . .

Politicus
(*Interrupting*) . . . or else it conceals the exploitation of the poor by powerful groups within the Church: the peasants are taught to love their sufferings.

Moderator
Well, yes. . . We are getting away from the play, aren't we? In a recent production I saw, I found it remarkable that *what is done* is more memorable than what is said. The Crucifixion is an icon of western civilization which we are used to seeing everywhere, whatever our own views. To see this enacted is for us an unusually moving experience.

The others, apart from Spectator, begin to converge on Moderator.

Christianus
Atheist!

Pius
Iconoclast!

Modernus
Christian!

Politicus
Sentimental capitalist scum!

They fall upon Moderator and tear him to pieces; Spectator licks his lips. . .

5 At this point you might like to relate your reactions to two pieces of historical information:
a There was a devotional tradition that the nail-holes already bored in the cross did not fit Christ's body (see Rosemary Woolf, *The English Mystery Plays*, p.258).
b The fifteenth century saw extreme forms of religious expressionism (see J. Huizinga, *The Waning of the Middle Ages*). Above right is a famous depiction of the Crucifixion.

I cannot predict your reactions, but would guess that some people who found the York Play 'cruel' might concede that it is not 'exceptionally cruel' in this historical context.

6 The author of this play is usually referred to as 'the York realist'. **Think back over the different styles of presentation in the Wakefield, Chester, and Brome plays. Do you see why the author is called this? Do you agree?** Whether we would now regard 'realism' as a particularly useful term is debatable: **in what sense is Christ's speech from the Cross 'realistic'?** I do not expect you to write a comparative value-judgement of the four plays; the point to grasp is the *variety* and *potentiality* in this drama.

The Crucifixion by Grunewald (c. 1512–16).

3   The York Corpus Christi play in its setting

7   Let us now move on from the York *Crucifixion* to discuss the York cycle of plays in its social and historical context. The aims and objectives of this section are
a   to show the social context of medieval 'miracle plays' by presenting a detailed study of one centre,
b   to illustrate this from original records.

8   The extracts from the charters have been taken from Canon John Purvis's *From Minster to Market Place*. I also acknowledge my indebtedness to Alexandra Johnston and Margaret Dorrell, 'The Doomsday pageant of the York mercers', and should like to thank Alexandra Johnston for corresponding helpfully with me.

Background

9   The four 'miracle plays' which you have been reading were not staged separately in the Middle Ages. Apart from the Brome play of *Abraham and Isaac*, you should remember that they are taken from play cycles, and that these cycles are referred to as 'the play' in medieval documents. The short episodes, referred to as 'pageants', were not thought of in isolation. Therefore, in order to understand this drama, you should try to envisage the pageants in their place in the cycle.

10   The Chester, York and Towneley cycles contained respectively twenty-five, forty-eight and thirty-two pageants. The *Ludus Coventriae* seems to be a conglomerate incorporating non-cycle plays, and if so it is not comparable. The York cycle happens to be the most comprehensive, and since it is the cycle with which you are most closely concerned, here is the list of its pageants as rendered by A. W. Pollard (*English Miracle Plays, Moralities and Interludes*) from the Latin of the *Ordo Paginarum* of 1415.

The order of the Pageants of the Play of Corpus Christi, in the time of the mayoralty of William Alne, in the third year of the reign of King Henry V., anno 1415, compiled by Roger Burton, town clerk.

1 Tanners	God the Father Almighty creating and forming the heavens, angels and archangels, Lucifer and the angels that fell with him to hell.
2 Plasterers	God the Father, in his own substance, creating the earth and all which is therein, by the space of five days.
3 Cardmakers	God the Father creating Adam of the clay of the earth, and making Eve of Adam's rib, and inspiring them with the breath of life.
4 Fullers	God forbidding Adam and Eve to eat of the tree of life.
5 Coopers	Adam and Eve and a tree betwixt them; the serpent deceiving them with apples; God speaking to them and cursing the serpent, and with a sword driving them out of paradise.
6 Armourers	Adam and Eve, an angel with a spade and distaff assigning them work.
7 Gaunters [Glovers]	Abel and Cain offering victims in sacrifice.
8 Shipwrights	God warning Noah to make an Ark of floatable wood.
9 Pessoners [Fishmongers] and Mariners	Noah in the Ark, with his wife; the three sons of Noah with their wives; with divers animals.
10 Parchment-makers Bookbinders	Abraham sacrificing his son Isaac on an altar, a boy with wood and an angel.
11 Hosiers	Moses lifting up the serpent in the wilderness; King Pharaoh; eight Jews wondering and expecting.
12 Spicers	A Doctor declaring the sayings of the prophets of the future birth of Christ. Mary; an angel saluting her; Mary saluting Elizabeth.
13 Pewterers Founders	Mary, Joseph wishing to put her away; an angel speaking to them that they go to Bethlehem.
14 Tylers	Mary, Joseph, a midwife; the Child born, lying in a manger betwixt an ox and an ass, and an angel speaking to the shepherds, and to the players in the next pageant.
15 Chandlers	The shepherds talking together, the star in the East; an angel giving the shepherds the good tidings of the Child's birth.
16, 17 Orfevers [Goldsmiths] Goldbeaters Monemakers	The three kings coming from the East, Herod asking them about the child Jesus; the son of Herod, two counsellors, and a messenger. Mary with the Child, a star above, and the three kings offering gifts.
41 [Misplaced in the MS.] Formerly the Hospital of St Leonards, now the Masons	Mary with the Child, Joseph, Anna, the midwife with young pigeons; Simeon receiving the Child in his arms, and two sons of Symeon.
18 Marshals [Shoers of horses]	Mary with the Child, and Joseph fleeing into Egypt at the bidding of an angel.
19 Girdellers Nailers Sawyers	Herod commanding the children to be slain; four soldiers with lances; two counsellors of the king, and four women lamenting the slaughter of the children.
20 Spurriers Lorymers [Bridlemakers]	The Doctors, the Child Jesus sitting in the Temple in their midst, questioning and answering them. Four Jews, Mary and Joseph seeking Him, and finding Him in the Temple.
21 Barbers	Jesus, John the Baptist baptizing Him.
Vinters [Omitted in the MS]	Jesus, Mary, bridegroom with bride, the Ruler of the Feast with his household, with six water-pots, in which the water is turned into wine.
22 Fevers [Smiths]	Jesus upon the pinnacle of the Temple, Satan tempting Him, with stones, and two angels ministering.
23 Curriers	Peter, James and John; Jesus ascending into the mountain and transfiguring Himself before them; Moses and Elias appearing, and a voice speaking from a cloud.
Ironmongers [Omitted in the MS]	Jesus, and Simon the Leper asking Jesus to eat with him; two disciples, Mary Magdalen washing the feet of Jesus with her tears and wiping them with her hair.
24 Plumbers Pattenmakers	Jesus, two Apostles, the woman taken in adultery, four Jews accusing her.
Pouchmakers Bottlers Capmakers	Lazarus in the tomb, Mary Magdalene, Martha, and two Jews in wonderment.
25 Skinners	Jesus upon an ass with its foal, xii Apostles following Jesus, six rich and six poor men, eight boys with branches of palms, singing

		Benedictus &c., and Zacchaeus climbing into a sycamore-tree.
26	Cutlers Bladesmiths Sheathers Scalers Bucklemakers Horners	Pilate, Caiaphas, two soldiers, three Jews, Judas selling Jesus.
27	Bakers	The paschal lamb, the Lord's supper, the xii Apostles, Jesus girt with a linen towel washing their feet; the institution of the Sacrament of Christ's Body in the New Law; the communion of the Apostles.
28	Cordwaners	Pilate, Caiaphas, Annas, fourteen armed soldiers, Malchus, Peter, James, John, Jesus, and Judas kissing and betraying Him.
29	Bowyers Fletchers [Arrow-featherers]	Jesus, Annas, Caiaphas, and four Jews persecuting and scourging Jesus. Peter, the woman accusing Peter, and Malchus.
30	Tapisers Couchers	Jesus, Pilate, Annas, Caiaphas, two counsellors and four Jews accusing Christ.
31	Littesters	Herod, two counsellors, four soldiers, Jesus and three Jews.
32	Cooks Waterleaders	Pilate, Annas, Caiaphas, two Jews, and Judas bringing back to them the thirty pieces of silver.
33	Tilemakers Millers Turners Hayresters [Workers in Horse Hair?] Bollers [Bowlmakers?]	Jesus, Pilate, Caiaphas, Annas, six soldiers carrying spears and ensigns, and four others leading Jesus from Herod, desiring Barabbas to be released and Jesus to be crucified, and then binding and scourging him, placing a crown of thorns upon his head; three soldiers casting lots for the vest of Jesus.
34	Tunners	Jesus, covered with blood, bearing His cross to Calvary; Simon of Cyrene, Jews compelling him to bear the cross; Mary, the mother of Jesus, the Apostle John informing her of the condemnation of her Son and of His journey to Calvary; Veronica wiping blood and sweat from the face of Jesus with the napkin on which is imprinted Jesu's face; and other women lamenting Jesus.
35	Pinners Latoners Painters	The Cross, Jesus stretched upon it on the earth, four Jews scourging and dragging Him with ropes, and afterwards uplifting the Cross and the body of Jesus nailed to it, on Mount Calvary.
36	Butchers Poulterers	The Cross, two thieves crucified, Jesus hung on the cross between them, Mary the mother of Jesus, John, Mary, James and Salome. Longeus with a lance, a slave with a sponge, Pilate, Annas, Caiaphas, a centurion, Joseph of Arimathea and Nicodemus laying Him in the tomb.
37	Sellers [Saddlers] Verrours [Glaziers] Fuystours [Makers of Saddle Trees]	Jesus despoiling Hell, twelve spirits, six good and six bad.
38	Carpenters	Jesus rising from the tomb, four soldiers armed and the three Maries lamenting. Pilate, Caiaphas [and Annas. A young man clad in white, sitting at the tomb, talking to the women].
39	Winedrawers	Jesus, Mary Magdalene with spices.
40	Broggours [Brokers] Woolpackers	Jesus, Luke and Cleophas in the guise of pilgrims.
42	Escriveners Luminers [Illuminators] Questors [Pardoners] Dubbers [Refurbishers of cloths]	Jesus, Peter, John, James and other apostles. Thomas feeling the wounds of Jesus.
43	Talliaunders [Tailors]	Mary, John the Evangelist, two Angels, and eleven Apostles; Jesus ascending before them and four angels carrying a cloud.
44	Potters	Mary, two Angels, eleven Apostles, and the Holy Spirit descending on them, and four Jews in wonderment.
45	Drapers	Jesus, Mary, Gabriel with two angels, two virgins and three Jews of the kindred of Mary, eight Apostles, and two devils.
	[Omitted in MS] Linen-weavers	Four apostles carrying the bier of Mary; Fergus hanging upon the bier, with two other Jews, [and one angel].
46	Weavers of Woollen	Mary ascending with a crowd of Angels, eight Apostles, and Thomas the Apostle preaching in the desert.
47	Hostlers	Mary, Jesus crowning her, singing with a crowd of angels.
48	Mercers	Jesus, Mary, twelve Apostles, four angels with trumpets and four with a crown, a lance and two scourges; four good spirits and four evil spirits, and six devils.

11   In the following pages we shall try to re-create a fifteenth-century performance of the York Corpus Christi play. From the many docu-

ments which have survived I have tried to select material which is typical rather than quaint, and useful rather than merely entertaining. Obviously the selection from documents is open to question, and from time to time more material becomes available. I think you should realize that some of the older books about these plays—up to say, 1955—tended to stress the 'folksy' and the childish aspects of this drama, calling it 'pre-Shakespearean' with all the attitudes that this implies. You can imagine the use that such books make of documents referring to 'a rib coloured red' (i.e. Adam's), or 'cakes and ale 4½d'. If you have absorbed similar attitudes and prejudices, please recognize them for what they are.

The City of York

12 In the fifteenth century York was the second city in England. It was a major fortress and the seat of an archbishop. It is difficult to obtain reliable figures for the population of medieval towns, but in the 1377 poll-tax, the tax-paying population amounted to 7,248. The walls of the town enclosed 263 acres, and besides houses, shops and warehouses, room was found for forty churches, nine chapels, four monasteries, four friaries, sixteen hospitals and nine guildhalls. It is difficult to calculate the proportion of the population engaged in productive industry. The names of the guilds indicate a wide variety of trading and manufacturing activities, but obviously on a very small scale compared to a modern industrial complex. York's economic status in the fifteenth century seems largely to have been related to the woollen industry, and declined when that passed to the towns of the West Riding.

The guilds

13 The various groups of workers, craftsmen and traders were organized in guilds[1]. In the late fourteenth century there was a strong social commitment to these organizations. While a great deal could be said about the way in which they regulated prices and wages and how they looked after their members in sickness or old age, two other areas of their activity are relevant to our study.

14 Each guild involved itself in *religious* activities. This is not to say that craftsmen were particularly pious; in the Middle Ages religion was simply a *given* basis of human life, and it would have been odd if such activities were omitted. Each craft had its patron saint, and, depending on its wealth, supported a chapel, hospital, or other charitable institution; even the smallest guild would maintain a shrine or an altar light. Craftsmen at Chester, on entering a guild, swore 'to maintain the Corpus Christi procession'; in York there are so many references to money for the Corpus Christi pageants[2] that

[1] These groups of craftsmen are also referred to as 'misteries'. The term 'mystery' (i.e. mystery play) is first recorded in English in the eighteenth century, but 'mystère' is used in medieval French to mean a 'miracle play'.

[2] e.g. Pelters Guild (i.e. Skinners) c. 1390: 'All fines to the craft to be divided, half to the Council Chamber and half to the craft, to maintain their pageant and light'.

The city of York from the late eighteenth century. The city had changed very little since medieval times—the outside walls and the minister are prominent features.

one might feel that the whole economy was arranged to support dramatic activities. But if the play is seen as a religious activity, which was probably supervised and certainly approved by the Church, such expenditure fits into the normal pattern of medieval life.

15 The guilds were powerful forces in *local government*. Although in theory the aldermen were responsible to the men of their wards, and collectively to the whole city, in practice it is usually aldermen with guild support who make up the city council. In York, as in other towns, there was potential conflict between guild and civic interests: the mayor and his council were responsible for the organization of trade, and could overrule the guilds. In the case of the Corpus Christi play the individual guilds seem to have lost control very early on, probably in the period of the Black Death. The right of the council to legislate and fine in this area of jurisdiction is supported by all the documents. I think we can see that, however remotely, this accounts for the feeling of wholeness about the York cycle. It is not a series of playlets, but a continuous play for which the whole city was collectively responsible.

16 The size and strength of individual guilds is important. The city would expect the largest guild to finance the most expensive pageants (the Mercers were given the Last Judgement). Other guilds expanded, shrank or coalesced, and the records show how pageants were combined or reassigned. The figures below were compiled from York documents by Canon Purvis:

In the early fifteenth century seven of the ten gilds connected with iron and metal could muster 79 members, which is an average of between 11 and 12 in a gild, while five gilds making or dealing in wool, cloth or fabrics showed for the same period 325, an average of 65 to a gild. Some figures for individual gilds at specified dates may be illuminating; all the dates fall within a fairly close time bracket. These figures are probably for Masters only, and do not include apprentices, who were no doubt roughly in proportion; many gilds restricted to one the number of apprentices whom a Master might take.

Tapiters'[1] Gild	57 members in the early fifteenth century
Weavers' Gild	50 members in 1395
Tailors' Gild	128 in 1386
Dyers' Gild	59 in 1390
Cordwainers'[2] Gild	59
Ironmongers' Gild	12 in 1342, 13 in 1419
Spurriers' and Lorimers'[3] Gild	17 in 1387
Pinners'[4] Gild	17

[1]Makers of carpets and tapestries.
[2]Shoemakers.
[3]Makers of spurs and other metal harness accoutrements.
[4]Makers of nails.

Founders' Gild	5 in 1396
Cutlers' Gild	10 in 1410
Joiners' Gild	10 c. 1410
Potters' Gild	12 c. 1410
Waxchandlers' Gild	6 in 1417
Saddlers' Gild	34 in 1398
Glovers' Gild	15

17 I would like to pause for a moment and ask you some questions. There have been a lot of facts and figures, and I am not asking you to spend too much time on them now, though you may need to refer to them later.

a What is the scale of this activity? Which of the following approximates to the size and population of fifteenth-century York?

i New York
ii a London borough
iii a large housing estate
iv a civic university

b In what ways do the following resemble a fifteenth-century guild?

i a trade union.
ii an employers' federation.
iii an Open University study centre committee.
iv a football supporters' club.
v a City of London livery company.

18 Here are some specimen answers.
a A large housing estate or a civic university are of about the same size and population as fifteenth-century York.

b i A guild was a *craft* union, looking after working conditions, etc.
ii It was a Masters' union, fixing wages and prices.
iii In size and dedication.
iv In enthusiasm.
v In love of ceremony. The livery companies are descended from the Merchants companies which succeeded the guilds in London in the sixteenth century.

The feast of Corpus Christi

19 The date on which the festival is celebrated varies from year to year. It is the first Thursday after Trinity Sunday, which falls in midsummer. For most of the population it would have been a public holiday. The feast was instituted in 1311 (see paragraph 2, p. 5) and was soon widely celebrated. It is in honour of the Blessed Sacrament, which is the body of Christ; it is also possible that the expression could refer to the Church, and all its members alive and dead, though this is not the usual meaning. Although the Papal Bulls do not require it, the festival was always associated with a procession, in which the Host (the consecrated wafer of the eucharist) was taken through the streets of a city; halts were made at various churches or shrines. The Host was followed by the clergy, members of religious organizations, and the laity. In many towns one of the craft guilds held a procession on Corpus Christi day; in York there was a special Corpus Christi Guild but this was a purely religious organization and had nothing to do with the play. In certain towns the Procession was followed by tableaux on carts, but it is not possible to assert that these tableaux *developed* into plays. Towns had either plays or tableaux, it seems.

20 The earliest reference to the Corpus Christi play at York is dated 1376: 'From one tenement in which three pageants of Corpus Christi are placed, yearly 2s'. (**What does 'pageant' mean?** It seems to refer to those physical elements of the plays which could be stored, i.e. the scenery, properties and possibly costumes. But in other contexts it means the stage to which the scenery was fixed, and the vehicle which transported it.) From other references in the late fourteenth century we may assume that by then the play was regarded as 'ancient'; it may have been in existence from about 1350, and it is even possible that it preceded the festival in some earlier form.

21 Some of you may already be wondering about practical difficulties. Would it be possible to hold a great procession and a play cycle of this size on one day? Does the religious procession precede the pageants as seems to be indicated? What happens when a halt is made to hear the play? Consider this document of 1425:

THE ARRANGEMENT FOR THE DATE OF THE PLAYS AND THE PROCESSION OF CORPUS CHRISTI FOLLOWING THE SERMON OF WILLIAM DE MELTON

By a custom used through many years and running of time, all the craftsmen of the city of York at their own expense every year have made certain sumptuous plays in divers pageants compiled in divers representations of the Old and New Testaments, through divers places of the city on the feast of Corpus Christi, and also at the same time similarly making a solemn procession for reverence of the Body of the Sacrament of Corpus Christi, beginning at the great gates of the Priory of the Holy Trinity, York, and so going in procession to the Cathedral Church of York, then to the Hospital of St Leonard of York, where they left the said Sacrament, there going before them a numerous light of torches and a great multitude of priests clothed in surplices and following them the Mayor and citizens of York with another great company of people flowing together. On which a certain very religious man, William Melton, of the Order of Friars Minor, Doctor of Divinity, a very famous preacher of the Word of God, coming to this city, in many divers sermons of his commended the aforesaid play to the people, affirming that it was good in itself and exceeding laudable. He said, however, that the citizens of this city and others foreigners on the said feast flowing together to it, not only on that play in that feast are much intent in eatings and drunkennesses and shouting and singing and other insolences, but pay very little attention to the service of the Divine Office of that day, and—what is to be deplored—for that reason lose the indulgences graciously granted in this behalf by Pope Urban IV of happy memory, namely to those faithful of Christ who shall be present in a church where that feast is celebrated 100 days, the same number [*to those who shall be present*] at the Mass, to those who shall be present at the First Vespers of that feast similarly 100, at the Second (Vespers) the same, to those who shall be present at the Offices of Prime, Terce, Sext, None and Compline for each of those Hours forty days, and to those who shall be present through the octaves of that feast at the Offices of Mattins, Vespers, Mass and those aforesaid Hours 100 days for each single day of those octaves, as in the Holy Canons issued therefore more fully is contained. And therefore it seemed healthful to the same Friar William, and he led the people of the city [*to accept*] this, that the play itself should be made on one day and the procession on another, so that the people could gather to the churches on the aforesaid feast and be present at the church service so as to obtain the indulgences. Wherefore the Mayor with the Mayor of the Staple of Calais, nine Aldermen, two Sheriffs, and twenty-one of the Twenty-four Council discussed the matter and decided to put it to the Commonalty for acceptance. Four days later, on 16 June 1426, the Commonalty agreed, and it was ordained by common consent that the solemn play which as aforesaid has been played by custom on the feast itself of Corpus Christi, hence forth shall be played every year on Wednesday the eve of the said feast, and that the procession shall be made always in solemn manner on the day of the feast itself, so that the whole then constituted in the said city may be devoutly free for Mattins, Mass, Vespers and other Hours of the same feast and participate in the indulgences graciously granted in that behalf by the said Pontiff of Rome Pope Urban IV.

22 **What points do you gather from this?**

a The Church is concerned about the disrespect shown by the holiday crowds to the religious festival. ('Foreigners' means people from outside the city.)

b 'The play' is not attacked; in fact it is praised by Melton. In general, it was the Lollards, and later the Puritans, who attacked plays in their sermons.

c The separation of play from procession does not seem to present any problem; i.e. the thing is not an integrated whole.

d The guilds are not asked for their opinion.

23 In fact, neither the Church nor the city council seem to have been able to carry this legislation through. Within a few years the play was back on Corpus Christi Day and the procession was held on the day following the play. I hope these preliminary details will help you to understand what follows. I have tried to lead you gently along a plank or bridge from

which we can make an imaginative jump into a very remote world.

A Corpus Christi festival in mid-fifteenth-century York

The eve of Corpus Christi

24 Wednesday evening. A proclamation is made. The mayor and city officers ride out accompanied by one member from each guild dressed in costume from the guild's own play. A *bayn* (hence 'banns') or messenger is charged to go twice round the city and announce:

Proclamacio ludi Corporis Christi facienda in vigiliis Corporis Cristi, Oiez etc., We command of the King's behalf and [of] the Mayor and Sheriffs of this city that no man go armed in this city with swords nor with Carlisle axes nor no other defences in disturbance of the King's peace and the play or hindering of the procession of Corpus Christi, and that they leave their harness [i.e. armour] in their Inns, saving knights and esquires of worship that ought to have swords borne after them, on payment of forfeiture of their weapons and imprisonment of their bodies. And that men that bring forth pageants that they play at the places that is assigned therefor and nowhere else, on pain of forfeiture to be raised that is ordained therefor, that is to say 40s. And that men of crafts and all other men that find torches, that they come forth in array and in the manner as it hath been used and accustomed before this time, not having weapons, carrying tapers of the pageant, and officers that are keepers of the peace on pain of forfeiture of their franchise and their bodies to prison. And all manner of craftsmen that bring forth their pageants in order and course by good players well arrayed and openly speaking, upon pain of losing 100s. to be paid to the Chamber without any pardon. And that every player that shall play be ready in his pageant at convenient time, that is to say, at the mid hour between four and five of the clock in the morning, and then all other pageants fast following each other one after other as their course is, without tarrying, under pain to be made to the Chamber 6s. 8d.

Corpus Christi day

25 Thursday 4.30 am. At the gate of the Priory of Holy Trinity in Micklegate—'at the Trinitie gaits where the Clerke kepys the regyster'—before dawn. A few short prayers and exchanges, to remind us that the Corpus Christi play, like the procession, has always started from this priory which is of right the first station. A scaffold is built against the wall, and the pageant wagon drawn up against it. There is also a hell-mouth at street level. Facing the gates are three tenement buildings; the windows are crowded with faces —'Nicholas Blakburn, William Beniland and others' have paid ten shillings 'for license to have the playing of the plays of Corpus Christi before

their tenements by the gates of Holy Trinity in Micklegate this year'. No doubt they have recouped themselves quite handsomely.

26 Tapers are lit. From somewhere high up God speaks:

Ego sum Alpha et Omega. . .
I am gracious and great, God without beginning

It is *The Creation, and the Fall of Lucifer,* presented by the Barkers (or Tanners). The choir of angels, all dressed in white, sing the *Te Deum.* A light shines out. God creates Lucifer (bearer of light). The Angels sing 'Holy, Holy, Holy, Lord God of Hosts'. Lucifer plans to rule, in Heaven— suddenly—'all goes down'. The bad angels fall, sliding down the scaffolding. Their white garments disappear, or are 'flipped over', so that they are changed to black. They are received into a gaping hell-mouth at street-level. Their light is withdrawn. In the third episode, again in heaven, God creates daylight as the dawn breaks.

27 4.50 am. The Barkers' Pageant moves on to the next station. The Plasterers present *The Creation, to the Fifth Day;* there will follow four plays about *Adam and Eve,* in which, following the greater plot within the whole cycle, the Fall of the Angels leads to the Fall of Man.

28 4.50 am–8.30 am. The Barkers' Pageant will continue to follow the scheduled route and will play at twelve stations according to the following map, and the document (of about 1399) on the next page.

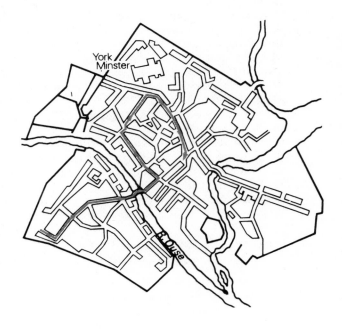

A map of York showing the route of the pageants, from Micklegate, near the walls, over the Ouse into the centre of the city, finishing at the Pavement.

To the honourable men the Mayor and the Aldermen of the city of York the Commons of the same city supplicate that as they make great expense and costs about the play and the pageants of Corpus Christi day which cannot be performed on the same day according as they ought to be because the plays aforesaid are played in so many places, to the great damage and discomfort to the said Commons and the strangers repairing to the city on the same day for the same cause, may it please you to consider that the said pageants are maintained and sustained by the Commons and Craftsmen of the city in honour and reverence of Our Lord Jesus Christ and the honour and profit of the city and to take order that the pageants be played in the places which were limited and assigned by you and the said Commons aforetime, which places are annexed in a schedule to this bill, or in other places each one at the disposition and will of the Mayor and Council of the Chamber, and that he or anyone who goes counter to the establishments and orders aforesaid shall make or incur a pain of 40s. to be forfeited to the Chamber of the Council of the city. And that if any of the pageants be late or delayed by the fault or negligence of the players, they shall incur a pain of 6s. 8d. to the same Chamber.

And they supplicate that these matters be performed or otherwise the said play be not played by the said Commons. And this they pray by God and in the cause of charity for the profit of the said Commons and of the strangers repairing to the city to the honour of God and the nourishing of charity amongst the Commons.

The places where the play of Corpus Christi shall be played. First at the gates of Holy Trinity in Mikelgate. Second at the door of Robert Harpham. Third at the door of John de Gyseburne. Fourth at Skeldergatehend and Northstretehend. Fifth at the end of Conyngstrete towards Castlegate. Sixth at the end of Jubretgate. Seventh at the door of Henry Wyman in Conyngstrete. Eighth at the end of Conyngstrete near the Common Hall. Ninth at the door of Adam del Brigg. Tenth at the gates of St Peter's Minster. Eleventh at the end of Girdlergate in Petergate. Twelfth on the Pavement. And it is ordered that the flags of the play with the city arms shall be delivered in the pageant of Corpus Christi to be placed in the places where the play of the pageants shall be; and that the flags themselves yearly on the morrow of Corpus Christi shall be brought back to the Chamber to the hands of the Mayor and Chamberlains of the city and there kept for the whole year following, on pain of 6s. 8d. to be paid to the use of the Commons by him and those who shall keep the flags beyond the morrow and not deliver them in the way aforesaid.

From this one can see that there had been variations from the ancient playing-places. These are now limited to twelve and each is marked with flags bearing the city arms. (The pageant-vehicles are also marked with the city arms, not the guild emblem—there is one exception to this as we shall see.)

29 9.30 am. By this time the streets are filled with 'strangers'. At the ninth station the Mayor and his guests are watching the sixth pageant,

Cain and Abel. There are topical references to paying tithes and Cain has a comic servant, but these do not distract from the typological point that this act prefigures the murder of Christ. The Shipwrights then present *The Building of the Ark,* and the Fishmongers and Mariners *Noah in the Ark*[1]. As in the Chester Play Noah's wife is reluctant to enter the Ark; the pageants affirm the promise and hope of salvation. The Parcheminers and Bookbinders appropriately present *Abraham and Isaac* (appropriately because of the ram caught in the thicket—animal skins were used in making books). Abraham says that Isaac is

Of *eelde*, to reken right   *age*
Thyrty year and more *sum dele*   *somewhat*

thus making clear the typological identification with God sacrificing Christ. The Old Testament plays end with *Moses and the Destruction of Pharao* (*sic*) in the Red Sea, which prefigures the destruction of the wicked and salvation of the blessed at the Harrowing of Hell.

30 11.15 am. At this point human endurance begins to give out. The sound of 'cooks and their boys crying "Hot Pies! Hot Pies! Fat pigs and geese; come and eat!" and inn keepers calling "White wine of Gascony! Red wine of Spain!"' (paraphrased from *Piers Plowman,* Langland) would ruffle the determination of even the most ascetic spectator. The streets are full of sideshows of all kinds, and one steps carefully to avoid a barber drawing a tooth in the open air.

31 11.45 am. On the way back from the tavern, having missed two plays at the ninth station, it is necessary to hurry towards the Pavement, the last station of all, to catch up with the New Testament pageants. However, is is evident that a brawl has developed in Petergate between the supporters of two pageants, similar to previous disturbances in 1419:

1419 on the morrow of the feast of Corpus Christi (16 June) in the year of Our Lord 1419 7 Henry V, before the Mayor, eight of the Twelve, one Sheriff and fourteen of the Twenty Four, where there came divers Craftsmen of the Skinners' Craft and made a serious complaint that divers Craftsmen of the Carpenters and Cobblers of the said City on the feast of Corpus Christi in the year aforesaid broke their [the Skinners'] torches lighted so that they might be carried in the procession of the said feast before the Body of Christ, and then attacked ['treated', *traxerunt*] them with their clubs and Carlisle axes which they carried there and committed other enormities to the grave disturbance of the peace of our Lord the King and hindering of the play of the procession of Corpus Christi. Because of which

[1] This means that there will be two Noahs. In the same way, there will be many actors playing Christ in the Passion sequence.

complaint there were taken and imprisoned Simon Calton and Benedict Williamson, carpenters, and Thomas Durem, cordwainer, and the said Simon and Benedict coming here before the Mayor and Council of the city in the Chamber and their said transgression being objected to them recognised that they had done the aforesaid things and put themselves in the mercy grace and order of the Mayor and Council of the Chamber of the city, and to do this the aforesaid Simon and Benedict and also John Mosse, William Hyrkeby, Richard Ferrour, William Cunsby, John Haxeby, Thomas Cunnysburgh and John Skathelok, wrights and citizens of York by their writings obligatory are bound in [?100] sterling as in the aforesaid more fully is contained.

32 12.15 pm. On arrival at the Pavement, it is still possible to take up the sequence with the first New Testament pageant. In other cycles there would usually be a special Prophets sequence, but at York this is used as a preface to *The Annunciation*. The Prologue, dressed as a Doctor of Divinity, reminds the audience of the story so far: how man

Was putte oute fro paradyse
And sithen what *sorouse sor warre seene*[1]
Sente unto to hym and to al his.
And how they lay *lange space*[2]
In helle.

The prophets are named down to John the Baptist, and the Annunciation to Mary is accompanied with three songs, concluding with the Magnificat.

33 1.30 pm. Three pageants later (the Shepherds having presented a brooch with a tin bell, two cob-nuts on a ribbon, and a horn spoon), we meet with Herod, a major character in all the cycles, representing the kings of this world. He worships Mahound (Mahomet), and rages at the news of the newborn king:

Kyng! in the devyl way, dogges, Fy!
Now I see wele *ye rothe and rave*[3].
Be ony *skymering*[4] of the skye
When ye shulde knawe othir Kyng or Knave?
Nay, I am Kyng and non but I.

The *Flight into Egypt,* and the *Massacre of the Innocents* follow. Christ is next seen *With the Doctors in the Temple.*

34 2.30 pm. Four short plays on the ministry of Jesus culminate in *The Transfiguration*. At one point '*Hic descendunt nubes, Pater in nube*': 'Here clouds descend, God the father in a cloud'.[1] We are now halfway through the cycle.

35 Pageants XXV–XXXIV present the Passion narrative in detail, leading up to the Crucifixion. This Passion sequence is the heart of the cycle. At each pageant's end, Christ is further tortured or humiliated. One unusual moment—from the Gospel of Nicodemus[2]—occurs in XXXIII, the *Second Trial before Pilate*, when the standard-bearers involuntarily salute Jesus by lowering the colours, and Pilate is forced to stand in his presence. This Pilate, again because of the influence of the Gospel of Nicodemus, is a closely-observed and changeable character who grows in interest throughout the sequence.

36 5.00 pm. Pageant XXXIV, *Christ led up to Cavalry,* begins with a plea for silence. Many of the pageants start like this to gain the audience's attention. This time the First Soldier commands the spectators

Uppon payne of emprisonment that noman appere
To supporte this *traytowe*[3], *be tyme ne be tyde*[4],
Noght are of this *pres*[5] . . .

But help me wholly, all that are here
This *kaitiffe care*[6] to increase

We are identified with the crowd in the streets of Jerusalem—*drawn into* the whole play—so that we are invited to share in the brutality of the *Crucifixion* by the Pinners (nail-makers)[7] which follows.

37 5.40 pm. The Butchers are given the *Death* and *Burial of Jesus,* which is followed by *The Harrowing of Hell*. Here again material is incorporated from the Gospel of Nicodemus. Christ descends into Hell; Adam and the prophets expect a joyful release, the fulfilment of the promises of the Old Testament.

Adam
Four thousand and six hundred year
Have we been here in this *stedde*[8].
Now see I signe of solace *seere*[9],
A glorious gleam to make us gladde.

---

[1] We do not know how this was done, but see no reason to suppose that it was botched. See Glynne Wickham, *Early English Stages,* Vol. 1 for details of special effects in tournaments and spectacles.

[2] An apocryphal gospel containing additional events said to have been witnessed by Nicodemus.

[3] traitor.
[4] at any time.
[5] crowd. .
[6] the sorrow of this wretch.
[7] i.e. the play printed on pp. 00–00.
[8] place.
[9] particular.

[1] woeful sorrows were seen.

[2] for a long time

[3] you are mad

[4] brightness

The devils (prison warders) cannot understand the noisy shouting of their captives. A voice cries out:

Attollite portas principes[1]
Open up ye princes of paynes seere
Et elevamini eternales[2]
Youre yendles gatis that ye have here.

Satan realizes that it is Jesus, who recently caused a deal of trouble about one Lazarus. If allowed to enter, he will ruin hell. But all the devils cannot bar the way, though Satan tells them to '*dynge*[3] that dastarde downe'. The great voice again cries out in the words of the psalm:

Principes, portas tollite,
Undo your gates, ye princes of pryde
Et introibit rex glorie[4]
The King of blysse comes in this tyde.

Satan, like Pharao, is defeated, and Jesus leads out his folk, leaving Cain and Judas and all tyrants in hell forever. Satan falls into a pit, and the patriarchs and prophets ascend to Paradise, David reasserting Psalm 16:

As I have said, yitt say I so:
Ne derelinquas, domine,
Animan meam in inferno[5],
Leave not my saule, lorde, aftir thee,
In depe helle. . .

and others singing '*laus tibi cum gloria*'[6].

38 6.00 pm. There follows a sequence of ten plays on the *Resurrection* and associated events. The angel at the sepulchre, saying 'Here in this place whom have ye sought?' recalls the liturgical origins of this drama (see paragraph 6, p. 6). *The Ascension* calls for more cloud-machinery and the whole cycle culminates, as darkness falls, in *The Last Judgement*.

39 9.00 pm. The five great banners of the Mercers are fixed in their places on the Pavement, replacing the city arms, for this is the only *royal* company. It is the richest guild and the final play is expected to be a magnificent spectacle. The Pageant-Masters (possibly directors?) have a large amount of equipment to organize as we can tell from the following indenture[7] of 1433 (here

presented in my translation of the medieval original belonging to the York Merchant Venturers, and first published in 1971).

This indenture made on the feast of Corpus Christi in the year of Our Lord God 1433 between Richard Louth, master of the Company of Mercers of the City of York, Nicholas Usflete and William Yarom Constables of the said Company on the one side, and William Bedale, William Holbeck, Henry Market and Thomas Curtays then Pageant Masters on the other side, bears witness that the said Master and Constables have delivered to the said Pageant Masters all their parcels [items of property] written below belonging to their pageant safely to keep and to govern for their time and those same parcels to deliver forth again in reasonable time to the next Pageant Masters that shall occupy [be in office] in the next year after and so all Pageant Masters to deliver forth according to this indenture to other Pageant Masters that shall occupy for the year while the Pageant gear lasts.

First: a Pageant with 4 wheels
Hell Mouth
3 garments for 3 devils
6 devils faces in 3 masks [2 faces on each mask]
Array for 2 evil souls that is to say:
    2 tunics
    2 pairs hose
    2 masks
    and 2 wigs
Array for 2 good souls that is to say:
    2 tunics
    2 pairs hose
    2 masks
    and 2 wigs
2 pairs of Angels' Wings with iron in the ends
2 trumpets of white plate and 2 reeds [pipes]
4 Albs for 4 Apostles
3 diadems with 3 masks for 3 Apostles
4 diadems with 4 blonde wigs for 4 Apostles
A cloud and 2 pieces of Rainbow made of wood
Array for God that is to say:
    A Tunic painted with wounds
    A diadem with a gilded mask
A large curtain of red damask painted for the back drop of the pageant
2 other smaller curtains for 2 sides of the Pageant
3 other curtains eleven [feet] broad for the sides of the pageant
A little curtain four-squared to hang behind God
4 Iron poles to support Heaven
4 Finial coterelles [brackets] and an Iron Pin [bolt]
A Brandreth [support] made of Iron for God to sit upon when he flies up to Heaven with 4 ropes at 4 corners
A Heaven of Iron with a wooden centre
2 pieces [of scenery] of red clouds and golden stars attached to Heaven
2 pieces of blue clouds painted on both sides
3 pieces of red clouds with sunbeams of gold and stars for the highest part of Heaven with a long thin border similarly decorated
7 great Angels holding the Passion of God
    One of them has a fane [pennant] of brass and a cross of Iron on his gilded head
4 small gilded Angels holding the Passion

[1] lift up your gates, princes (of hell)
[2] and be lifted up the eternal (gates)
[3] knock.
[4] and the King of glory shall come in.
[5] do not leave, Lord, my soul in hell.
[6] praise to thee with glory.
[7] An agreement between two parties. The two halves were torn apart, leaving jagged edges on both, which could be brought together at a later date to establish authenticity.

9 smaller Angels painted red to move about in the Heaven
A long string to enable the Angels to run about
Two short wooden rollers to get the Pageant out

Endorsement

Item: One banner of red buckram embroidered with gold with the Trinity and with ostrich feathers and with 1 long streamer
Item: 4 small banners with the Trinity on them and coloured red.   1433.

40   The full technical implications of all this are not clear, but the broad indications are that the pageant-wagon was built up with four iron posts bearing a heaven made of iron and wood. This had to carry a great deal of mechanical gear to work the nine smaller angels and God's flying swing. Hell-mouth was placed below, in the street.

41   The pageant begins with a recapitulation by God of the main events of the cycle—Creation, Fall, Passion, and Harrowing of Hell. The Angels are commanded to blow their trumpets. Good and bad souls rise up, and are divided—good to the right of God, bad to the left. God descends to earth. In the second scene God mounts the Judgement Seat to the sound of angels singing. He takes the apostles with him into the pageant-wagon. He then displays the wounds of Christ to the souls below—the angels hold up the symbols representing the Passion. As the scene ends the bad souls are dispatched to hell, and the good received into heaven. To the sound of the angelic choir God flies up into the highest heaven.

42   10.00 pm. The day ends with a feast given by the mayor and council for the distinguished guests. The money spent on this, together with 'presents' to other notable persons 'for the honour of the city' is many times that spent by the Mercers, for example, on the supper for their twenty-one actors:
1433 Chamberlain's Accounts: In presents of bread, wine and fruit, £3–1–2.
1472 Mercers' Accounts: Item to the said players and their fellows for the supper, 10d.

The day after Corpus Christi

43   Friday. On this day the religious procession is held, ending with a sermon in York Minster. The representatives of the guilds march behind their banners; most of the laity and the strangers have already returned to work. The holiday is over.

Comments and questions

44   Such a reconstruction can easily be faulted in particular details, but I have held back from quoting documents to support every statement. A number of queries must be faced, however.

a   How could forty-eight plays of between 200 and 400 lines each possibly be got through in one day? Even at Chester with twenty-five plays, three days were allowed for performance.

b   How many actors were required? Where were they found? Exactly what does payment to actors imply? What about rehearsals?

c   Who wrote this cycle? For whom is it written?

d   What historical judgement can we now reach about the whole affair?

a   Duration

45   Martial Rose, in his introduction to *The Wakefield Mystery Plays,* says of the York cycle:

The playing of 273 lines, including the music and movement, would take about 15 minutes. At the first station, allowing five minutes for the time taken between the end of one pageant and the beginning of another, the whole cycle would last for about 15 hours; if it was started at 4.30 a.m. it would finish at 7.30 p.m.

Even so, there are innumerable difficulties. No wonder that some scholars do not agree that the cycles were presented processionally. See, for example, A. H. Nelson, in *The Medieval English Stage,* pp. 15–81. At one time I felt that only a short selection of scenes could have been staged on any one occasion; this is because there were two other York cycles, now lost, which alternated with the Corpus Christi play in the sixteenth century. The Creed Play is thought to have contained thirteen scenes, and dealt with similar material; the Paternoster Play was probably a series of moralities on the seven deadly sins, and seems to have been the same length as the Creed Play. But would a short selection from the forty-eight plays make sense? It must be said that internal evidence of 'the grand design' of the York cycle would not allow much to be cut. I suspect that some of the pageants in the register were occasionally omitted, but the documents make it clear that heavy fines were levied if guilds did not produce pageants. Poorer guilds asked for permission to be relieved or subsidised, e.g. consider this undated document of about 1421:

The Goldsmiths complain that they used to bear a heavy burden and excessive expenses for producing two pageants in the Corpus Christi play, and now the world is altered with them and they are made more than ordinary poorer in goods: they ask for a subsidy to relieve their unbearable burdens, or to be discharged of one pageant with the unbearable burdens which daily increase by reason of it.

46   It is evident also from the following (dated

1421–2) that there were originally two plays instead of the present York *Crucifixion,* and that it was felt sensible to cut one out.

He who is ignorant of nothing knows and the whole people complains that the play on the day of Corpus Christi in that city, of which the institution was made of ancient time for the sake of great devotion and the extirpation of vices and reformation of morals, alas, is hindered more than usual by the multitude of pageants, and unless a swifter and better caution be provided, it is feared in the shortest process of time will be much more hindered; and the craftsmen of the Painters, Stainers, Pinners and Latoners[1] of the said city, being previously assigned to play separately two pageants in the said play, namely, one of the Stretching and Nailing of Christ to the Cross and the other of the Raising of the Crucifix on the Hill, understanding that by the abbreviation of the matter both pageants could be included together in one pageant and the oracles could be shewn to the people who hear more conveniently to the players, agreed for themselves and their fellow-craftsmen in future that one of their pageants should be deleted and the other kept, accordingly as the Mayor and the Council of the Chamber might wish to order. And on this the searchers and craftsmen of the said crafts came before Richard Russell Mayor of York, the Aldermen and other worthy men here in the Council Chamber situated on Ouse Bridge on the last day of January 9 Henry V, and showed their desire and intention in the above, namely (*15 men named*) of the Pinners' craft, (*4 named*) of the Painters' craft and (*6 named*) of the Stainers' craft. Wherefore the said Mayor, Aldermen and worthy men kindly accepting this and the said craftsmen and commending them for their laudable proposal for themselves and all the craftsmen decreed and ordered by counsel that from this day forward the pageant of the Painters and Stainers shall be removed completely from the said play, and that the craftsmen of the Pinners and Latoners shall take on themselves the burden of playing in their pageant the matter of speeches which formerly was played in their own pageant and the pageant of the Painters and Stainers, and that the Painters and Stainers every year shall collect among them of the men of their craft five shillings sterling and shall pay them to the Masters of the pageant of the Pinners and Latoners for the time being yearly on the eve of Corpus Christi. For failure to pay this, the Mayor and Chamberlains of the city may compel them to pay 40s. to the wardens of the pageant of the Pinners and Latoners for the time being on the Sunday next after the said feast. The Mayor for the time being may take and have one half of the said 40s. to the use of the community, and the pageant wardens of the Pinners' and Latoners' Gild for the time being the other half to the use and upkeep of their said pageant. The representatives of the Painters bound themselves and their craft similarly, provided always that the said craftsmen of the Painter craft and the Stainers shall not meddle at all henceforth with the pageant of the Pinner craft nor with their accounts.

The general weight of the York documentary evidence does imply that somehow most of the forty-eight pageants were performed on Corpus Christi day. Evidently medieval audiences were tougher than today's. They were also more enthusiastic—when would they see any other drama, or indeed entertainment of any kind?

b   Actors

47   There are 320 speaking parts in the York cycle. The Mercers pageant, with its twenty-one actors in all, gives us evidence of the number of non-speaking parts which could be required. So we must allow another 400 for walk-on parts, 'stage managers', pageant masters, and those policing or controlling the movement of the wagons. This is roughly a tenth of the estimated population of York. Records from about 1476 tell us:

It is ordained and established by the full consent and authority of the Council the day and year within written from this day perpetually to be observed and kept that is to say that yearly in the time of Lent there shall be called before the Mayor for the time being four of the most cunning [skilful] discreet and able players within this city to search hear and examine all the plays and players and pageants throughout all the artificers belonging to Corpus Christi play, and all such as they shall find sufficient in person and cunning to the honour of this city and the worship of the crafts to admit and enable, and all other insufficient persons either in cunning voice or person to discharge, amove and avoid. And that no player that shall play in the Corpus Christi play shall be conducted and retained to play twice[1] on the day of the play, and that he or they so playing over twice the said day upon pain of 40s. to forfeit to the Chamber so often as he or they be found at fault in the same.

('Conducted' means hired: an apparently unique reference to the hiring of players.)

48   Tradition has it that the actors were unpaid. Some payments may have been hard-lying money, e.g. for having one's face gilded. It is evident from recent research that special actors were hired for certain plays, e.g. The Mayor's play of the *Coronation of the Virgin.* The following Mercers' accounts of 1467 seem to indicate the payment of expenses rather than fees.

These are the costs paid about the pageant.
Item first paid to William Clark and his players for rehearsing 10d. Item to John Lyster for going with us 2d. Item paid 11d. (for) pikes and great nails for the axletree and boards and nails and workmanship to the great pageant 20d. Item paid for (*lost*) and 2 English boards and double spikings and (workman-)ship the 'lyles' 13d. Item for mending of an angel coat. . . Item paid to William Clarkson for a pair of gloves and half a

---

[1] Workers in brass and other metals.

[1] It is not clear how someone could play twice.

yard of linen... Item paid for soap and (gr)ease for the pageant wheels... Item for washing of... Item paid to William (Clarkeson for) playing of the play... Item paid to William Clarke(-son) and John Lyster for setting up and taking down what belongs... Item of putting home of the pageant...

Item putting the pageant about on the morn 6d. Item spent at ale divers times on William Clerke and John Lyster and Malum 6d. Item that we have spent at divers times about the town and our drinking and our supper on Corpus Christi day at even 3s. 6d. Sum of the costs 33s. 0½d. and in the master hand 13d.

It is not clear what kind of rehearsals are envisaged in this passage. It has been suggested that part of the social effect of the performance came from knowing that it was William Clark or whoever up there (compare 'our team' in football) and that little illusionist acting would be needed.

c Author and audience

49 It used to be assumed that the plays were written by the guilds. Modern scholars, however, suggest that there was a learned author, possibly a cleric; later, whole plays and groups of plays were rewritten. Since the audience included kings from time to time (Richard II, Richard Duke of York, Richard III, possibly Henry VIII) as well as the common people, one cannot specify a particular

social group as audience. Records show that the plays continued for 200 years, and they probably existed for fifty years before that—ample evidence of their popularity and power. Even Shakespeare is not really comparable, since no single play of his has been produced every year in one place for a similar length of time. The comparison is with something like Handel's *Messiah*, or Bach's *Saint Matthew Passion*.

d Conclusion: the cycle as the focus for a culture

50 Whatever else we may feel, must this not have been a major aesthetic experience (if not the greatest) in the life of a York citizen of the fifteenth century? Manuscript illustrations were only seen by a few, the poems of Chaucer and Langland were written down and presumably not often read aloud in public. Sermons, wall-paintings and stained glass, even the great east window of York Minster, were part of the general educative and cultural experience provided by the Church, but many Church authorities believed that drama could teach even more effectively. The play cycle created by the people of York, combining drama, scenic effects, moving pageantry and music, retelling the myth by which its audience lived, could never be equalled by any other experience in that culture.

4 The last performances of the York cycle

51 All over Europe, in Catholic as well as Protestant countries, the regular celebration of the Corpus Christi festival by the performance of cycle plays began to decline from the mid-sixteenth century onwards. There are various reasons: the obvious one, as far as England is concerned, is that they were associated with the Roman Catholic faith, and were therefore opposed by the reformers and the new established Church. But everywhere, the spread of Renaissance ideas and sensibilities, the increase in literacy following the invention of printing, and the development of a vigorous secular drama which catered for all classes, probably combined to make the traditional religious drama seem old-fashioned and even offensive. Among other things, the cycles caused considerable expense to civic authorities and guilds, and disrupted commercial life in the big cities, and this helped to bring about their eventual abandonment.

52 The sequence of events in York is as follows:

1548–9 (Reign of Edward VI) Three pageants of Our Lady omitted.

1553–4 (Accession of Mary) Three omitted pag-

eants restored. General revival of interest in the pageants.

1558 (Accession of Elizabeth) Plays suspended for two years.

1561 Pageants of Our Lady excised. N.B. 'And for as much as the late feast of Corpus Xti is not now celebrated and kept holy day as it was accustomed it is therefore agreed that on Corpus even my Lord Mayor and Aldermen shall in making the proclamation accustomed go about in seemly sad apparel and not in scarlet.'

1562 Attempt to move the play 'until St Barnabe day on the apostle', but the commons insist on the proper day.

1563 Play again performed. Suspension till 1567.

1568 Creed Play suppressed—'boke delivered in' to Church authorities i.e. Dean Hutton.

1569 (Rebellion in the north). Possibly a 'corrected' version of Corpus Christi play is played.

1570	Archbishop Grindal appointed to See of York.
1572	Last performance of Paternoster Play. Book handed in to archbishop.
1575	Attempt by aldermen to get books back from the archbishop.
1579	Corrected text of Corpus Christi Play requested from archbishop.
1580	Commons ask mayor for the Corpus Christi play 'this year'. No further records of religious plays.
1580s	Playing of interludes by noblemen's companies i.e. travelling companies. Davies, the original editor of the York records comments:

> None of these entertainments seem to have afforded the same gratification . . . as the Corpus Christi pageants for which they seem to have been substituted.

THE CASTLE OF PERSEVERANCE

1 Introduction

1 *The Castle of Perseverance* is one of three morality plays found in the fifteenth-century manuscripts collected by the Rev. Cox Macro of Bury St Edmunds (1683–1767); they were subsequently bound into a single volume generally described as *The Macro Moralities*. This is the title of the Early English Text Society edition (ed. Mark Eccles), to which you should refer if you want to go into textual and linguistic matters which are hardly touched upon in this study material. There is general agreement that the play in its present form dates from the first quarter of the fifteenth century, and it seems from the quality of the language and from one or two references within the play that it is connected with the northern part of East Anglia, possibly Lincoln. However, Mark Eccles notes the regular occurrence of linguistic forms connected with Norfolk, which suggests to him the possibility that a Norfolk man was the scribe (*The Macro Moralities*, p. xi). But the language as a whole is east Midlands, with a strong northern element.

2 For an immediate idea of the nature and subject of *The Castle of Perseverance*, read the Banns (lines 1–156, pp. 77–80), the public announcement made by the two flag-bearers in a town about a week before the performance. At this first contact with the text, savour the language and the verse form, because they will be the prime means by which the whole play works; and get a firm idea of the course of the action and its implied religious message. Owing to its length, you will be asked to work in detail only on the central part of the play, beginning with the musical celebration of the Virtues' initial triumph in getting Mankind into the Castle of Perseverance (1705), and concluding with the Bad Angel's assumption of triumph after the death of Mankind (3129). In the Banns, this part of the play is summarized in lines 55–120.

The difference between cycle and morality plays

3 Turning thus from the cycle plays to *The Castle of Perseverance*, you will find something completely different, although you will recognize in it the medieval frames of mind and reference with which you have already become familiar. To list the main structural differences:

a To the medieval mind, the cycle plays are fundamentally historical, that is, dramatizations of parts of the Bible. But *The Castle of Perseverance* is an original dramatic creation which, though based upon many aspects of medieval Christian thinking and tradition, has as its single theme the progress of the soul from birth to death, and then to the hereafter. If you compare its theme with *Everyman* (A201, Units 5–6)[1], you will see that the theme of *Everyman* is holy dying, while in *The Castle* holy dying is treated only from line 2778 ff., after Mankind's life-long struggle with good and evil.

b The huge scope of a cycle play, taking the religious history of the universe from the Fall and the Creation right through to the Last Judgement, we call *macrocosmic*. The scope of *The Castle of Perseverance*, which takes the single soul, in its relation to the universal and eternal scheme of things, we call *microcosmic*. The macrocosm is the great world, the microcosm is the little world.

[1] The Open University (1972) A201 *Arts: Renaissance and Reformation*, Units 5–6, *The Mediaeval Inheritance and the Revival of Classical Learning*, The Open University Press.

Shakespeare's Gentleman in *King Lear* describes the old King in the storm

Striving in his *little world of man* to outscorn
The to-and-fro conflicting wind and rain.
(III. i.10)

c   The characters in the cycle plays are actual people from history. Those in *The Castle* are abstractions. Even the central figure of the play, who is worked upon by good and evil forces and is faced by choices and moulded by powers of growth and decay ordained by God, is not a particular person like Dr Faustus, but an abstraction representing the essence—body and soul—of any human being.

d   The conduct of events in a pageant from a cycle play is recognizably realistic: real individual people are in conflict in specific individual circumstances. The conduct of events in *The Castle* proceeds by debate among abstractions—a debate which from time to time moves into both symbol and allegory, and at crucial points moves into physical conflict—battles, sieges, and individual fights, which all over medieval Europe were staple resorts of the moral drama. (If you took our second level course A201, *Renaissance and Reformation,* you will remember your work on medieval allegory [pp.56–68 of Units 5–6], of which the first two pages are particularly relevant to your present study. If you did not take that course, do not worry; in studying the play, you will make the necessary discoveries in a strictly dramatic context.) It is direct religious and moral teaching about life, conducted at a fairly sophisticated level, and is therefore a different kind of dramatized sermon from a typical cycle pageant. The latter usually consisted of an *exemplum* (the name medieval preachers gave to the instance from real life upon which they wished to moralize), and a short piece of direct religious and moral teaching in the form of the lesson to be drawn from the exemplum, stated by an Expositor or Doctor.

Staging the play

4   *The Castle of Perseverance* manuscript contains fairly full instructions for mounting the play. There is a diagram of the whole layout as envisaged by the artist, accompanied by an interesting detailed rubric. Diagram and rubric have been discussed and interpreted by Richard Southern, upon whose book, *The Medieval Theatre in the Round,* the following summary is largely based. The drawing on p. 74 conflates the original with Dr Southern's findings, and I have modernized the original wording. But I also print the objections of Glynne Wickham (*The Medieval*

Theatre, pp.116–7) to Richard Southern's placing of the audience. Natalie Crohn Schmitt ('Was there a medieval theatre in the round? A re-examination of the evidence'), also challenges Southern's reconstruction.

5   The theatre was circular and of fairly substantial diameter. Dr Southern, finding that the presentation envisaged compares well with what we know of Cornish medieval theatre in the round, and noting that the theatre at St Just had a diameter of 126 feet, suggests 110 feet and estimates that the audience would be of perhaps 3000 people. On the circumference was a raised ring of earth, on the inside of a ditch. 'To dig a ditch in a plain is to provide two things—a hollow and a hill.' (*op.cit.* p.51)[1]. Already we have a physical barrier to gate-crashers (there are medieval illustrations of theatres in the round enclosed by high wattle fences which would have served the same purpose) and a raised circular viewpoint for spectators on the perimeter. There were five 'scaffolds', that is, raised covered booths facing inwards, big enough for action to take place inside them (i.e. not so small that only a few standing figures could use them for acting—see *Theatres and Staging*, p. 18) and accessible to the central playing area within the circle by means of ladder or stairway. (Both ladder and stairway appear in medieval illustrations of other theatre scaffolds: probably considerations of the action would determine which means was used for each scaffold.) Scaffolds would have to be about eight feet high if all spectators in 'the place' were to see the action. If part of this height were obtained by their being mounted on the mound, construction problems would be eased, and sight-lines would be better all round. This arrangement also makes it possible for a scaffold to have two levels, one at ground level and another on top of it (see hell-mouth in the Fouquet miniature on the cover of this study block). Probably (necessarily for performing convenience, I should say) there was access to the scaffolds round the perimeter at the back. Almost certainly each scaffold had a curtain across the front, to conceal or reveal what was within. You will remember that dramatic revelation by means of a curtain was used in the nativity sequence in the Rouen liturgy. God's late and decisive appearance at 3597 would certainly gain by the quality of instant revelation.

---

[1] Natalie Crohn Schmitt questions the whole idea of a ditch being specially dug for mound-boundary purposes, which would entail vast labour. She suggests that the ditch is the moat of the Castle. Lines 2300–2400 seem to indicate that water-fights happen in the play which could scarcely take place beyond the perimeter containing the audience. Nevertheless, if a circular water barrier is *within* the place, it would have to be bridged in several places, and there is no supporting evidence for anything of the kind.

6 The main acting area was within the circle, where the Castle itself (twelve or thirteen feet high, I suggest) dominated the scene. Dr Southern thinks that there were also spectators within the circle who were controlled by the *stytelers*, or marshals. You will see from the drawing below that if the audience were disposed as Southern suggests, there would be access from every scaffold to the central playing area, clear sight-lines from audience to wherever the action was, and an ample, permanently clear acting area in the middle, in and around the Castle—an area from which, as you will see from the original instructions, spectators should be absolutely excluded. If the Castle were mounted on four long legs, as the original diagram (see *Theatres and Staging*, p. 20) seems to suggest, then the audience could also see through the Castle at ground level in the middle, but not through it if the action happened to be taking place on a scaffold directly

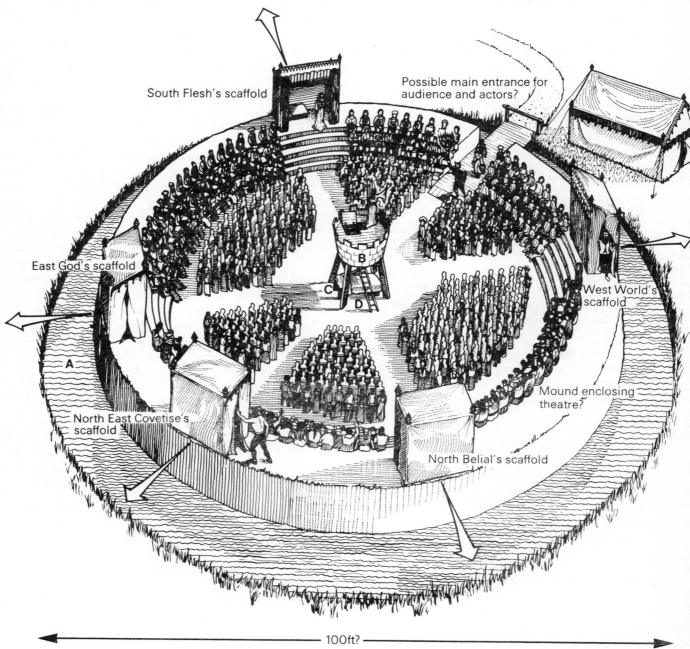

South Flesh's scaffold

Possible main entrance for audience and actors?

East God's scaffold

West World's scaffold

A

Mound enclosing theatre?

North East Covetise's scaffold

North Belial's scaffold

— 100ft? —

A reconstruction of the theatre for *The Castle of Perseverance*. The letters on the drawing indicate the position of inscriptions on the medieval plan for the staging of the play (see *Theatres and Staging*, p. 20). The inscriptions were as follows:

A This is the water about the place, if any ditch be made where it shall be played, or else that it be strongly barred all about, and let not overmany stytelers be within the place.

B This is the Castle of Perseverance that standeth in the midst of the place, but let no man sit there, for letting of sight, for there shall be the best of all.

C Covetise's cupboard by the bed's feet shall be at the end of the Castle.

D Mankind's bed shall be under the Castle and there shall the soul lie under the bed till he shall rise and play.

beyond the Castle from them. The action being far away, they could move to one side or the other to get a better view—hence one function of the *stytelers*. Another function, which Dr Southern suggests might be the main one, would be to control the ground immediately in front of a scaffold upon which action was taking place: spectators would tend to flock there, and it would be essential both to control flocking generally, for the sake of good order, and to keep an access lane open to that scaffold.

7 Here is Glynne Wickham's objection to the audience being within the round:

Richard Southern in *The Medieval Theatre in the Round* provides a detailed analysis of the staging of this play; but as he fails to notice the parallel so carefully drawn by the playmaker with this most popular and spectacular form of tournament and elects without much warrant to fill the *platea* with spectators, little confidence can be placed in this analysis. As one of the most elementary rules of any *ludus,* athletic or mimetic, is a well-defined *separation* of the areas reserved respectively for performers and spectators, it seems more prudent to read the ground-plan of this manuscript, along with those of the Cornish plays, as meaning what they say, and thus accepting the lack of any provision for an audience *in* the ground-plan as indication that provision was made for it *outside* the acting-area. A recent production of the Cornish Cycle in St Piran's 'Round' has at least proved conclusively that with scaffolds set on the top of the bank and ladders connecting the scaffolds to the *platea*, ample room remains to accommodate spectators in an orderly fashion on terraces on the inner side of the bank and to supply them all with a full and unimpeded view of all the action both on the scaffolds and in the arena.

8 A theatre in the round such as was evidently used in the Middle Ages in Cornwall as well as in the East Midlands has an extraordinary potential for audience involvement, as well as for varied styles of performance based upon either stasis or movement, the intimate or the public, the universal or the particular in both time and space. The average distance of a member of the audience from the action is much less than in any other kind of theatre, and the mere fact that action can be almost all round any spectator (to an extent of at least 180 degrees for everybody, and up to 310 degrees for many) makes for intensification of the theatre experience, and makes it harder for anybody present to detach himself mentally or emotionally from the action. It is not surprising that a number of modern drama companies have revived this kind of theatre, complete with scaffolds. Two French companies seen in London in 1972, both of which came to the Roundhouse, perhaps the only theatre building in London able to house such shows (although the Albert Hall would also do very well), used it effectively. One was Ariane Mnouchkine's Le Théâtre du Soleil,

which presented a seriocomic documentary of the French Revolution called *1789,* and the other was Le Grand Magic Circus et Ses Animaux Tristes, which presented *Robinson Crusoe—Twenty years of Love and Adventure*, the scenario and direction of which were by Jerome Savary; a satire on modern loneliness and reactionary political activity. Both engendered scenes of extraordinary enthusiasm among their audiences. (Both, in my opinion, could have done with *stytelers* at all those times when the action was slowed down because actors were fighting their way through standing spectators or hopping over sitting ones. Perhaps that was part of the fun—but it would have been out of place had the tone been lofty and serious, as it mostly is in *The Castle of Perseverance*.)

9 Dr Southern's dedication of his book on *The Castle of Perseverance* 'to the memory of Bertolt Brecht and to the Berliner Ensemble in recognition of a theatrical experience among the greatest of our time' effectively helps me to make my point: you are not being asked now to study a curiosity of the medieval theatre for its own sake alone (though that would be well worthwhile), but so that you may take into your knowledge and experience an aspect of the universal development of the stage from which the foremost modern practitioners of drama are constantly learning.

10 In much of the work that I shall ask you to do when reading *The Castle,* it will be essential for you to have the staging plan which I have described absolutely clear in your mind. **To strengthen your impression of medieval theatre in the round, look again at the Fouquet miniature on the unit cover. Note the wattle fence round 'the place', and the height and different functions of the scaffolds. Then look at Norman Clark's drawing (on facing page) of an impression of a performance of 'The Castle'. Note the tent outside the ditch—the base and green room of the acting company.**

The Characters

11 Each of the three enemies of the soul of Mankind—the World, the Flesh and the Devil (Belial)—has a trio 'with him'. All six attached to Belial and Flesh remain throughout the play, being six of the Seven Deadly Sins. But the two vices attached to the World, Lust-Liking and Folly, drop out, and Lechery, who alone of the Seven Deadly Sins is represented as a woman, takes on the sensual aspect of Lust-Liking for the rest of the play. Covetise (covetousness), the remaining sin of the Seven, has a key role in the action, and is therefore independent of an infernal supervisor; he also has his own scaffold, into which he lures the ageing Mankind. However, when the Virtues win the first stage of the battle,

Covetise is beaten by World for his share of the blame, which attaches him to World in some degree; and that is appropriate.

12 Of the Virtues, Dr Southern writes (*The Medieval Theatre in the Round*, p. 13):

... these Seven Virtues are an oddly assorted choice. The orthodox Seven are the Three Christian Virtues—Faith, Hope and Charity—plus the Four Platonic Virtues—who are, approximately, Prudence, Justice, Fortitude and Temperance... Save for Charity and perhaps Temperance under the name of Soberness [Abstinence], we have in the Seven Virtues of *The Castle* none of the accepted Seven.

But I think Dr Southern misses a point here: the Virtues are chosen because they are opposite qualities to the Seven Deadly Sins, against whom they fight in the great battle, *viz.* Meekness against Pride, Patience against Wrath, Charity against Envy, Abstinence against Gluttony, Chastity against Lechery, Industry against Sloth, and Generosity against Covetousness. Concerning the four daughters of God, Mercy, Truth, Righteousness and Peace, it is important to know that the reference is to Psalm 85, 10: 'Mercy and truth are met together; righteousness and peace have kissed each other'—a fertile source of religious allegory and personification in all ages: it is only because they meet together and kiss in the play that the fate of Mankind's soul is determined according to the best orthodox teaching.

The text and explanatory matter on it

13 With regard to the text of the play, to which we now come, please note:

a   The original stage directions, most of which are in Latin, I have translated without comment.

b   As in the previous texts in this study, I have italicized marginal glosses on the meaning of the English text and translations of the Latin quotations which figure in the text. Scholars disagree on this point, but my view is that when the Latin is extrametrical, it was not spoken as part of the play—except of course, when accompanied by a musical direction, in which case it was sung. Since the Latin quotations function as mottoes for different parts of the action, in a modern production it might be fun, for completeness' sake, to display them on banners during the action they summarize.

c   I have added a number of suggested stage directions which are clearly marked by being enclosed in square brackets. These suggestions of mine are very sparse; where the work requires it, you will want to add stage directions and indeed other production suggestions of your own.

14   Now a note by way of introduction, to smooth your way through the language, and to help you to assess it as a dramatic instrument. As far as comprehension is concerned, late medieval English presents few problems that cannot be solved by recourse to a dictionary—which I provide in the margin. If you are interested in the language, you will find a summary statement in Eccles, *The Macro Moralities*, pp. xi–xv. I do not deal with grammatical problems, but some of the auxiliary verbs are tricky: the ones you will meet most often will be *do* and *gin* in their various tenses. *Do* carries either of our present meanings—i.e. to intensify the force of a verb, as in 'he did go', and to perform; but it also has the meaning 'impel' or 'bring about' (e.g. 1970, 'to do those damsels dote'—i.e. to make those girls afraid). *Gin* sometimes means 'begin', but mostly, in its past form *gan*, acts as a simple auxiliary (e.g. 1762, 'To yon castle he gan creep'—i.e. he crept). Sometimes both functions are present (e.g. 1832, 'Now will I gin forth to go').

15   Lastly the verse. The author uses a thirteen-line alliterative stanza with four stresses per line and usually allots a whole stanza to each speaker; though he does vary it from time to time, and then usually divides the stanza after the ninth line; or, especially in action passages, he allots a speaker just a quatrain. There are occasional other variants. The main effects of choosing complex stanzaic verse as the basis of stage dialogue are

a   to make the speech more formal and rounded, thus weakening (or perhaps deliberately eradicating?) the relation of what is said to ordinary speech,

b   to assume the power of poetry. After all, prose did exist as a literary medium at the time, but poetry was thought of as automatically more lofty and memorable; medieval religious drama is in essence a poetic artefact.

You will have to decide for yourself how successful the author is in transcending his poetic medium when he needs to, in the name of action or passionate exchange, and how successful he is when he capitalizes on the resources of the grand convention he is following (try 1767–82 for the former and 2777–842 for the latter). The alliterative aspect of that convention dominated English verse for so long that it permanently affected the language; it is so all-pervading a characteristic that to write about it would be to range much more widely than is here proposed. But you will notice the many alliterative phrases, some of which are poetically and dramatically apt and powerful (e.g. 1878), while others are mere line-fillers (e.g. 1839, 2718). And you will prove on your pulses, especially if you read some of the dialogue aloud, the capacity of alliteration to determine the structure of the verse and reinforce its meaning, tone and rhythm. Yet for all the difficulty of managing alliterative rhyming verse, the poet generally achieves logical sentence structure and sound dramatic speech order. There is nothing rigid or artificial about the dialogue, and the play has been very effective when performed in modern times.

Reading and working on the play

16 I want you to be quite clear on this point: I do not *require* you to read the whole play, because in the planning of your work I must give higher priority to your working in detail on the best part of it. You can rely on the summary in the Banns for the first 1700 and the last 500 lines; but if you *can* manage to read the whole play, if only cursorily, then that will be an advantage.

Working on lines 1705–3129

While reading the play, I suggest you concentrate on the following:

a Lines 1705–1876. Identify main production problems.

b Lines 1878–2409. Discuss the prelude to the battle and the battle itself in terms of properties and movement, the properties precisely, the movement generally in terms of principle.

c Lines 2414–2543, 2700–2778. Write notes on Covetise, who is evidently the dramatic and moral key to the whole play. Do not forget the actual death of Mankind.

d Write notes on
i Death (2779–2848)
ii Boy (2895–2968)

Now please read the set part of the play, making notes as you proceed. At the end, read your notes reflectively, improving them if necessary, before reading my discussion notes.

2 The text of *The Castle of Perseverance*

[After the diagram at the front of the manuscript, the following instructions also appear.]

And he that shall play Belial look that he have gunpowder burning pipes in his hands and in his ears and in his arse when he goeth to battle.

The four daughters shall be clad in mantles, Mercy in white, Righteousness in red altogether, Truth in sad [i.e. full, sober] green, and Peace in black, and they shall play in the place altogether till they bring up the soul.

Here are the names of the players
First, two flag-bearers
World, and with him Lust-Liking, Folly and Boy
Belial, and with him Pride, Wrath and Envy
Flesh, and with him Gluttony, Lechery and Sloth
Mankind, and with him Good Angel and Bad Angel
Covetise, Backbiter
Shrift, Penance
Meekness, Patience, Charity, Abstinence, Chastity, Industry, Generosity
Death
The Soul
Mercy, Truth Righteousness and Peace
The Father enthroned
Total xxxvi players

The Banns

FIRST FLAG BEARER	Glorious God, in all degrees lord most of might,
	That heaven and earth made of nought, both sea and land,
	The angels in heaven him to serve bright
	And Mankind in middle-earth he made with his hand,
	And our lovely Lady, that lantern is of light,

Save our liege lord the King, the leader of this land,
And all the royal of this realm, and *rede* them the right,   counsel
And all the good commons of this town that before us stand
    In this place.
We muster you with *menship*   honour   10
And *freyn* you of *frely* friendship!   ask   nobly
Christ save you all from *schenship*   ignominy
    That knowen will our case.

SECOND
FLAG
BEARER

The *case* of our coming you to declare,   reason
Every man in himself forsooth he it may find:
How Mankind into this world born is full bare,
And bare shall buried be at his last end.
God him giveth two angels full *yepe* and full *yare,*   alert   active
The Good Angel and the Bad to him for to lend.
The Good teacheth him goodness, the Bad sin and *sare.*   misery   20
When the t'one hath the victory, the t'other goeth behind,
    By *skill.*   reason
The Good Angel coveteth evermore Man's salvation
And the Bad *besetteth* him ever to his damnation,   assails
And God hath given Man free arbitration
    Whether he will himself save or his soul *spill.*   destroy

FIRST FLAG
BEARER

Spilt is Man *spetously* when he to sin assent.   destroyed   cruelly
The Bad Angel then bringeth him three enemies so stout,
The World, the Fiend, the foul Flesh so *jolly* and *gent.*   gay   courteous
They leaden him full lustily with sins all about.   30
Pight with Pride and Covetise, to the World is he went.   placed
To maintain his manhood: all men to him *lout.*   bow
After Ire and Envy the Fiend hath to him lent   afterwards
Backbiting and *Indicting* with all men for to *rout*   accusation   gad about
    Full even.   as much as possible
But the foul Flesh, *homeliest* of all,   most familiar
Sloth, Lust and Lechery *gun* to him call,   have begun
Gluttony and other sins both great and small.
    Thus Man's soul is soiled with sins more than seven.

SECOND
FLAG
BEARER

When Man's soul is soiled with sin and with *sore,*   misery   40
Then the Good Angel maketh *mickle* mourning   much
That the lovely likeness of God should be *lore*   lost
Through the Bad Angel's false enticing.
He sendeth to him Conscience, *pricked* full poor,   dressed
And clear Confession with Penance-doing.
They moven Man to mendment that he misdid before.
Thus they call him to *cleanness* and to good living,   purity
    Without *distance.*   doubt
Meekness, Patience and Charity,
Soberness, Busyness and Chastity,   50
And *Largity,* virtues of good degree,   generosity
    Man calleth to the Castle of good Perseverance.

FIRST FLAG
BEARER

The Castle of Perseverance when Mankind hath *tan,*   taken
Well armed with virtues and overcome all vices,
There the Good Angel maketh full merry then;
That Mankind hath overcome his *ghostly* enemies.   spiritual
The Bad Angel mourneth that he hath missed Man.
He calleth the World, the Fiend and the foul Flesh *iwis*   certainly
And all the seven sins to do *that* they can   what
To bring Mankind again to *bale* out of bliss   torment   60
    With wrong.
Pride assaileth Meekness with all his might,
Ire against Patience full fast *gan* he fight.   begins

Envy against Charity striveth *full right*,   *to the utmost*
    But Covetise against *Largity* fighteth overlong.   *generosity*

SECOND
FLAG
BEARER
Covetise Mankind ever coveteth for to *quell*.   *destroy*
He gathereth to him Gluttony against Soberness,
Lechery with Chastity fighteth full *fell*,   *fiercely*
And Sloth in God's service against Busy-ness.
Thus vices against virtues fighteth full *snell*.   *vigorously*   70
Every busketh to bring Man to distress.   *everyone prepares*
But Penance and Confession with Mankind will *mell*,   *concern themselves*
The vices are full likely the virtues to oppress,
    Sans doubt;   *without*
Thus in the Castle of good Perseverance
Mankind is *maskered* with *mickle variance*.   *bewildered great conflict*
The Good Angel and the Bad be ever *at distance*;   *in opposition*
    The Good holdeth him in, the Bad would bring him out.

FIRST FLAG
BEARER
Out of good Perseverance when Mankind will not come,
Yet the Bad Angel with Covetise him *gan* assail,   *begins to*   80
Finding him in poverty and penance so *benome*   *consumed*
And bringeth him in belief in default to fail[1].
Then he proffereth him *good* and gold so great a sum,   *goods*
That if he will come again and with the World *dayle*,   *dally*
The Bad Angel to the World *tolleth* him down   *entices*
The Castle of Perseverance to flee from the *vale*   *benefit*
    And bliss.
Then the World beginneth him to restore;
Have he never so mickle, yet he would have more.
Thus the Bad Angel *lereth* him his *lore*:   *teaches lesson*   90
    The more a man ageth, the harder he is.

SECOND
FLAG
BEARER
Hard a man is in age and covetous by *kind*.   *nature*
When all other sins man hath forsake,
Ever the more that he hath the more is in his mind
To gather and get *good* with woe and with *wrake*.   *goods persecution*
Thus the Good Angel cast is behind
And the Bad Angel Man to him taketh,
That *wringeth* him *wrenches* to his last end   *inflicts treacheries*
Till Death cometh full dolefully and lodgeth him in a *lake*   *pit*
    Full low.   100
Then is Man on *molde maskered* in mind;   *earth bewildered*
He sendeth after his *secutors*, full *fickle* to find,   *executors untrustworthy*
And his heir afterward cometh ever behind:
    I Wot Not Who is his name, for he *him not know*.   *does not know him*

FIRST FLAG
BEARER
Man know not who shall be his heir and govern his *good*;   *possessions*
He careth more for his *catel* than for his cursed sin.   *property*
To put his good in governance he mengeth his mood[2],
He would that it were *skifted* among his nigh kin.   *distributed*
But there shall come a *lither* lad with a torn hood,   *rascally*
I Wot Never Who shall be his name, his clothes be full thin,   110
Shall herit the heritage that never was of his blood,
When all his life is *lighted upon* a little pin   *dwindled to*
    At the last.
On live he may no longer *lende*,   *alive remain*
Mercy he calleth at his last end:
'Mercy God! Be now my friend!'
    With that Man's spirit is past.

[1] 82   And makes him believe that he will be disabled through poverty.

[2] 107   He worries about the arrangements for disposing of his possessions.

SECOND FLAG BEARER

When Man's spirit is past, the Bad Angel full fell
Claimeth that *for* covetise Man's soul should be his   *because of*
And for to bear it full *boystously* with him into hell.   *violently*   120
The Good Angel saith nay, the spirit shall to bliss
For at his last end *of mercy he gan spell*   *for mercy he called out*
And therefore of mercy he shall not miss,
And our lovely Lady if she will for him *mell,*   *speak*
By mercy and by *menys* in Purgatory he is,   *mediation*
        In full bitter place.
Thus mouth's confession
And his heart's contrition
Shall save Man from damnation
        By God's mercy and grace.   130

FIRST FLAG BEARER

Grace if God will grant us of his mickle might,
These *parcels* in *properties* we purpose to play   *roles   stage properties*
This day seven night before you in sight
At . . . . .[1] on the green in royal array.
Ye haste you then thitherwards, sirs, *hendly in height*;   *graciously*
All good neighbours full specially we you pray,
And look that ye be there *betime,* lovely and *light,*   *early   willingly*
For we shall be *onward by undern of the day,*   *moving on by noon*
        Dear friends.
We thank you of all *good dalliance,*   *courtly conversation*   140
And of all your *special sportance,*   *exceptionally good welcome*
And pray you of good countenance
        To our lives' ends.

SECOND FLAG BEARER

As our lives we love you, thus taking our leave.
Ye manly men of . . . . .[1], *there* Christ save you all!   *may*
He maintain your mirths and keep you from grief,
That born was of Mary mild in an ox stall.
Now merry be all . . . . .[2] and *well might ye cheve!*   *may you thrive*
All our faithful friends, there fair may ye fall!
Yea, and welcome be ye when ye come *price for to preve*   *our worth to prove*   150
And worthy to be *worshipped* in bower and in hall   *honoured*
        And in every place.
Farewell, fair friends,
That *lovely* will listen and *lend.*   *willingly   attend*
Christ keep you from fiends!
        Trump up and let us *pace*!   *depart*

The Play

WORLD
(in his scaffold)

Worthy *wights* in all this world wide,   *people*
By wild wood *wones* and every *way-went,*   *dwellings   highways*
Precious *prinse, pricked* in pride,   *princes   dressed up*
Through this proper *plain* place in peace be ye bent!   *open*   160
Busk you, bold *bachelors,* under my banner to abide   *prepare   young knights*
Where bright *bassinets* be battered and backs are *schent.*   *helmets   broken*
Yea, sirs seemly, *all same sitteth on side,*   *all you who are sitting at the side*
For both by sea and by land my *sondes* I have sent,   *messengers*
        All the world my name is *meant.*   *proclaimed to*
All abouten my *bane* is blow,   *summons*
In every coast I am know,
I do men ravin in rich row   *I make a lot of men act madly*
        Till they be *dight* to Death's *dent.*   *put   stroke*

Assyria, Achaia and *Almayne,*   *Germany*   170
Cavadoyse, Capadoyse and *Cananee,*   *Calvados   Cappadocia   Canaan*

---

[1] Here the name of the town where the play was to be performed was inserted, e.g. Lincoln.

[2] e.g. men of Lincoln.

Babylone, Brabant, *Burgoyne* and Britain,   *Burgundy*
Greece, *Galys* and to the Greekish Sea;   *Galicia*
I move also Macedone in my *mickle main,*   *great power*
France, Flanders and Friesland, and also Normandy,
Pyncecras[1], Paris and long *Pygmayne,*   *land of the Pygmies*
And every town in *Trage*, even to the Dry Tree[2],   *Thrace?*
     Rhodes and rich Rome.
All these lands *at mine avise*   *under my orders*
Are *casten to* my worldly *wise.*   *governed by ways*   180
My treasurer, Sir Covetise,
     Hath seized them wholly to me.

Therefore my game and my glee grow full glad.
There is no *wight* in this world that my wit will me *werne.*   *person obstruct*
Every rich reigner *rapeth him full rad*   *hurries fast*
In lusts and in likings my laws to learn.
With fair folk in the field freshly I am *fed*;   *nourished*
I dance down as a doe by dales full *derne.*   *secretly*
What *boy* biddeth battle or *debateth with blade,*   *fellow fights*   190
Him were better to be hangen high in hell *herne*   *it were better for him nook*
     Or burnt *on light levin.*   *by bright lightning*
Whoso speaketh against the World
In a prison he shall be *sparred*   *locked up*
Mine *hest* is *holden* and *heard*   *command obeyed attended to*
     Into high heaven.

BELIAL   Now I sit, Satan, in my sad sin,
(in his   As devil doughty, in *draff* as a *drake.*   *filth dragon*
scaffold) I champ and I chafe, I *chock on* my chin,   *stick out*
         I am *boystous* and bold, as Belial the black.   *fierce*
         What folk that I *grope*, they gapen and grin,   *grasp*   200
         Iwis from Carlisle into Kent my *carping* they take,   *words*
         Both the back and the buttock bursteth all *on brenne,*   *burning*
         With works of *wreche* I work them *mickle wrake.*   *vengeance much ruin*
             In woe is all my *wenne.*   *delight*
         In *care* I am cloyed   *sorrow*
         And foul I am annoyed
         But Mankind be stroyed   *unless*
             By *dykes* and by *den.*   *ditches valley*

         Pride is my prince in pearls *i-pight*;   *arrayed*
         Wrath, this wretch, with me shall *wawe*;   *travel*   210
         Envy into war with me shall walken *wyth*;   *quickly*
         With these *faytours* I am fed, in faith I am *fawe.*   *deceivers joyful*
         As a *dyngne* devil in my den I am *dight.*   *worthy equipped*
         Pride, Wrath and Envy, I say in my *saw,*   *speech*
         Kings, kaisers and *kempys* and many a *keen* knight,   *warriors bold*
         These lovely lords have *learned* them my law.   *taught*
             To my den they will *draw.*   *come*
         All wholly Mankind
         To hell *but* I win,   *unless*
         In *bale* is my *bin,*   *torment stall*   220
             And *shent* under *shaw.*   *ruined the earth*

         On Mankind is my trust, in country *i-knowe,*   *well-known*
         With my *tire* and with my *tayl* tightly to *tene,*   *accoutrements speech vex*
         Through Flanders and Friesland fast I gan flow
         Fele folk on a flock to *flappen* and to *flene.*   *many beat flay*
         Where I grasp on the ground, *grim* there shall grow,   *cruelty*
         Gather you together, ye boys, on this green!

[1] Land of the Pincenarii in Thrace.
[2] The Dry Tree was the tree in Eden which withered when Adam ate the apple.

On this broad bugle a blast when I blow,
All this world shall be *wood iwis* as I ween,   *mad   certainly*
   And to my bidding bend.   230
Wythly on side   *quickly*
On bench will I bide
To *tene, this tide,*   *harm   on this occasion*
   All wholly Mankind.

FLESH
*(in his
scaffold)*

I bide as a broad bursten-gut aboven on these towers.
Everybody is the better that to mine bidding is bent.
I am Mankind's fair Flesch, flourished in flowers.
My life is with lusts and liking *i-lent.*   *fixed*
With *tapets* of taffeta I timber my towers.   *tapestries*
In mirth and in melody my *mende* is *i-ment.*   *mind   disposed*   240
Though I be clay and clod, clapped under *clowrys,*   *ground*
Yet would I that my will in the world went,
   Full true I you *behight.*   *promise*
I love well mine ease
In lusts me to please;
Though sin my soul seize,
   I give not a mite.

In gluttony gracious now am I grow;
Therefore he sitteth seemly here by my side.
In Lechery and Liking *lent* am I low,   *settled*   250
And Sloth, my sweet son, is bent to abide.
These three are noble, truly I trow,
Mankind to *tenen* and tricken *a tide.*   *injure   at some time*
With many *berdys* in bower my blasts are blow,   *girls*
By ways and by woods, through this world wide,
   The truth for to sayn.
But if Man's Flesh fare well   *unless*
Both at meat and at meal,
Dight I am in great *dell*   *set   misery*
   And brought into pain.   260

And after good *fare in faith* though *I fell,*   *eating and drinking   indeed   died*
Though I *drive* to dust, in dross for to *drepe,*   *am forced   droop*
Though my *sely* soul were harried to hell,   *miserable*
Whoso will do these works, iwis he shall weep
   Ever withouten end.
Behold the World, the Devil and me!
With all our *mights* we kings three   *powers*
Night and day busy we be
   For to destroy Mankind
   If that we may.   270
Therefore on hill
Sitteth all still
And seeth with good will
   Our rich array.

Enter Good and Bad Angel. They raise Mankind from his bed.[1]

MANKIND

After our *form-father's kende*   *first father's manner*
This night I was of my mother born.
From my mother I walk, I wend,
Full faint and feeble I *fare* you *beforn.*   *walk   before*
I am naked of limb and *lend*   *loin*
As Mankind is shapen and shorn.   280
I *not* whither to go ne to *lend*   *know not   stay*
To help myself *midday nor morn.*   *i.e. at any time*
   For shame I stand and *schende.*   *am confounded*

[1]Possibly Mankind is brought into 'the place' by Good and Bad Angel.

I was born this night in bloody *ble*;   *condition*
And naked I am, as ye can see.
Ah Lord God in trinity,
    How Mankind is *unthende*!   *feeble*

Whereto I was to this world brought
I *ne wot,* but to woe and weeping   *know not*
I am born and have right nought   290
To help myself in no doing.
I stand and study all full of *thought*;   *wonder*
Bare and poor is my clothing.
A *sely chrisom* mine head hath caught   *miserable christening-cloth*
That I took at my christening.
    Certes I have no more.   *certainly*
Of earth I came, I wot right well.
And of earth I stand this *sele*.   *moment*
Of Mankind it is great *dele*.   *for anguish*
    Lord God, I cry thine *ore!*   *mercy*   300

Two angels been assigned to me:
The t'one teacheth me to good;
On my right side ye may him see;
He came from Christ that died on *Rood*.   *the cross*
Another is ordained here to be
That is my foe, by fen and flood;
He is about in every degree
To draw me to those devils *wood*   *mad*
    That in hell been thick.
Such two hath every man *on live*   *alive*   310
To rulen him and his wits five.
When Man doth evil, the t'one would *shrive*,   *hear his confession*
    The other draweth to *wick*.   *wickedness*

But since these angels be to me *fall*,   *allotted*
Lord Jesu, to you I *bid a boon*,   *ask a favour*
That I may follow *by street and stall*   *everywhere*
The angel that came from heaven throne.
Now Lord Jesu in heaven hall,
Hear when I make my moan.
Curious Christ, to you I call.   *caring*   320
As a grisly ghost I *grucche* and groan,   *complain*
    I ween, right full of thought.
Ah Lord Jesu, whither may I go?
A *chrisom* I have and no *mo*.   *christening-cloth*   *more*
Alas, men may be wonder woe
    When they be first forth brought.

GOOD   Yea, forsooth, and that is well seen.
ANGEL   Of woeful woe man may sing,
    For each creature helpeth himself *bedene*   *at once*
    Save only man at his coming.   330
    Nevertheless turn thee from *teen*   *harm*
    And serve Jesu, heaven king,
    And thou shalt, by groves green,
    Fare well in all thing.
        That Lord *thy life hath lent*.   *has given you life*
    Have him alway in thy mind
    That died on *Rood* for Mankind   *the cross*
    And serve him to thy life's end
        And certes thou shalt not want.

BAD ANGEL   Peace, Angel! Thy words are not wise.   340
    Thou counselest him not aright.

He shall him drawen to the World's service
To dwell with kaiser, king and knight,
    That in land be him none *liche*.   *like*
Come on with me, still as stone.
Thou and I to the World shall goen,
And then thou shalt see anon
    How soon thou shalt be rich.

GOOD   Ah peace, Angel! Thou speakest folly.
ANGEL   Why should he covet World's *good*,   *goods*   350
Since Christ in earth and his *meiny*   *retinue*
All in *povert* here they stood?   *poverty*
World's *weal by street and stye*   *well-being i.e. everywhere*
Faileth and fadeth as fish in flood,
But *heveryche* is good and *trye*   *the kingdom of heaven trusted*
Where Christ sitteth bright as blood
    Withouten any distress.
To the World would he not flit,   *he would not follow the way of the world*
But forsook it every whit.
Example I find in holy writ,   360
    He will bear me witness.

Divicias et Paupertates ne dederis michi, Domine
('Give me neither riches nor poverty, Lord'—from Proverbs 30, 8)

BAD ANGEL   Yah, yah, Man, *leve* him not,   *believe*
But come with me, *by stye and street.*   *i.e. everywhere*
Have thou a gobbet of the World caught,   *if you take a morsel of the world*
Thou shalt find it good and sweet.
A fair lady thee shall be *taught*   *given*
That in bower thy *bale* shall *bete*.   *suffering cure*
With rich rents thou shalt be fraught,
With *silk sendal* to sit in seat.   *fine robe*
    I *rede,* let *bedes* be!   *advise prayers*   370
If thou wilt have well thine *heal*   *health*
And fare well at meat and meal,
With God's service may thou not deal,
    But come and follow me.

MANKIND   Whom to follow *witen I ne may.*   *do not know*
I stand and study and gin to *rave*.   *behave madly*
I would be rich in great array
And fain I would my soul save.
    As wind in water I *wave*.   *waver*
Thou wouldest to the World I me took,   380
And he would that I it forsook.
Now so God me help and the holy book,
    I *not* which I may have.   *know not*

BAD ANGEL   Come on, Man, wherefore hast thou care?
Go we to the World, I *rede* thee, *blyve,*   *counsel immediately*
For there thou shalt *mow* right well fare.   *be able to*
In case if thou think for to thrive
    No Lord shall be thee *lyche*.   *like*
Take the World to thine intent   *pay heed to the world*
And let thy love be thereon lent.   390
With gold and silver and rich rent
    Anon thou shalt be rich.   *immediately*

MANKIND   Now since thou hast *beheten* me so,   *promised*
I will go with thee and *assay*.   *try*
I *ne let* for friend nor foe,   *will not stop*
But with the World I will go play
    Certes a little *throw*.   *while*

	In this World is all my trust		
	To live in liking and in lust.		
	Have he and I once *cust*	*kissed*	400
	We shall not part, I trow.		

GOOD
ANGEL

Ah nay Man, for Christ's blood,
Come again, by street and stile!
The World is wicked and full *wood*   *mad*
And thou shalt liven but a while.
        What covetest thou to win?
Man, think on thine ending day
When thou shalt be closed under clay,
And if thou think of that *array,*   *state*
        Certes thou shalt not sin.   410

Homo, memento finis et in eternum non peccabis.
('Man, remember your end, and for ever you shall not sin'—varied from
Ecclesiasticus 7, 40)

BAD ANGEL

Yes, on thy soul thou shalt think *all betime.*   *early enough*
Come forth Man, and take no heed.
Come on, and thou shalt *holden him in.*   *keep possession of it*
Thy flesh thou shalt foster and feed
        With lovely life's food.
With the World thou mayst be bold
Till thou be sixty winters old.
When thy nose waxes cold
        Then thou mayst draw to good.

MANKIND

I vow to God and so I may   420
Make merry a full great throw.
I may liven many a day;
I am but young as I trow
        For to do *that I should.*   *as I ought*
Might I ride by swamp and *syke*   *rivulet*
And be rich and lordlike,
Certes then should I be *fryke*   *energetic*
        And a merry man on *molde.*   *earth*

BAD ANGEL

Yes, by my faith thou shalt be a lord,
And else hang me by the *hals*!   *neck*   430
But thou must be *at mine accord.*   *in agreement with me*
Otherwhile thou must be false
        Among kith and kin.
Now we go forth *swythe anon,*   *quickly at once*
To the World us must goen,
And bear thee manly *ever* among   *always*
        When thou comest out or in.

MANKIND

Yes, and else have thou my neck
But I be manly by down or dyke;
And though I be false, I *ne recke*   *care not*   440
With so that I be lordlike.   *provided*
        I follow thee as I can.
Thou shalt be my *bote of bale,*   *remedy for misery*
For were I rich *of holt and hale*   *in woods and hall*
Then would I give never *tale*   *reckoning*
        Of God ne of good man.

[Bad Angel takes Mankind towards the World's scaffold]

GOOD
ANGEL

I wail and wring and make moan!
This man with woe shall be *pilt.*   *thrown out*
I sigh sore and grisly groan
For his folly shall make him *spilt.*   *destroyed*   450

          I *not* whither to goen;   *do not know*
     Mankind hath forsaken me.
     Alas Man, for love of thee!
     Yea, for this game and this glee
          Thou shalt *grucchen* and groan.   *lament*

     Pipe up music (in English)

WORLD   Now I sit in my seemly *sale,*   *hall*
          I trot and *tremle* in my true throne;   *move quickly about*
          As a hawk I hop in my *hende hale;*   *noble hall*
          King, knight and kaiser to me maken moan.
          Of God ne of good man give I never *tale*.   *take account*   460
          As a *liking* lord I *leyke* here alone.   *joyful*   *sport*
          Whoso *brawl* any boast, by down or by dale,   *brag*
          Those *gadlings* shall be ghasted and grisly groan iwis.   *base fellows*
          Lust, Folly and Vainglory,
          All these are in my memory.
          Thus beginneth the noble story
               Of this world's bliss.

          Lust-Liking and Folly,
          Comely knights of renown,   470
          Belyve through this land do cry   *at once*
          All abouten in tower and town.
          If any man be far or nigh
          That to my service will *busk him boun,*   *make himself ready*
          If he will be *trost* and *trye*   *trusty   constant*
          He shall be king and wear the crown
               With richest robes *in res.*   *immediately*
          Whoso to the World will draw
          Of God ne *of* good man *giveth he not a hawe,*   *for   if he will not give a hawthorn berry*
          Such a man by landes law   480
               Shall sitten on my dais.

LUST–LIKING   Lo, me here ready Lord, to *faren* and to *flee,*   *travel about   hurry*
          To seeken thee a servant *dynge* and dear.   *worthy*
          Whoso will with Folly ruled be
          He is worthy to be a servant here
               That draweth to sins seven.
          Whoso will be false and covetous
          With this world he shall have land and house.
          This world's wisdom giveth not a louse
               Of God nor of high heaven.   490

          Then he descends into the place at the same time

          Peace, people, of peace we you pray:
          Sythe and *sethe* well to my *saw.*   *sit   attend   advice*
          Whoso will be rich and in great array
          Toward the World he shall draw.
          Whoso will be false all that he may,
          Of God himself he hath none awe
          And liven in lusts night and day,
          The World of him will be right *fawe*   *delighted*
               To dwell in his house.
          Whoso will with the World have his dwelling   500
          And ben a lord of his clothing
          He must needs *over all thing*   *above all*
               Evermore be covetous.

          Non est in mundo dives qui dicit 'habundo'
          ('There is not a rich man in the world who says "I have enough"')

FOLLY   Yea, covetous he must be

86

And me, Folly, must *have in mende,*   *be disposed towards*
For whoso will alway Folly flee
In this world shall *be unthende.*   *not thrive*
Through World's wisdom of great degree
Shall never Man in world *moun wende*   *prosper*
But he have help of me   *unless*   510
That am Folly fair and *hende;*   *courteous*
    He must hangen on my hook.
Worldly wit was never nought
But with folly it were fraught.   *unless*
Thus the wise man hath taught
    Abouten in his book.

Sapiencia penes Domini
('Wisdom is in the power of God'—adapted from Ecclesiasticus 1, 1)

LUST–LIKING   Now all the men that in this world would thrive,
For to riden on horse full high,
Come speak with Lust and Liking *belyve*   *at once*
And his *fellow,* young Folly.   *companion*   520
    Let see who will us know.
Whoso will draw to Liking and Lust
And as a fool in Folly rust,
On us two he may trust
    And liven lovely, I trow.

BAD ANGEL   Ho, Lust-Liking and Folly,
Take to me good intent!   *pay attention*
I have brought *by downs dry*   *across the dry uplands*
To the World a great present.
I have guiled him full quaintly,   530
For since he was born I have him *blent.*   *blinded*
He shall be servant good and *try:*   *trusty*
Among you his will is lent.
    To the World he will him take.
For since he could *wit* I understand   *reason*
I have him ticed in every land.
His Good Angel, by street and strand,
    I have *done* him forsake.   *made*

Therefore Lust, my true *fere,*   *companion*
Thou art ready alway iwis   540
Of worldly laws thou him *lere*   *teach*
That he were brought in worldly bliss.   *so that he will be*
    Look he be rich, the sooth to tell.
Help him fast he *gin* to thrive,   *begin*
And when he weeneth best to live
Then shall he die and not be *shrive,*   *shriven*
    And go with us to hell.

LUST–LIKING   By Satan, thou art a noble knave
To *techen* men first from good.   *guide*
Lust and Liking he shall have,   550
Lechery shall be his food,
    Meats and drinks he shall have *trye.*   *choice*
With a *liking* lady *of lofte*   *pleasant   on high*
He shall sit in *sendal* soft   *rich silk*
To catchen him to hell *croft*   *enclosure*
    That day that he shall die.

FOLLY   With rich rents I shall him blind
With the World till he be *pit*   *fixed*
And then shall I long ere his end
Make that *caitiff* to be *knit*   *wretch   bound*   560

       On the World when he is *set sore.*   *to*   *settled in his mind*
  Come on Man, thou shalt not rue
  For thou wilt be to us true.
  Thou shalt be clad in clothes new
       And be rich evermore.

MANKIND   *Marry* fellow, *gramercy*!   *by our Lady* *many thanks*
  I would be rich and of great renown.
  I give no tale truly   *I do not worry*
  So that I be lord of tower and town,   *provided*
      By bushes and banks brown.   570
  Since that thou wilt make me
  Both rich of gold and fee,
  Go forth, for I will follow thee
      By dale and every town.

Trump up. Then shall go Lust-Liking, and Folly, Bad Angel and Mankind to World, and shall say

LUST–LIKING   How Lord, look out! for we have brought
  A servant of noble fame.
  Of worldly *good* is all his thought,   *possessions*
  Of lust and folly he hath no shame.
      He would be great of name.
  He would be at great honour   580
  For to rule town and tower.
  He would have to his paramour
      Some lovely *dynge* dame.   *noble*

WORLD   Welcome sir, seemly in sight!
  Thou art welcome to worthy *wede,*   *clothing*
  For thou wilt be my servant day and night,
  With my service I shall thee foster and feed.
  Thy back shall be beaten with bezants bright[1].
  Thou shalt have *byggyngs* by banks *brede;* *buildings* *broad*
  To thy *corse* shall kneel kaiser and knight   *person*   590
  Where that thou walk, by *sty* or by street,   *path*
      And ladies lovely *on lere.*   *of complexion*
  But God's service thou must forsake
  And wholly to the World thee take
  And then a man I shall thee make
      That none shall be thy peer.

MANKIND   Yes, World, and thereto here mine hand
  To forsake God and his service.
  To meeds thou give me a house and land   *as reward*
  That I reign richly at mine *emprise.*   *power*   600
  So that I fare well by street and strand
  While I dwell here in worldly wise,
  I reckon never of heaven *wand*   *rod i.e. of punishment*
  Nor of Jesu, that gentle justice.
      Of my soul I have no *ruth.*   *pity*
  What should I reckon of Doomsday
  So that I be rich and of great array?   *provided*
  I shall make merry while I may,
      And thereto *here my truth.*   *I give my pledge*

WORLD   Now certes sir, thou sayst well.   610
  I hold thee true from top to the toe.
  But thou were rich it were great *dele*   *unless* *pity*
  And all men that will fare so.
  Come up, my servant true as steel.

[1] (The clothing on) your back shall be in beaten gold (of bezants).

88

Then ascendeth Mankind to World

Thou shalt be rich, whereso thou go.
Men shall serven thee at meal
With minstrelsy and *bemys'* blow,   *trumpets'*
    With meats and drinks *trye.*   *choice*
Lust and Liking shall be thine ease
Lovely ladies thee shall please.   620
Whoso do thee any *dis-ease*   *harm*
    He shall be hangen high.

Liking, *belyve*   *quickly*
Let clothe him *swythe*   *immediately*
In robes *ryve*   *ample*
    With rich array.
Folly, thou *fond,*   *fool*
By street and strand,
Serve him at hand   630
    Both night and day.

LUST–LIKING   Trustily,
Lord, ready,
Je vous prie,   *I pray you, i.e. after you!*
Sir I say.
In liking and lust
He shall rust
Till death's dust
    Do him to *day.*   *die*

FOLLY   And I, Folly,
Shall *hyen* him high   *uplift*   640
Till some enemy
    Him *overgo.*   *conquer*
In world's wit
That in Folly sit,
I think yet
    His soul to *slo.*   *kill*

Trump-up.
[Lust-Liking and Folly take off Mankind to dress him. Enter Backbiter]

BACKBITER   All things I cry against the peace
To knight and knave, this is my *kind.*   *nature*
Yea, *dynge* dukes on their dais   *worthy*
In bitter *bales* I them bind.   *woes*   650
Crying and care, chiding and *ches*   *quarrelling*
And sad sorrow to them I send.
Yea, loud *leasings latched in les*   *lies tied with a leash*
Of tales untrue is all my *mend.*   *inclination*
    Man's *bane* abouten I bear.   *ruin*
I will that ye witen, all those that be here,
For I am known far and near,
I am the World's messenger,
    My name is Backbiter.

With every wight I walk and wend   660
And every man now loveth me well.
With loud *leasings under lende*   *lies under lime trees, or kept in store*
To death's *dint* I *dress and deal.*   *blow prepare and arrange for*
To speak fair before and foul behind
Amongst men at meat and meal
Truly, lords, this is my *kind.*   *nature*
Thus I run upon a wheel,
    I am *feller* than a fox.   *fiercer*

Flittering and flattering is my lesson;
With *leasings* I *tene* both tower and town   *lies*   *harm*   670
With letters of defamation
      I bear here in my box.

I am *light* of leaps through every land,   *nimble*
Mine holy *haps* may not be hid;   *successes*
Two may not together stand
But I, Backbiter, be the third.   *unless*
I shape yon boys to shame and *schonde*,   *disgrace*
All that will *bowen* when I them bid.   *bow down*
To law of land in faith I *fonde*.   *put test*
When tales untrue are *betid*   *current*   680
      Backbiter is wide *sprung*.   *spread*
Through the world by down and dales
All abouten I brew *bales*.   *torments*
Every man telleth tales
      After my false tongue.

Therefore I am made messenger
To leapen over lands *leye*   *fallow*
Through all the world far and near
Unsaid *saws* for to say.   *sayings*
In this *holt* I hunt here   *copse, i.e. place*   690
For to spy a *privy play,*   *secret trick*
For when Mankind is clothed *clear*   *handsomely*
Then shall I teachen him the way
      To the deadly sins seven.
Here shall I abiden *with my peace*   *silently*
The wrong *to do him for to chese*   *to make him choose*
For I think that he shall *lese*   *lose*
      The light of high heaven.

[Enter Lust-Liking and Folly, with Mankind richly clothed]

LUST–LIKING   Worthy World, in wealths *wound*!   *arrayed*
Here is Mankind *full fair in fold*.   *well dressed on earth*   700
In bright bezants he is bound
And *boun* to bow to you so bold.   *ready*
He liveth in lusts every *stound*;   *moment*
Wholly to you he hath *him yold*;   *submitted himself*
For to maken him gay on ground,
Worthy World, thou art *behold*.   *beholden*
      This world is well *at ease*.   *satisfied*
For to God I make a vow
Mankind had *liefer* now   *rather*
Grieve God with sins *row*   *many*   710
      Than the World to displease.

FOLLY   Displease thee he will for no man.
On me, Folly, is all his thought.
Truly Mankind *nought ne can*   *cannot*
Think on God that hath him *bought*.   *redeemed*
Worthy World, white as swan,
In thy love *leally is he laught*.   *loyally is he attached*
Sithen he could and *first began*   *since*   *came into existence*
Thee forsaken would he not,
      But give him to Folly.   720
And sithen he hath to thee be true,
I *rede* thee forsaken him for no new.   *advise*
Let us pleasen him till that he rue
      In hell to hangen high.

WORLD	Now Folly, fair thee befall,	
	And Lust, blessed be thou *ay!*	*for ever*
	Ye have brought Mankind to mine hall	
	Certes in a noble array.	
	With world's wealths within these walls	
	I shall him *feoff* if that I may.	*endow*	730
	Welcome Mankind! to thee I call,	
	Cleaner clothed than any clay	*more finely clad than any mortal*
	By down, dale and ditch.	
	Mankind, I rede that thou rest	
	With me, the World, as it is best.	
	Look thou hold mine *hende hest*	*courteous command*
	And ever shalt thou be rich.	
MANKIND	How should I *but* I *thy hests helde?*	*unless obey your commands*
	Thou workest with me wholly my will.	
	Thou feoffest me with fen and field	*you endow*	740
	And high hall, by *holts* and hill.	*copses*
	In worldly *weal* my wit I wield,	*wealth*
	In joy I *jet* with jewels *gentill,*	*strut noble*
	On blissful bank my bower is build,	
	In vainglory I stand still.	
	I am *keen* as a knight.	*bold*
	Whoso against the World will speak	
	Mankind shall on him be *wreke*;	*avenged*
	In strong prison I shall him *steke*	*shut up*
	Be it wrong or right		750
WORLD	Ah Mankind, well thee betide	
	That thy love on me is set!	
	In my bowers thou shalt abide	
	And yet fare *mickle the bet.*	*much the better*
	I feoff thee in all my *wones* wide	*dwellings*
	In *dale of dross* till thou be *det*	*the grave put*
	I make thee lord of mickle pride,	
	Sir, *at thine own mouth's mette.*	*to your own desire*
	I find in thee no treason.	
	In all this world, by sea and sand,		760
	Parks, places, *laund* and land,	*glade*
	Here I give thee with mine hand,	
	Sir, an open *seisin.*	*possession*
	Go to my treasurer, Sir Covetous;	
	Look thou tell him as I say.	
	Bid him make thee master in his house	
	With pence and pounds for to play.	
	Look thou give not a louse	
	Of the day that thou shalt die.	*for*
	Messenger, do now thine *use*;	*job*	770
	Backbiter, teach him the way.	
	Thou art sweeter than mead.	
	Mankind, take with thee Backbiting;	
	Leave him for no manner thing.	
	Flippergibbet with his flattering	
	Standeth Mankind in stead.	
BACKBITER	Backbiting and Detraction	
	Shall go with thee from town to town.	
	Have done, Mankind, and come down.	
	I am thine own page.		780
	I shall bear thee witness with my might	
	When my lord the World it *behight.*	*commands*

[Covetise is revealed in his scaffold]

Lo, where Sir Covetise sit
    And bideth us in his stage.

MANKIND   Sir World, I wend
In Covetise to *chasen my kend.*   *pursue my inclination*

WORLD   *Have him in mende*   *bear him in mind*
And iwis then shalt thou be right *thende.*   *prosperous*

GOOD ANGEL   Alas Jesu, gentle justice,
Whither may Man's Good Angel wend?   790
Now shall *careful* Covetise   *wretched*
Mankind truly all *schend.*   *destroy*
His *sely* ghost may sore *agryse*;   *miserable*   *shudder with fear*
Backbiting bringeth him in bitter bond.
Worldly wits, ye are not wise!
Your lovely life amiss ye spend
    And *that* shall ye sore smart.   *for that*
Parks, ponds and many pence
They seemen to you sweeter than sense,
But God's service nor his commandments   800
    Standeth you not at heart.

BAD ANGEL   Yah! When the fox preacheth, *keep well* your geese!   *watch out for*
He speaketh as it were a holy Pope.
Go fellow, and pick off the lice
That creep there upon thy cope!
Thy part is played all at the dice
That thou shalt have here, as I hope.
Till Mankind falleth to *podys* price   *toad's*
Covetise shall him *gripe and grope*   *seize and tear*
    Till some shame him *schend*   *disgrace*   810
Till Man be *dight* in death's *dow*   *put*   *dough, i.e. grave*
He saith never he hath enow.
Therefore good boy, come blow
    At my nether end!

BACKBITER   Sir Covetise, God thee save,
Thy pence and thy pounds all!
I, Backbiter, thine own knave,
Have brought Mankind unto thine hall.
The World bade thou shouldst him have
And *feoffen* him, whatso befall.   *endow*   820
In green grass till he be *grave*   *buried*
Put him in thy *precious pall,*   *rich robe*
    Covetise, it were else *ruth.*   *a pity*
While he walketh in worldly *wold*   *ground*
I, Backbiter, am with him *hold.*   *bound in obligation*
Lust and Folly, those barons bold
    To them he hath *plight his truth.*   *given his pledge*

COVETISE   Oh Mankind, blessed might thou be!
I have loved thee dearworthly many a day,
And so I *wot* well that thou dost me;   *know*   830
Come up and see my rich array.
It were a great point of pity
But Covetise were to thy *pay.*   *satisfaction*
Sit up right here in this *see.*   *seat*
I shall thee *lere* of worldly's *lay*   *teach*   *law*
    That fadeth as a flood.
With *good* enow I shall thee store,   *possessions*
And yet our game is but *lore*   *lost*

But thou covet mickle more   *unless*
    Than ever shall do thee good.   840

Thou must give thee to simony,
Extortion and false *asyse*.   *measure*
Help no man *but* thou have *why*;   *unless   cause, i.e. of self-interest*
Pay not thy servants their service.
Thy neighbours look thou destroy
Tithe not on none wise.   *on no account pay your tithes*
Hear no beggar though he cry,
And then shalt thou full soon rise.
    And when thou *usest merchandise*   *practise trade*
Look that thou be subtle of sleights,   850
And also swear all by deceits,
Buy and sell by false weights,
    For that is *kind* covetise.   *natural*

Be not aghast of *the great curse*;   *i.e. excommunication*
This lovely life may long *lest*.   *last*
Be the penny in thy purse,   *so long as there is*
Let them cursen and do their best.
What devil of hell art thou the worse
Though thou breakest Goddes *hest?*   *command*
Do after me, I am thy nurse.   860
Always gather and have none rest.
    In winning be all thy work.
To poor men *take none intent,*   *pay no attention*
For that thou hast long time *hent*   *accumulated*
In little time it may be spent;
    Thus saith Cato, the great *clerk.*   *scholar*

Labitur exiguo quod partum tempore longo
('That which was produced in a long while falls away in a short time')

MANKIND   Ah, Avarice, *well thou speed!*   *may you prosper*
Of worldly wit *thou canst* iwis   *you know*
Thou wouldst not I had need
And shouldst be wroth if I fared amiss.   870
I shall never beggar *bede*   *offer*
Meat nor drink, by heaven bliss;
Rather ere I should him clothe or feed
He should *starve* and stink iwis   *die*
    Covetise, as thou wilt I will do,
Whereso that I *fare*, by fen or flood,   *go*
I make avow by God's blood
Of Mankind getteth no man good
    But if he sing *'si dedero'*[1].   *unless*

COVETISE   Mankind, that was well sung.   880
Certes now thou *canst* some skill.   *know*
Blessed be thy true tongue!
In this bower thou shalt bide and *bill*.   *have a dwelling*
More sins I would thou *underfong*;   *undertook*
With covetise thee *feoff* I will: *endow*
And then some pride I would sprung
High in thy heart to holden and *hill*   *remain*
    And abiden in thy body.
Here I feoff thee in mine heaven
With gold and silver *light as levin*.   *bright as lightning*   890
The deadly sins all seven
    I shall *do comen in hy*.   *make come in haste*

---

[1] 'If I give' (i.e. I expect money back with interest).

Pride, Wrath and Envy,
Come forth, the Devil's children three!
Lechery, Sloth and Gluttony,
To man's flesh ye are fiends *free*.   *noble*
Driveth down our dales dry,
Be now blithe as any be,
Over hill and *holts* ye you hie   *woods*
To come to Mankind and to me   900
          From your *doughty* dens.   *worthy*
As dukes doughty ye you dress.
When the six be come, I guess
Then we be seven and no less
          Of the deadly sins.

[Enter Pride, Wrath and Envy on Belial's scaffold]

PRIDE   Wonder high *houtes* on hill heard I hout—   *shouts*
          Covetise cryeth, his *carping* I *ken*.   *voice*   *recognize*
          Some lord or some *lordeyn lely* shall *lout*   *rascal*   *loyally*   *bow*
          To be *pight* with pearls of my proud *pen*.   *adorned*   *store*
          Boun I am to bragging and busking about   *prone*   910
          Rapely and readily on *rout* for to *ren*.   *hurriedly*   *rush*   *run*
          By down, dales nor dens no duke I *doubt,*   *fear*
          Also fast for to *fog,* by floods and by fen,   *jog along*
                    I roar when I rise.
          Sir Belial, bright of *ble,*   *complexion*
          To you I recommend me.
          Have goodday, my father *free,*   *noble*
                    For I go to Covetise.

WRATH   When Covetise cried and *carped* of *care*   *complained*   *sorrow*
          Then must I, *wood* wretch, walken and wend   *mad*   920
          High over holts, as hound after hare.
          If I *let* and were the last, he should me sore *schend.*   *delayed*   *revile*
          I *busk my bold baston* by banks full bare;   *get ready my staff*
          Some boy shall be beaten and brought under bond;
          Wrath shall him *wreken* and *weighen his ware.*   *assault*   *measure his goods*
          Forlorn shall all be *for* lusty *layks* in land   *destroyed*   *because of*   *games*
                    As a *lither page.*   *good-for-nothing*
          Sir Belial black and blue,
          Have goodday, now I go
          For to fell thy foe   930
                    With wicked *wage.*   *payment*

ENVY   When Wrath ginneth walk in any wide *wones*   *dwellings*
          Envy flits as a fox and followeth on fast.
          When thou stirrest or starest or stumble upon stones
          I leap as a lion; me is loth to be the last.
          Yea, I breed bitter *bales* in body and in bones.   *torments*
          I fret mine heart and in *care* I me cast.   *sorrow*
          Go we to Covetise all three at once
          With our grisly gear a *groom* for to *ghast.*   *man*   *terrify*
                    This day shall he die.   940
          Belzabub, now have good day,
          For we will wenden in good array
          All three *in fere* as I thee say,   *together*
                    Pride, Wrath and Envy.

BELIAL   Farewell now, children fair to find!
          Do now well your old use!
          When ye come to Mankind
          Make him wroth and envious.
          Leveth not lightly under *linde*;   *leave*   *lime tree*

94

To his soul breweth a bitter juice.   950
When he is dead I shall him bind
In hell, as cat doth the mouse.
　　　Now *busk* you forth *on brede*.　　*hurry*　*far and wide*
I may be blithe as any bee,
For Mankind in every country
Is ruled by my children three,
　　　Envy, Wrath and Pride.

[Enter Gluttony, Lechery and Sloth on Flesh's scaffold]

GLUTTONY　A *groom* gan *greden* gaily on ground;　　*boy*　*called loudly*
　　　Of me, gay Glutton, gan all his *gale*.　　*song*
　　　I stamp and I start and *stint upon stound*,　　*stop in a moment*　960
　　　To a staunch death I stagger and *stale*.　　*decline?*
　　　What boys with their bellies in my bonds been bound,
　　　Both their back and their blood I brew all to *bale*.　　*torment*
　　　I *fese* folk to fight till their flesh *fond*.　　*stir up*　*founder*
　　　When some have drunken a draught they *drepen* in a dale;　　*droop*
　　　　　In me is their mind.
　　　Man's flourishing flesh
　　　Fair, frail and fresh,
　　　I *rape* to rule in a rush　　*hurry*
　　　　　To *cloy* in my kind.　　*to get in the way, as my manner is*　970

LECHERY　In Man's *kith* I *cast me* a castle to keep.　　*loins*　*propose*
　　　I, Lechery, with liking am loved in each a land.
　　　With my *suckles* of sweetness I sit and I sleep.　　*honeysuckles*
　　　Many *berdes* I bring to my bitter bond.　　*girls*
　　　In woe and in *wrake* wicked wits shall weep　　*pain*
　　　That in my *wones* wild will not out wend.　　*dwellings*
　　　When Mankind is casten under *clourys* to creep　　*the sod*
　　　Then the *ledrouns* for their liking I shall all *to-schend*,　　*rascals*　*shatter*
　　　　　Truly to tell.
　　　Sir Flesh, now I wend　　　　　　　　　　　　　　980
　　　With Lust in my *lend*　　*loin*
　　　To catchen Mankind
　　　　　To the Devil of hell.

SLOTH　Yea, what sayst thou of Sir Sloth, with my *sour syth*?　　*dull appearance*
　　　Mankind loveth me well, *wis* as I ween;　　*certainly*
　　　Men of religion I rule *in my right*;　　*according to my standards*
　　　I *let* God's service, the truth may be seen.　　*impede*
　　　In bed I *breed brothel* with my *berdes* bright;　　*become lecherous*　*girls*
　　　Lords, ladies and *ledrouns* to my lore lean.　　*rascals*
　　　Mickle of Mankind in my cloaks shall be knit　　　　　990
　　　Till death driveth them down in dales *bedene*.　　*quickly*
　　　　　We may no longer abide.
　　　Sir Flesh, comely king,
　　　In thee is all our breeding.
　　　Give us now thy blessing,
　　　　　For Covetise hath cried.

FLESH　Gluttony and Sloth, farewell *in fere*!　　*together*
　　　Lovely in land is now your *lesse*;　　*comfort*
　　　And Lechery, my daughter so dear,
　　　Dapperly ye dress you so *dyngne* on dais.　　*nobly*　1000
　　　All three my blessing ye shall have here.
　　　Goeth now forth and give ye no *fors*.　　*regard*
　　　It is no need you for to *lere*　　*teach*
　　　To catchen Mankind to a *careful close*　　*miserable confinement*
　　　　　From the bright bliss of heaven.　　*away from*
　　　The World, the Flesh and the Devil are *know*　　*recognized as*

Great Lords, as we well *owe*,   *ought to be*
And through Mankind we *setten* and sow   *sit*
    The deadly sins seven.

Then go Pride, Wrath, Envy, Gluttony, Lechery and Sloth to Covetise and Pride says

PRIDE   What is thy will, Sir Covetise?   1010
    Why hast thou after us sent?
    When thou criedest we gan *agryse*   *shudder with fear*
    And come to thee now *par assent*,   *willingly*
        Our love is on thee lent.
    I, Pride, Wrath and Envy,
    Gluttony, Sloth and Lechery,
    We are come all six for thy cry
        To be at thy commandment.

COVETISE   Welcome be ye, brethren all,
    And my sister, sweet Lechery!
    Wit ye why I gan to call?   *know*   1020
    For ye must me help and that *in hy*.   *in haste*
    Mankind is now come to mine hall
    With me to dwell by downs dry.
    Therefore ye must, whatso befall,
    Feoffen him with your folly,   *endow*
        And else ye do him wrong.   *or*
    For when Mankind is *kendly* covetous,   *thoroughly*
    He is proved wrathful and envious;
    Gluttons *slaw* and lecherous   *lazy*
        They are *otherwhile* among.   *also sometimes*   1030

    Thus every sin *tilleth in* other   *attracts*
    And maketh Mankind to be a fool.
    We seven *fallen on a fodyr*   *all rush together*
    Mankind to chase to *pining's stool*.   *the seat of punishment*
    Therefore Pride, good brother,
    And brethren all, take ye your tool.
    Let each of us take at other
    And set Mankind on a stumbling stool
        While he is here *on lyve*.   *living*   1040
    Let us lull him in our lust
    Till he be driven to damning dust.
    Cold care shall be his crust
        To death when he shall drive.

PRIDE   In glee and game I grow glad.
    Mankind, take good heed
    And do as Covetise thee bad,
    Take me in thine heart, precious Pride.
    Look thou be not *over-led*,   *dominated*
    Let no *bachelor* thee *misbede*.   *young knight*   *ill-treat*   1050
    Do thee to be doubted and dread,   *Make yourself feared*
    Beat boys till they bleed,
        Cast them *in careful kettys*,   *into wretched carrion*
    Friend, father and mother dear,
    Bow them not in manner,
    And hold no manner man thy peer,
        And use these new *jettis*.   *fashions*

    Look thou blow mickle boast
    With long *crakows* on thy shoes.   *points*
    Jag thy clothes in every *cost*   *slash*   *manner*   1060
    And else men shall *let* thee but a goose.   *or*   *consider*
    It is thus, Man, well thou *wost*,   *knowest*
    Therefore do as no man does

And every man *set at a thost*   count a turd
And of thyself make great *ros.*   boasting
    Now *see thyself on every side.*   look around
Every man thou shalt *schende and schelfe*   hurt and push aside
And hold no man better than thyself.
Till death's *dint* thy body *delf*   stroke   pierces
    Put wholly thine heart in Pride.   1070

MANKIND   Pride, by Jesu thou sayest well.
Whoso suffer is over-led all day.   who allows it is dominated
While I rest on my *running wheel*   i.e. the wheel of fortune?
I shall not suffer, if that I may.
Much mirth at meat and meal
I love right well, and rich array.
Truly I think, *in every sele,*   at all times
On ground to be *graythed* gay   dressed
    And of myself to take good guard.
Mickle mirth thou wilt me make,   1080
Lordly to live by land and lake.
Mine heart wholly to thee I take
    Into thine own award.

[Pride ascends Covetise's scaffold to join Mankind]

PRIDE   In thy bower to abide
I come to dwell by thy side.

MANKIND   Mankind and Pride
Shall dwell together every tide.

WRATH   Be also wroth as thou were *wood.*   mad
Make thee be dread, by dales *derne*!   secret
Whoso thee *wrethe* by fen or flood,   enrage   1090
Look thou be avenged *yerne.*   quickly
Be ready to spill man's blood.
Look thou him fear, by fields *ferne.*   make him afraid   far-off
Always, Man, be full of *mood.*   aggressive spirit
My *loathly* laws look thou learn,   horrible
    I rede for anything.   I counsel in all circumstances
Anon take vengeance, man, I rede,
And then shall no man thee *over-lead,*   dominate
But of thee they shall have dread
    And bow to thy bidding.   1100

MANKIND   Wrath, for thy counsel *hende*   courteous
Have thou God's blessing and mine.
What *caitiff* of all my *kende*   wretch   race
Will not bow, he shall *abyn.*   pay for it
With mine vengeance I shall him *schende*   harm
And *wreken* me, by God's *eyne.*   avenge   eyes
Rather ere I should bow or bend
I should be sticked as a swine
    With a loathly lance.
Be it early or late,   1110
Whoso make with me debate
I shall him hitten on the pate
    And taken anon vengeance.

Wrath ascends Covetise's scaffold

WRATH   With my *rewly* rudder,   hurtful
I come to thee, Mankind my brother.

MANKIND   Wrath, thy fair *fothyr*   company
Maketh each man to be venged on other.

ENVY	Envy with Wrath must drive		
	To *haunt* Mankind also.	*accompany*	
	When any of thy neighbours will thrive		1120
	Look thou have Envy thereto.		
	On the high name I charge thee *belyve*	*in God's name*	*at once*
	Backbite him, howso thou do.		
	Kill him anon withouten knife		
	And speak him some shame where thou go		
	By dale or downs dry.		
	Speak thy neighbour mickle shame,		
	Put on him some false fame,		
	Look thou undo his noble name		
	With me, that am Envy.		1130

MANKIND	Envy, thou art both good and *hende*	*courteous*
	And shalt be of my counsel chief.	
	Thy counsel is knowen through Mankind	
	For *ilke* man calleth other whore and thief.	*each*
	Envy, thou art *root and rind*	*i.e. source*
	Through this world of mickle mischief.	
	In bitter *bales* I shall them bind	*torments*
	That to thee putteth any *reprefe*.	*reproach*
	Come up to me above.	
	For more envy that is now reigning	1140
	Was never since Christ was king.	
	Come up, Envy, my dear darling:	
	Thou hast Mankind's love.	

ENVY	I climb from this croft	
	With Mankind to sitten *on loft*.	*on high*

MANKIND	Come, sit here soft,
	For in abbeys thou dwellest full oft.

GLUTTONY	In gay Gluttony a game thou begin;	
	Ordain thee meat and drinks good.	
	Look that no treasure thou part *atwin*	*in two*
	But thee *feoff* and feed with all kinds food.	*endow*
	With fasting shall man never heaven win;	
	These great fasters I hold them *wood*.	*mad*
	Though thou eat and drink, it is no sin.	
	Fast no day! I *rede*, by the *Rood,*	*advise* *cross*
	Thou chide these fasting churls.	
	Look thou have spices of good odour	
	To feoff and feed thy fleshly flower	
	And then mayst thou *bulten* in thy bower	*fornicate*
	And *serden* gay girls.	*fuck*

1150

1160

MANKIND	Ah Gluttony, well I thee greet.	
	Sooth and *sad* it is, thy *saw*.	*solemn* *advice*
	I am no day well by stye nor street	
	Till I have well filled my maw.	
	Fasting is felled under feet.	
	Though I never fast I *ne reck an haw*.	*care not a hawthorn berry*
	He serveth of nought, by the Rood I *let,*	*it serves me'nothing* *consider*
	But to *do* a man's gut to *gnaw*.	*make* *suffer*
	To fast I will not *fonde*.	*attempt*
	I shall not spare, so have I rest,	
	To have a morsel of the best.	
	The longer shall my life *mow lest*	*be able to last*
	With great liking in land.	

1170

GLUTTONY	By banks *on brede*	*broad*
	Otherwise to spew *thee speed!*	*sometimes* *make haste*

MANKIND   While I life lead
With fair food my flesh shall I feed.

LECHERY   Yea, when thy flesh is fair fed
Then shall I, lovely Lechery,
Be *bobbed* with thee in bed;   *bounced up and down*   1180
Hereof serve meat and drinkes *trye*.   *therefore*   *choice*
In love thy life shall be led;
Be a lecher till thou die.
Thy needs shall be the better *sped*   *satisfied*
If thou give thee to fleshly folly
    Till death thee down *drepe*.   *strike*
Lechery since the world began
Hath advanced many a man.
Therefore, Mankind, my *leve lemman*,   *darling lover*
    In my cunt thou shalt creep.   1190

MANKIND   Ah Lechery, well thee be!
Man's seed in thee is sow.
Few men will forsake thee
In any country that I know.
Spouse-breach is a friend right *free,*   *noble*
Men use that more than enow.
Lechery, come sit by me.
Thy *banns* be full wide *y-know,*   *summons*   *known*
    Liking is in thy *lend*.   *lust*   *loins*
One nor other, I see no wight   1200
That will forsake thee day nor night.
Therefore come up, my *berd bright*   *beautiful girl*
    And rest thee with Mankind.

LECHERY   I may sooth sing
'Mankind is caught in my sling'.

MANKIND   For any earthly thing
To bed thou must me bring.

SLOTH   Yea, when ye be in bed both
Wrapped well in worthy *weed,*   *bedclothes*
Then I, Sloth, will be wroth   1210
But two *brothels* I may breed.   *lechers*
When the mass-bell goth
Lie still man, and take none heed.
Lap thine head then in a cloth
And take a sweat, I thee *rede,*   *counsel*
    Church-going thou forsake.
Losengerys in land I *lift*   *flatterers*   *exalt*
And *dyth* men to *mickle unthrift*.   *lead*   *great dissoluteness*
Penance enjoined men in shrift
    Is undone, and that I *make*.   *cause*   1220

MANKIND   Oh Sloth, thou *sayst me skill*.   *speakest wisely*
Men use thee *mickle, God it wot*.   *much*   *God knows*
Men love well now to lie still
In bed to take a *morrow swot*.   *morning sweat*
To churchward is not their will;
Their beddes they thinken good and hot.
Harry, Jeffrey, Joan and Jill
Are laid and lodged *in a lot*   *in turn*
    With thine *unthende* charms.   *profitless*
All mankind, by the holy Rood,   1230
Are now slow in works good.
Come near therefore, mine fair *food,*   *nurse*
    And lull me in thine arms.

SLOTH	I make men, I trow, In God's service to be right slow.
MANKIND	Come up this throw. Such men thou shalt finden enow.

Mankind I am called by *kind*   *nature*
With cursedness in *costs* knit. *habits*
In sour sweetness my *syth* I send *seeing*   1240
With seven sins *sad* beset.[1] *seriously*
Mickle mirth I move in mind
With melody at *my mouth's met*. *my desire*
My proud power shall I not *pend* *limit*
Till I be put in pain's pit
  To hell *hent* from hence. *seized*
In dale of dole till we are down
We shall be clad in a gay gown.
I see no man *but* they use some *unless*
  Of these seven deadly sins.   1250

For commonly it is seldom seen
Whoso now be lecherous
But of other men he shall have disdain
And be proud or covetous.
  In sin each man is found.
There is poor nor rich by land nor lake
That all these seven will forsake,
But with one or other he shall be take
  And in their bitter bonds bound.

GOOD
ANGEL
	So mickle the worse, *weleawoo*, *woe!* 1260
	That ever Good Angel was ordained thee.
	Thou art ruled after the Fiend that is thy foe
	And nothing certes after me.
	Weleaway! Whither may I go? *woe!*
	Man doth *me bleyken bloody ble*. *makes pale my ruddy complexion*
	His sweet soul he will now *slo*. *slay*
	He shall weep all his game and glee
	  At one day's time.
	Ye see well all soothly in sight
	I am about both day and night 1270
	To bring his soul into bliss bright,
	  And himself will it bring to *pine*. *torment*

BAD ANGEL	No Good Angel, thou art not in season,
	Few men in thee faith they find.
	For thou has skewed a *bald reason*; *feeble argument*
	Good sir, come blow my hole behind.
	Truly man hath no *chesun* *cause*
	On thy God to *grede* and *grind*, *call out* *gnash his teeth*
	For *that* should con Christ's lesson *he that*
	In penance his body he must bind 1280
	  And forsake the World's mind.
	Men are loath on thee to cry
	Or do penance for their folly.
	Therefore have I now mastery
	  Wellnigh over all mankind.

GOOD ANGEL	Alas, Mankind Is *bobbed* and *blent* as the blind; *mocked* *deceived* In faith I find

[1] Possibly translate these two lines: 'In bitter sweetness I observe that my vision is seriously assailed by seven sins'; or, 'I set my heart on a bitter kind of sweetness, being hard put to it by (the) seven sins'.

To Christ he cannot be kind.
Alas, Mankind   1290
Is soiled and sagged in sin.
He will not *blin*   cease
Till body and soul part *atwin*.   *in two*
Alas, he is *blended*,   *blinded*
Amiss man's life is i-spended,
With fiends *fended*.   *by   attacked*
Mercy, God, that man were amended!

[Enter Shrift and Penance]

SHRIFT   What, man's Angel good and true,
Why sighest thou and sobbest sore?
Certes sore it shall me rue   1300
If I see thee make mourning more.
May any *bote thy bale brew*   *remedy relieve thy grief*
Or anything thy state *astore?*   *restore*
For all fellowships, old and new
Why makest thou *groching under gore*   *lamentation*
          With *pining points* pale?   *tormenting pricks*
Why was all this *greting gun*   *weeping begun*
With sore sighing under sun?
Tell me and I shall if I cun
          Brew the *bote of bale*.   *remedy for suffering*   1310

GOOD   Of bitter bales thou mayst me *bete*,   *cure*
ANGEL   Sweet Shrift, if that thou wilt.
For Mankind it is that I *grete*;   *weep*
He is *in point to be spilt*.   *about to be destroyed*
He is set in seven sins' seat
And will, certes, till he be killt.
With me he thinketh nevermore to meet;
He hath me forsake, and I have no guilt.
          No man will him amend.
Therefore, Shrift, so God me speed,   1320
But if thou help at this need,
Mankind getteth never other *meed*   *reward*
          But pain withouten end.

SHRIFT   What, Angel! Be of comfort strong,
For thy Lord's love that died on tree.
On me, Shrift, it shall not be long
And that thou shalt the sooth see.
If he will be *aknow* his wrong   *confess*
And nothing *hele*, but tell it me,   *hide*
And do penance soon among,   1330
I shall him steer to *gamen and glee*   *mirth and joy*
          In joy that ever shall last.
Whoso shrive him of his sins all
I *behete* him heaven hall.   *promise*
Therefore go we hence whatso befall
          To Mankind fast.

Then they go to Mankind and he says

SHRIFT   What, Mankind, how goeth this?
What dost thou with these devils seven?
Alas, alas man, all amiss!
Bliss in the name of God in heaven   *rejoice*   1340
          I *rede,* so have I rest.   *advise*
These loathly *lordeyns* away thou lift   *villains*
And come down and speak with Shrift

And draw thee *yerne* to some thrift.   *quickly*
　　Truly it is the best.

MANKIND　Ah Shrift, thou art well *be note*   *known*
Here to Sloth that sitteth herein.
He saith thou mightest a come to man's *cote*   *house*
On Palm Sunday *all betime.*   *early enough*
　　Thou art come all too soon.   1350
Therefore Shrift, by thy *fay,*   *faith*
Go forth till on Good Friday.
Tend to thee then well I may;
　　I have now else to doen.

SHRIFT　Oh, that harlot is now bold;
In *bale* he bindeth Mankind *belyve.*   *torment quickly*
Say Sloth I prayed him that he would   *tell*
Find a charter of thy life.   *get a guarantee*
Man, thou mayst be under *mold*   *ground*
Long ere that time, killed with a knife,   1360
With *podys* and *forskys* many-fold.   *toads frogs*
Therefore shape ye now to shrive
　　If you wilt come to bliss.
Thou sinnest; ere sorrow thee *ensense,*   *arouse*
Behold thine heart, thy privy *spense*   *store-room*
And thine own conscience,
　　Or certes thou dost amiss.

MANKIND　Yea, Peter, so do *mo*!   *more people*
We have eaten garlic everyone[1].
Though I should to hell go   1370
I *wot* I shall not go alone,   *know*
　　Truly I tell thee.
I did never so evil truly
But other have done as evil as I.
Therefore sir, let be thy cry
　　And go hence from me.

PENANCE　With point of penance I shall him *prene*   *pierce*
Man's pride for to fell.
With this lance I shall him *lene*   *lend*
Iwis a drop of *mercy well.*   *mercy's fountain*   1380
Sorrow of heart is that I mean;
Truly there may no tongue tell
What washeth souls more clean
From the foul fiend of hell
　　Than sweet sorrow of heart.
God that sitteth in heaven on high
Asketh no more ere that thou die
But sorrow of heart with weeping eye
　　For all thy sins *smart.*   *vigorous*

They that sigh in sinning   1390
In sad sorrow for their sin,
When they shall make their ending,
All their joy is to begin.
Then *meddleth* no mourning,   *mingles*
But joy is joined with gentle *gynne.*   *skill*
Therefore Mankind, in this tokening,
With *spete* of spear to thee I *spin*;   *point move quickly*
　　God's laws to thee I learn.
With my *spud* of sorrow *swote*   *knife sweet*

[1] Probably 'We are all tarred with the same brush'.

102

I reach to thine heart root.   1400
All thy bale shall turn thee to *bote*.   *cure*
    Mankind, go shrive thee *yerne*.   *quickly*

[Pricks Mankind with his lance]

MANKIND   A *sete* of sorrow in me is set;   *plant*
Certes for sin I sigh sore.
Moan of mercy in me is met;
For World's mirth I mourn more.
In weeping woe my weal is wet.
Mercy, thou must mine state *astore*.   *restore*
From our Lord's light thou hast me *let*,   *obstructed*
Sorry sin, thou *grisly gore*!   *filthy lout*   1410
    Out on thee, deadly sin!
Sin, thou hast Mankind *schent*.   *ruined*
In deadly sin my life is spent.
Mercy, God omnipotent!
    In your grace I begin.

For though Mankind have done amiss,
And he will fall in repentance,
Christ shall him bringen to bower of bliss
If sorrow of heart latch him with lance.
Lordings, ye see well all this,   1420
Mankind hath been in great *bobbaunce*.   *worldly pomp*
I now forsake my sin iwis
And take me wholly to Penance.
    On Christ I cry and call.
Ah mercy, Shrift! I will no more.
For deadly sin my heart is sore.
Stuff Mankind with thine store
    And have him to thine hall.

SHRIFT   Shrift may no man forsake.
When Mankind crieth I am ready.   1430
When sorrow of heart he hath take
Shrift profiteth verily.
Whoso for sin will sorrow make
Christ him heareth when he will cry.
Now Man, let sorrow thine sin slake
And turn not again to thy folly,
    For that maketh *distance*.   *discord*
And if it hap thee turn again to sin,
For God's love lie not long therein!
He that doth alway evil and will not *blin*,   *cease*
    That asketh great vengeance.   1440

MANKIND   Nay certes that shall I not do,
Shrift, thou shalt the sooth see;
For though Mankind be wont thereto
I will now amend me.

Then he descends to Shrift

I come to thee Shrift, all wholly lo!
I forsake you, sins, and from you flee.
Ye *shapen to* man a sorry show;   *contrive for*
When he is beguiled in this degree
    Ye *bleykyn* all his *ble*.   *make pale*   *complexion*   1450
Sin, thou art a *sorry store*.   *wretched treasure*
Thou makest Mankind to sink sore.
Therefore of you will I no more.
    I ask Shrift for charity.

SHRIFT	If thou wilt *be aknow* here *confess*	
	Only all thy trespass,	
	I shall thee shield from hell fire	
	And put thee from pain unto precious place.	
	If thou wilt not make thine soul clear	
	But keep *them* in thine heart case, *i.e. trespasses*	1460
	Another day they shall be raw and *rere*. *rare, i.e. partly raw*	
	And sink thy soul to Satanas	
	In ghastful glowing *gleed*. *coal*	
	Therefore man, in *mody* moans, *grieving*	
	If thou wilt wend to worthy *wones* *places*	
	Shrive thee now all at once	
	Wholly of thy misdeed.	

MANKIND	Ah yes, Shrift, truly I trow	
	I shall not spare for odd nor even	
	That I shall reckon all *on a row* *in order*	1470
	To *latch me up to life's leaven*. *bring myself to the light of eternal life*	
	To my Lord God I *am aknow* *confess*	
	That sitteth aboven in high heaven	
	That I have sinned many a *throw* *time*	
	In the deadly sins seven,	
	Both in home and hall.	
	Pride, Wrath and Envy,	
	Covetise and Lechery,	
	Sloth and also Gluttony,	
	I have them used all.	1480

The ten commandments broken I have
And my five *wits spent them amiss*.   *senses   abused*
I was then *wood* and gan to rave.   *mad*
Mercy God! Forgive me this!
When any poor man gan to me crave
I gave him nought and that *forthinketh* me iwis   *repenteth*
Now Saint Saviour, ye me save
And bring me to your bower of bliss,
    I cannot all say.
But to the earth I kneel adown   1490
Both with *bede* and orison   *prayer*
And ask my absolution,
    Sir Shrift, I you pray.

SHRIFT	Now Jesu Christ, God holy,	
	And all the saints of heaven *hende*, *loving*	
	Peter and Paul apostoly,	
	To whom God gave power to loose and bind,	
	He forgive thee thy folly	
	That thou hast sinned with heart and mind.	
	And I *up my power thee assoly* *according to my power absolve thee*	1500
	That thou hast been to God unkind,	
	Quantum peccasti. *all that you have sinned*	
	In Pride, Ire and Envy,	
	Sloth, Gluttony and Lechery	
	And Covetise continually	
	Vitam male continuasti. *you have lived continually in sin*	

I thee *assoil* with good intent   *absolve*
Of all the sins that thou hast wrought
In breaking of God's commandment
In word, *work*, will and thought.   *deed*   1510
I restore to thee sacrament
Of penance which thou never *rowt*;   *took heed of*
Thy five wits mis-dispent

In sin, the which thou shouldest not,
 Quicquid gesisti *whatever you have done*
With eyes seen, ears hearing,
Nose smelled, mouth speaking,
And all thy body's bad working,
 Vicium quodcumque fecisti. *whatever sin you have committed*

  I thee assoil with mild mood   1520
Of all that thou hast been full mad
In forsaking of thine Angel Good,
And thy foul Flesh that thou hast fed,
The World, the Devil that is so *wood,* *mad*
And followed thine angel that is so bad.
To Jesu Christ that died on Rood
I restore thee again full *sad.* *solemnly*
 Noli peccare! *do not sin*
And all the good deeds that thou hast done
And all thy tribulation   1530
Stand thee in remission. *be valid*
 Posius noli viciare. *do not sin any more*

MANKIND Now Sir Shrift, where may I dwell
To keep me from sin and woe?
A comely counsel ye me spell *give me good advice*
To fend me now from my foe.
If these seven sins here tell
That I am thus from them go,
The World, the Flesh and the Devil of hell
Shall seeken my soul for to *slo* *kill*   1540
 Into *bale's* bower. *torment*
Therefore I pray you put me
Into some place of surety
That they may not harmen me
 With no sins sour.

SHRIFT To such a place I shall thee *ken* *direct*
Where thou mayst dwell *withouten distance* *undoubtedly*
And alway keep thee from sin,
Into the Castle of Perseverance.
If thou wilt to heaven win   1550
And keep thee from worldly *distance,* *discord*
Go to yon castle and keep thee therein,
For it is stronger than any in France.
 To yon castle I thee send.
That castle is a precious place,
Full of virtue and of grace;
Whoso liveth there his life's space
 No sin shall him *schend.* *confound*

MANKIND Ah Shrift, blessed may thou be!
This castle is *here but at hand.* *very close by*   1560
Thither *rapely* will I *tee* *quickly* *go*
Secure over this sad sand.
Good perseverance God send me
While I live here in this land.
From foul filth now I flee,
Forth to faren now I *fonde* *go*
 To yon precious *port.* *refuge*
Lord, what! Man is in merry live
When he is of his sins shrive!
All my *dole* adown is drive. *grief*
 Christ is mine comfort.   1570

BAD ANGEL   Eh, what devil, Man? *Whither shalt?*   *where are you going*
    Wouldest draw now to holiness?
    Go fellow, thy good *gate,*   *course*
    Thou art forty winter old, as I guess.
    Go again, the Devil's mate,
    And play ye a while with Sarah and Ciss.
    She would not else, yon old *trat,*   *hag*
    But put thee to penance and to *stress,*   *hardship*
        Yon foul *feterel fyle.*   *deceiving wretch*   1580
    Let men that are on the *pit's* brink   *grave*
    Forbearen both meat and drink
    And do penance as them good think;
        And come and play thee a while.

GOOD   Yea, Mankind, wend forth thy way
ANGEL   And do nothing after his *rede.*   *counsel*
    He would thee lead over *lands lay*   *fallow earth*
    In *dale of dross* till thou were dead.   *valley of worthless matter, i.e. the grave*
    Of cursedness he keepeth the key
    To baken thee a bitter bread.   1590
    In dale of dole till thou shouldst die
    He would draw thee to cursedhead,
        In sin to have mischance.
    Therefore speed now thy pace
    Pertly to yon precious place   *quickly*
    That is all growen full of grace,
        The Castle of Perseverance.

MANKIND   Good Angel, I will do as thou wilt
    In land while my life may last,
    For I find well in holy writ   1600
    Thou counselest ever for the best.

[Leaf of manuscript missing. It probably contained speeches by Meekness and Patience, as well as the end of Mankind's speech. The play resumes with Mankind being lectured by the Seven Moral Virtues in front of the Castle]

CHARITY   To Charity, Man, have an eye
    In all thing, man, I rede.
    All thy doing as dross is dry
    But in Charity thou doth thy deed.   *unless*
    I destroy alway Envy;
    So did thy God when he gan bleed;
    For sin he was hangen high
    And yet sinned he never in deed,
        That mild mercy *well.*   *fountain*   1610
    Paul in his *'pistle* putteth the *prefe:*   *epistle*   *proof*
    'But Charity be with thee chief'.   *1 Corinthians 13, 1–3*
    Therefore, Mankind, be now *lief*   *desirous*
        In Charity for to dwell.

ABSTINENCE   In abstinence lead thy life,
    Take but *skilful reflection*;   *moderate refreshment*
    For Glutton killeth withouten knife
    And destroyeth thy *complexion.*   *constitution*
    Whoso eat or drink *overblyve,*   *too eagerly*
    It *gathereth to corruption.*   *generates corrupt matter*   1620
    This sin brought us all in strife
    When Adam fell in sin down
        From precious Paradise.
    Mankind, learn now of our lore.
    Whoso eat or drink more
    Than skilfully his state *astore,*   *(to) restore*
        I hold him nothing wise.

CHASTITY   Mankind, take *keep* of Chastity   *heed*
And *move thee* to maiden Mary.   *appeal*
Fleshly folly look thou flee
At the reverence of Our Lady.   1630

Quia qui in carne vivunt Domino placere non possunt
('Because those who live in the Flesh cannot please the Lord')

That courteous queen, what did she?
Kept her clean and steadfastly,
And in her was trussed the Trinity.
Through *ghostly* grace she was worthy,   *spiritual*
    And all *for* she was chaste.   *because*
Whoso keepeth him chaste and will not sin,
When he is buried *in bank's brim*   *on the brink of a slope*
All his joy is to begin.
    Therefore to me *take taste*.   *give affection*   1640

INDUSTRY   In busyness, Man, look thou be,
With worthy works good and thick.
To Sloth if thou cast thee
It shall thee draw to thoughts *wykke*.   *wicked*

Osiositas parit omne malum
('Idleness gives rise to all evil')

It putteth a man to poverty
And pulleth him to pain's prick.
Do somewhat alway for love of me
Though thou shouldest but *thwyte* a stick.   *whittle*
    With *bedes* sometime thee bless;   *prayers*
Sometime read and sometime write   1650
And sometime play at thy delight.   *i.e. always be busy*
The Devil thee waiteth with despite
    When thou art in idleness.

GENEROSITY   In *Largity*, Man, lay thy love;   *generosity*
Spend thy *good*, as God it sent.   *goods*
In worship of him that sit above
Look thy goodes be dispent.
In *dale of dross* when thou shalt *drove,*   *i.e. the grave be forced*
Little love is on thee *lent.*   *fixed*
The *sekatours* shall say: 'It is their *behove*   *executors duty*   1660
To make us merry, for he is went
    That all this *good gan owle*!'   *possessions got together*
Lay thy treasure and thy trust
In place where no *ruggynge* rust   *corrosive*
May it destroy to dross ne dust,
    But all to help of soul.

MANKIND   Ladies in land, lovely and *lyt,*   *bright*
Liking lelys, ye be my *leech*!   *pleasant lilies physician*
I will bow to your bidding bright;
True tokening ye me teach.   1670
Dame Meekness, in your might
I will *me wryen* from wicked *wreche.*   *turn aside vengeance*
All my purpose I have *pight,*   *set*
Patience, to do as ye me preach;
    From Wrath ye shall me keep.
Charity, ye will to me attend;
From foul Envy ye me defend.
Man's mind ye may amend
    Whether he wake or sleep.

Abstinence, to you I trust;
From Gluttony ye shall me draw.   1680

In Chastity to liven *me list,*   *I wish*
That is Our Lady's law.
Busyness, we shall be *cyste*;   *kissed, i.e. joined*
Sloth, I forsake thy *sleper saw.*   *deceitful saying*
Largity, to you I trust,
Covetise to *don of dawe.*   *put to death*
    This is a courteous company.
What should I more moneys make?
The seven sins I forsake   1690
And to these seven virtues I me take.
    Maiden Meekness, now mercy!

MEEKNESS   Mercy may mend all thy moan;
Come in here at thine own will.
We shall thee fend from thy *fon*   *enemies*
If thou keep thee in this castle still.

Cum sancto sanctus eris, et cetera
('With the pure thou shalt be pure'—Psalm 18, 26)
Then he enters (the Castle)

Stand herein as still as stone;
Then shall no deadly sin thee *spill.*   *destroy*
Whether that sins come or goen
Thou shalt with us thy bowers *bylle,*   *build*   1700
    With virtues we shall thee *vaunce.*   *lift up*
This castle is of so quaint a *gynne*   *design*
That whoso ever hold him therein
He shall never fall in deadly sin;
    It is the Castle of Perseverance.

Qui perseveraverit usque in finem, hic salvus erit.
('He who perseveres till the end shall be saved'—Matthew 24, 13)
Then they sing 'Eterne rex altissime' ('Eternal King most high')

MEEKNESS   Now blessed be Our Lady, of heaven Empress!
Now is Mankind from folly fall
And is in the castle of goodness.
He haunteth now heaven hall
    That shall bringen him to heaven.   1710
Christ that died with dying *dose*   *potion*
Keep Mankind in this castle close
And put alway in his purpose
    To flee the sins seven!

BAD ANGEL   Nay, by Belial's bright bones
There shall he nowhile dwell.
He shall be won from these *wones*   *dwellings*
With the World, the Flesh and the Devil of hell.   *by*
    They shall my will *a-wreke,*   *carry out*
The sins seven, the kings three,   1720
To Mankind have enmity.
Sharply they shall helpen me
    This castle for to break.

How, *Flippergibbet,* Backbiter!   *a chattering fiend*
Yerne our message look thou make!   *eagerly*
Blithe about look thou bear!   *swiftly*
Say Mankind his sins hath forsake.
With yon wenches he will him *were,*   *guard*
All to holiness he hath him take.
In my heart it doth me *dere,*   *injure*
The boast that those *mothers crack*;   *common girls   brag*   1730
    My *gall* ginneth to *grind.*   *gall-bladder   torment*

Flippergibbet, run *upon a rasche*;   *in a rush*
Bid the World, the Fiend and the Flesh
That they come to fighten fresh
    To win again Mankind.

BACKBITER   I go, I go on ground glad
Swifter than ship with rudder.
I make men mazed and mad
And every man to killen other   1740
    With a *sory chere*.   *sad expression*
I am glad, by Saint James of *Galys,*   *Galicia*
Of schrewdnes to tellen tales   *out of wickedness*
Both in England and in Wales,
    And faith I have many a *fere*.   *accomplice*

Then he goes to Belial

Hail, set in thine *selle*!   *seat*
Hail, *dynge* Devil in thy *delle*!   *worthy   low place*
Hail, low in hell!
I come to thee tales to tell.

BELIAL   Backbiter, boy,   1750
Alway by *holts and hothe,*   *woods and heath*
Say now, I say,
What tidings? Tell me the sooth.

BACKBITER   *Teneful* tales I may thee say,   *painful*
To thee no good, as I guess.
Mankind is gone now away
Into the Castle of Goodness.
There he will both liven and die
In *dale of dross* till death him *dress*;   *i.e. the grave   put*
Hath thee foresaken, forsooth I say   1760
And all thy works more and less;
    To yon castle he *gan to* creep.   *did*
Yon mother Meekness, sooth to sayn,
And all yon maidens on yon plain
For to fighten they be full fain
    Mankind for to keep.

Then he calls Pride, Envy and Wrath

PRIDE   Sir King, *what wit?*   *what is your plan*
We be ready throats to cut.

BELIAL   Say, *gadelyngys*—have ye hard grace   *base fellows*
And evil death may ye die!—   1770
Why let ye Mankind from you pass
Into yon castle from us away?
    With *tene* I shall you *tay*.   *pain   punish*
Harlots, at once   *low persons of either sex*
From this *wonys*!   *dwelling*
By Belial's bones,
Ye shall *abeye,*   *pay the penalty*

And he beats them down to (or over) the ground

BACKBITER   Yea, *for* God, this was well *go*   *before   done*
Thus to work with backbiting.
I work both wrack and woe   1780
And make each man other to *dynge*.   *beat*
I shall go about and maken *mo*   *more*
Rappys for to rout and *ring*.   *strokes   roar*
Ye backbiters, look that ye do so.
    Make debate abouten to spring

                    Between sister and brother.
            If any backbiter here be *lafte,*   *remaining*
            He may *lere me of* his craft.   *learn from me*
            Of God's grace he shall be reft,
                    And every man to killen other.   1790

            To Flesh

            Hail, King, I call!
            Hail, Prince, *proud pricked in pall*!   *richly attired in a robe*
            Hail, *hende* in hall!   *gracious*
            Hail, Sir King, fair thee befall!

FLESH   Boy Backbiting,
            Full ready in robes to *rynge,*   *reign*
            Full glad tiding,
            By Belial's bones, I trow thou bring.

BACKBITER   Yea, *for* God, out I cry   *before*
            On thy two sons and thy daughter *yynge*:   *young*   1800
            Glutton, Sloth and Lechery
            Hath put me in great mourning.
            They let Mankind go up high
            Into yon castle at his liking
            Therein for to live and die,
            With those ladies to make ending,
                    Those flowers fair and fresh.
            He is in the Castle of Perseverance
            And put his body to penance.
            Of hard hap is now thy chance,   *your fortunes are now in a bad way*
                    Sir King, Mankind's flesh.   1810

            Then Flesh calls to Gluttony, Sloth and Lechery

LECHERY   Say now thy will.
            Sir Flesh, why criest thou so shrill?

FLESH   Ah Lechery, thou *skallyd* mare!   *scurvy*
            And thou Glutton, God give thee woe!
            And vile Sloth, evil *mote* thou fare!   *may*
            Why let ye Mankind from you go
                    In yon castle so high?
            Evil grace come on thy snout!
            Now I am *dressed in great doubt.*   *made very fearful*   1820
            Why *ne* had ye looked better about?   *not*
                    By Belial's bones, ye shall *abye.*   *pay the penalty*

            Then he beats them in the place

BACKBITER   Now by God, this is good game!
            I, Backbiter, now bear me well.
            If I had lost my name
            I vow to God it were great *del.*   *grief*
            I shape these shrews to mickle shame;
            Each rappeth on other with *rowtynge rele.*   *roaring rushing about*
            I, Backbiter, with false *fame*   *rumour*
            Do breaken and bursten hoods of steel.   1830
                    Through this country I am know.
            Now will I gin forth to go
            And make Covetise have a knock or two,
            And then *iwis* I have do   *certainly*
                    My *dever,* as I trow.   *duty*

            To the World

            Hail, *stiff in stound*!   *strong in attack*
            Hail, gaily girt upon ground!

Hail, fair flower ifound!
Hail, Sir World, worthy in *weeds* wound!   *clothes*

WORLD   Backbiter, *in rout*   *in my retinue*   1840
Thou tellest tales of doubt
So stiff and stout.
What tidings bringest thou about?

BACKBITER   Nothing good that shalt thou *wit*.   *know*
Mankind, Sir World, hath thee forsake.
With Shrift and Penance he is smit
And to yon castle he hath him take
          Among yon ladies white as *lake*.   *fine linen*
Lo, Sir World, ye *moun agryse*   *have cause to shudder with fear*
That ye be served on this wise.   1850
Go play you with Sir Covetise
          Till his crown crack.

Then he (World) blows a horn to [summon] Covetise

COVETISE   Sir *Bolning Bowd,*   *swelling malt-worm*
Tell me why blow ye so loud!

WORLD   *Lewd losel,* the Devil thee burn!   *good-for-nothing*
I pray God give thee *a foul hap!*   *misfortune*
Say, why lettest thou Mankind
Into yon castle for to scape?
          I trow thou ginnest to *rave*.   *behave madly*
Now for Mankind is went   1860
All our game is *schent*.   *spoilt*
Therefore a sore driving *dent,*   *blow*
          Harlot, shalt thou have.   *rogue*

Then he beats him

COVETISE   Mercy, mercy! I will no more.
Thou hast me rapped with *rewly routs*!   *pitiful blows*
I snore, I sob, I sigh sore.
Mine head is *clattered all to clouts*.   *shattered to bits*
In all your state I shall you *store*   *restore*
If ye abate your dintes *dowtes*   *fearful*
Mankind that ye have *forlore*   *lost*   1870
I shall *do* come out from yon *skowtes*   *make*   *trulls*
          To your *hende* hall.
If ye will no more beaten me
I shall do Mankind come out free.
He shall forsake, as thou shalt see,
          The fair virtues all.

WORLD   Have do then, the Devil thee tear!
Thou shalt be hangen in hell *herne*.   *nook*
Bylyve my banner up thou bear   *quickly*
And besiege we the castle *yerne*   *at once*   1880
          Mankind for to steal.
When Mankind groweth good
I, the World, am wild and *wood*.   *mad*
Those bitches shall *bleryn* in their blood   *stream*
          With *flaps* fell and *fele*.   *blows*   *many*

Yerne let *flapper* up my *fane*   *flutter*   *banner*
And *shape* we shame and *schonde*.   *prepare*   *disgrace*
I shall bring with me those bitches' bane;
There shall be no virtues dwellen in my land.
Meekness is that mother that I mean,   1890
To her I brew a *bitter bond*.   *cruel domination*
She shall die upon this green

111

If that she come all in my hand,
　　Yon *rappokis* with their rumps.　　*wretches*
I am the World. It is my will
The Castle of Virtue for to *spill*.　　*destroy*
Howteth high upon yon hill, *blow loudly*
　　Ye traitors, *in your trumps*.　　*on your trumpets*

Then World, Cupidity and Folly (Southern proposes Covetous and Backbiter for the last two) *go to the Castle with their banner and the Devil says*

BELIAL
I hear trumpets *trebelen* all of *tene*.　　*sounding shrilly　anger*
The worthy World walketh to war　　1900
For to cleaven yon castle clean,
Those maidens' minds for to mar.
Spread me pennon upon a *prene*　　*spike*
And strike we forth now *under star*.　　*i.e. the sky*
Shapeth now your shields *sheen*　　*prepare　bright*
Yon *skalled skoutes* for to scare　　*scurvy trulls*
　　Upon yon green *grese*.　　*grass*
Busk you now boys, *belyve*,　　*get ready　quickly*
For ever I stand in mickle strife.
While Mankind is in clean life　　1910
　　I am never well at ease.

Make you ready all three
Bold battles for to *bede*!　　*offer*
To yon field let us flee
And bear my banner forth *on brede*.　　*abroad*
To yon castle will I *tee*;　　*go*
Those *mammering* mothers shall have their *meed*.　　*muttering　reward*
But they yield up to me　　*unless*
With bitter *bales* they shall bleed:　　*torments*
　　Of their rest I shall them *reve*.　　*rob*　　1920
In woeful waters I shall them wash.
Have done, fellows, and take your *trash*　　*course*
And wend we thither in a rush
　　That castle for to cleave.

PRIDE
Now, now, now, go now!
On high hills let us *howte*,　　*shout*
For in Pride is all my *prow*　　*advantage*
Thy bold banner to bear about.
To Goliath I make avow
For to shooten yon each *skowte*.　　*trull*　　1930
On her arse *ragged and row*　　*torn and rough*
I shall both clatter and clout
　　And give Meekness mischance.
Belial bright, it is thine hest
That I, Pride, go the next
And bear thy banner before my breast
　　With a comely countenance.

FLESH
I hear an hideous hooting on height.
Belyve bid my banner forth to blaze!　　*quickly*　　1940
When I sit in my saddle it is a *selkowth* sight;　　*marvellous*
I gape as a Gogmagog[1] when I gin to *gaze*.　　*stare*
This worthy wild world I *wag* with a weight;　　*set moving*
Yon *rappokys* I *rubble* and all to-raze;　　*wretches　crush*
Both with shot and with sling I cast with *a sleight*　　*crafty technique*

---

[1] Gog and Magog were evil giants of mythology, whose descendants were killed off by Brutus, the mythological founder of Britain. Their names derive from the Bible (see Genesis 10, 2 and Ezekiel 38, 2).

With care to yon castle to cracken and to *crase*   *shatter*
       In flood.   *with force*
I am Man's Flesh; where I go
I am Man's most foe;
Iwis I am ever woe   *certainly*
       When he draweth to good.   1950

Therefore ye bold boys, busk you about.
Sharply on shields *your shafts ye shiver*!   *splinter your lances*
And Lechery *ledron,* shoot thou a *skoute*!   *rascal trull*
Help we Mankind from yon castle to *kever,*   *recover*
       Help we mun him win.   *help us to regain him*
Shoot we all at a shot
With gear that we can best *note*   *use*
To chase Mankind from yon *cote*   *dwelling*
       Into deadly sin.

GLUTTONY   Lo, Sir Flesh, how I fare to the field   1960
             With a faggot in mine hand for to setten on a fire.
             With a *wreath* of the wood well I can *me wield*;   *twisted piece acquit myself*
             With a long lance those *losels* I shall *lere.*   *good-for-nothings teach*
                    Go we with our gear.
             Those bitches shall *bleykyn and blodyr*;   *blench and blubber*
             I shall maken such a powder
             Both with smoke and with *smodyr*   *fumes*
                    They shall shitten for fear.

             Then they descend into the place
             Bad Angel says to Belial

BAD ANGEL   *Aux armes!* As an herald, high now I *howte.*   *to arms call*
             Devil *dight thee* as a *duke* to do those damsels *dote.*   *appoint yourself leader fear*
             Belial, as a bold boy thy *brodde* I bere about;   *bannered spike*   1970
             Help to catch Mankind from caitiffs *cote.*   *dwelling*
             Pride, put out thy pennon of rags and of *rout*!   *riot*
             Do this mother Meekness melten to *mote*!   *make speck of dust*
             Wrath, *preve* Patience, the *skallyd skowte*!   *put to the test scurvy trull*
             Envy, to Charity shape thou a shot
                    Full *yare.*   *readily*
             With Pride, Wrath and Envy,
             These devils by downs dry
             As comely kings I descry,   1980
                    Mankind to *catchen to care.*   *ensnare in anguish*

             To Flesh

             Flesh, frail and fresh, *frely* fed,   *generously*
             With Glutton, Sloth and Lechery Man's soul thou *slo*!   *kill*
             As a duke doughty *do thee to be dread*;   *make yourself feared*
             Gear thee with *gears* from top to the toe.   *weapons*
             Kyth this day thou art a king frely fed!   *make known*
             Glutton, slay thou Abstinence with wicked woe.
             With Chastity, thou Lecher, *be not overled*!   *do not be daunted*
             Sloth, beat thou Busyness on buttocks blue.
                    Do thou thy craft *in coste to be know*!   *so that it may be known*   1990

             To the World

             Worthy, witty and wise, wounden in *weed,*   *clothing*
             Let Covetise carpen, cryen and *grede*!   *call loudly*
             Here be bold *bachelors* battle to *bede*   *young knights offer*
                    Mankind to *tene,* as I trow.   *injure*

MANKIND   That *dynge* Duke that died on *Rood*   *noble the cross*
             This day my soul keep and save!

When Mankind draweth to good
Behold what enemies he shall have!
The World, the Devil, the Flesh are *wood*;   *mad*
To men they *cast a careful cave*;   *prepare a cavern full of grief*   2000
Bitter *bales* they brewen *on brode*   *torments*   *everywhere*
Mankind in woe to *welter and wave,*   *make (him) roll and plunge*
      Lordings, sooth to say.
Therefore each man beware of this,
For while Mankind clean is
His enemies shall tempten him to do amiss
      If they might by any way.

Omne gaudium existimate cum variis temptacionibus insideritis
('Count it all joy when you fall into various temptations'—James 1, 2)

Therefore lordes, be now glad
With almsdeed and orison
For to do as Our Lord bade,   2010
Stiffly withstand your temptation.
With this foul fiend I am near mad.
To battle they *busk them bown.*   *make ready*
Certes I should be *overled,*   *dominated*
But that I am in this castle town,
      With sins sore and smart.
Whoso will liven out of distress
And leaden his life in cleanness
In this castle of virtue and of goodness
      Him must have whole his heart.   2020

Delectare in Domino et dabit tibi peticiones cordis tui
('Delight in the Lord and he will give you your heart's desires'—Psalm 37, 4)

GOOD   *Ah Meekness, Charity and Patience,*
ANGEL   *Primrose playeth parlasent.*[1]
    Chastity, Busyness and Abstinence,
    My hope, ladies, in you is *lent.*   *fixed*
    Succour, paramours, sweeter than *cense,*   *incense*
    Red as rose on *rys i-rent*!   *branch*   *torn off*
    This day ye *dight* a good defence!   *perform*
    While Mankind is in good intent
      His thoughts are *unhende.*   *unfitting*
    Mankind is brought into this wall   2030
    In frailty to faden and fall.
    Therefore, ladies, I pray you all,
      Help this day Mankind.

MEEKNESS   God that sitteth in heaven on high
    Save all Mankind by sea and sand!
    Let him dwellen here and be us by
    And we shall putten to him helping hand.
    Yet forsooth never I see
    That any fault in us he found
    But that we saved him from sin sly   2040
    If he would by us stiffly stand
      In this castle of stone.
    Therefore dread ye not, Man's angel dear!
    If he will dwellen with us here
    From seven sins we shall him *were*   *guard*
      And his enemies each one.

[1] 'Ah, the primrose enacts Meekness, Charity and Patience, as is acknowledged', *or* 'Play at primrose with one accord', i.e. disseminate grace in the spirit of the Passion (of which the primrose is a symbol).

Now my seven sisters sweet,
This day falleth on us the lot
Mankind for to shield and *schete*   *make secure*
From deadly sin and shamely shot.   2050
His enemies strayen in the street
To *spill* Man with *spetous* spot.   *destroy* *shameful*
Therefore our flowers let now *flete*   *fly*
And keep we him, as we have *het,*   *promised*
    Among us in this hall.
Therefore, seven sisters *swote,*   *sweet*
Let our virtues *rain on rote.*   *fall like rain on roots*
This day we will be Man's *bote*   *remedy*
    Against these devils all.

BELIAL   This day the *vaward* will I hold.   *vanguard*   2060
    Advance my banner, precious Pride,
    Mankind to catch to *cares* cold.   *sorrows*
    Bold battle now will I *bide.*   *undertake*
        Busk you, boys, *on brede*!   *get ready* *abroad*
    All men that be with me *wytholde,*   *kept as retainers*
    Both the young and the old,
    Envy, Wrath, ye boyes bold,
        To *round raps ye rape,* I rede.   *hurry to hard blows*

PRIDE   *Aux armes,* Meekness! I bring thee bane   *to arms*
    All with pride painted and *pight.*   *adorned*   2070
    What sayst thou, *faytour?* By mine fair *fane,*   *deceiver* *banner*
    With robes *round* arrayed full right,   *hard*
    Great goose, I shall thee *gane.*   *overcome*
    To mar thee, Meekness, with my might
    No worldly *wits* here are *wane.*   *strategems* *lacking*
    Lo, thy castle is all beset!
        Mothers, how shall ye do?   *girls*
    Meekness, yield thee to me, I *rede.*   *advise*
    Mine name in land is precious Pride.
    Mine bold banner to thee I *bede.*   *show*   2080
        Mother, what sayst thereto?

MEEKNESS   Against thy banner of pride and boast
    A banner of meekness and mercy
    I put against pride, well thou *wost,*   *knowst*
    That shall *schende* thy *careful* cry.   *overthrow* *harmful*
    This meek King is known in every coast
    That was *crossed* on Calvary.   *crucified*
    When he came down from heaven host
    And *lighted* with meekness *in* Mary,   *descended* *into*
        This Lord thus lighted low.   2090
    When he came from the Trinity
    Into a maiden lighted he,
    And all was for to destroy thee,
        Pride, this shalt thou know.

    Deposuit potentes de sede et cetera
    ('He hath put down the powerful from their seats etc.' ['. . . and exalted them of
    low degree']—Luke 1, 52)

    For when Lucifer to hell fell,
    Pride, thereof thou were *chesun;*   *cause*
    And thou, devil, with wicked will
    In paradise trapped us with treason.
    So thou us bound in bales ill,
    This may I prove by right reason;   2100
    Till this *Duke* that died on hill   *leader*

In heaven man might never have *seisin,*   *possession*
    The gospel thus declared.
For whoso love him shall be high;
Therefore thou shalt not comen us nigh,
And though thou be never so sly,
    I shall *fell* all thy *fare.*   *strike down   boasting*

Qui se exaltat humiliabitur et cetera
('Who exalts himself shall be humbled etc.'—i.e. and who humbles himself shall
be exalted—after Matthew 23, 12)

WRATH	Dame Patience, what sayst thou to Wrath and Ire?	
	Put Mankind from thy castle clear,	
	Or I shall tappen at thy *tire* *headdress*	2110
	With stiff stones that I have here.	
	I shall sling at thee many a *vyre* *bolt from crossbow*	
	And been avenged hastily here.	
	Thus Belzebub, our great sire,	
	Bade me burn thee with wild fire,	
	Thou bitch black as coal!	
	Therefore fast, foul *skowte,* *trull*	
	Put Mankind to us out,	
	Or of me thou shalt have *doubt,* *fear*	
	Thou mother, thou *motyhole*! *moth-hole?*	2120

PATIENCE   From *thy doubt* Christ me shield   *fear of you*
    This each day, and all mankind!
    Thou wretched Wrath, *wood* and wild,   *mad*
    Patience shall thee *schend.*   *overthrow*

Quia ira viri justiciam Dei non operatur
('Since the wrath of man does not promote the justice of God'—James 1, 20)

For Mary's son meek and mild
Rent thee up root and rind
When he stood meeker than a child
And let boys him beaten and bind;
    Therefore, wretch, be still.
For those *pelourys* that gan him *pose*   *despoilers   treat roughly*   2130
He might have driven them to dross,
And yet to casten him on the cross
    He suffered all their will.

Thousands of angels he might have had
To a *wroken* him there *full yerne,*   *avenge   at once*
And yet to *dien* he was glad   *die*
Us patience to teach and learn.
Therefore boy, with thy *boystous* blade   *violent*
Fare away by fields *ferne.*   *far-off*
For I will do as Jesus bade,   2140
Wretches from my *wonys werne*   *dwelling   ward off*
    With a *dyngne* defence   *noble*
If thou *fond* to comen aloft   *attempt*
I shall thee *cacche* from this croft   *drive*
With these roses sweet and soft
    Painted with patience.

ENVY   Out, my heart ginneth to break,
    For Charity that standeth so stout.
    Alas, mine heart ginneth to *wreke:*   *seek vengeance*
    Yield up this castle, thou whore-clout.   2150
    It is mine office foul to speak,
    False slanders to bear about.
    Charity, the Devil may thee *cheke*   *choke*

| | *But* I thee rap with *rewly rout,* | *unless* | *grievous blow* |
| | Thy *targe* for to tear. | *shield* | |

Let Mankind come to us down
Or I shall shooten to this castle town
A full foul defamation.
      Therefore this bow I bear.

CHARITY   Though thou speak *wycke* and false *fame,*   *wicked   rumour*   2160
The worse shall I never do my deed.
Whoso *peyreth* falsely another man's name   *injures*
Christ's curse he shall have *to meed.*   *as reward*

Ve homini illi per quem scandalum venit
('Woe to the man through whom offence comes'—Matthew 18, 7)

Whoso will not his tongue tame—
Take it sooth as mass creed!—
Woe, woe to him and *mickle* shame!   *much*
In holy writ this I read.
      For ever thou art a shrew.
Though thou speak evil, I ne give a *gres*;   *blade of grass*
I shall do never the worse   2170
At the last the *sooth verse*   *true verse, i.e. gospel*
      Certes *himself shall shew.*   *he (i.e. Christ) will reveal*

Our lovely Lord *withouten lack*   *free from fault*
Gave example to charity,
When he was beaten blue and black
For trespass that never did he.
In sorry sin he had no *tak*   *spot*
And yet for sin he bled bloody *ble.*   *colour*
He took his cross upon his back,   2180
Sinful man, and all for thee.
      Thus he made defence.
Envy with thy slanders thick,
I am *put at* my Lord's *prick;*   *mindful of   suffering*
I will do good against the *wycke*   *wicked people*
      And keep in silence.

BELIAL   What, for Belial's bones,
Whereabouten chide ye?   *what are you arguing about*
Have done, ye boys, all at once.
Lash down these mothers all three!
Work wreck to this *wonys!*   *place*   2190
The *vanward* is granted me!   *vanguard*
Do these *mothers* to make moans.   *common girls*
Your doughty deeds now let see.
      Dash them all to *daggys!*   *shreds*
Have do, boys, blue and black!
Work these wenches woe and wrack!
Clarions, cryeth up *at a krake,*   *with sudden din*
      And blow your broad *bags!*   *bagpipes*

Then they shall fight for a long time

PRIDE   Out, my proud back is bent!
Meekness hath me *al forbeat.*   *thoroughly beaten*   2200
Pride with Meekness is *forschent.*   *utterly overcome*
I wail and weep with woundes wet;
      I am beaten in the head.
My proud pride adown is driven;
So sharply Meekness hath me *shriven*   *beaten*
That I may no longer liven;
      My life is me bereft.

117

ENVY All mine enmity is not worth a fart;
     I shit and shake all in my sheet.
     Charity, that sour *swart,*   *dark person*   2210
     With fair roses my head gan break.
       I breed the *malaunder.* *scabby horse infection*
     With worthy words and flowers sweet
     Charity maketh me so meek
     I dare neither cry nor creep,
       Not a shot of slander.

WRATH I Wrath may sing *weleawo:* *woe*
     Patience me gave a sorry *dint.* *blow*
     I am all beaten black and blue
     With a rose that on Rood was rent.   2220
       My speech is almost spent.
     Her roses fell on me so sharp
     That mine head hangeth as a harp.
     I dare neither cry nor carp,
       She is so patient.

BAD ANGEL Go hence, ye *do* not worth a turd. *are*
     Foul fall you, all four!
     Yerne, yerne, *let fall on bord,* *quickly attack*
     Sir Flesh, with thine eyen sour.
       For care I *cukke* and cower. *with anguish shit* 2230
     Sir Flesh, with thine company,
     Yerne, yerne, make a cry. *quickly*
     Help we have no *velony,* *disgrace*
       That this day may be our!

FLESH *War, war!* Let Man's Flesh go to! *look out*
     I come with a company.
     Have do, my children, now have do,
     Glutton, Sloth and Lechery.
     Each of you *winneth a sho*! *win honour*
     Let not Mankind win mastery.   2240
     Let sling him in a foul *slo* *bog*
     And *fond* to *feoff* him with folly. *try endow*
       Doth now well your deed.
     Yerne let see how ye shall *gin* *rapidly begin*
     Mankind to tempten to deadly sin.
     If ye *must* this castle win *are able to*
       Hell shall be your *meed.* *reward*

GLUTTONY *War!* Sir Glutton shall maken a *smeke* *look out smoke*
     Against this castle, I vow.
     Abstinence, though thou *bleyke* *blench*   2250
     I look on thee with bitter brow.
     I have a *faggot in my neck* *bundle on my shoulder*
     To setten Mankind *on a lowe.* *on fire*
     My foul *leye* shalt thou not *let,* *law abandon*
     I vow to God as I trow.
       Therefore put him out here.
     In *measling* gluttony *causing festers*
     With good meats and drinkes *trye* *choice*
     I nourish my sister Lechery
       Till man runneth on fire.   2260

ABSTINENCE Thy meats and drinkes are *unthende* *unhealthy*
     When they are out of measure take.
     They maken man mad and out of *mende* *mind*
     And worken them both woe and *wrake.* *ruin*
     That for thy fire though thou here kindle,

Certes I shall thy weal *a-slake*   *satisfy*
With bread that brought us out of hell
And on the cross suffered *wrake*:   *anguish*
      I mean the sacrament.
That *iche* blissful bread   *same*   2270
That hung on hill till he was dead
Shall temper so mine maidenhead
      That thy purpose shall be spent.

In abstinence this bread was brought
Certes, Mankind, and all for thee.
Of forty days ate he not   *for*
And then was nailed to a tree.

Cum jejunasset quadraginta diebus et cetera
('When he fasted forty days etc.'—Matthew 4, 2)

Example us was betaught,
In soberness he bade us be.
Therefore Mankind shall not be caught,   2280
Gluttony, *with thy degree.*   *in your condition*
      The sooth thou shalt see.
To *nourish fair* though thou be *fawe*   *eat well*   *eager*
Abstinence it shall withdraw
Till thou be *shut under shaw*   *banished to the woods, or buried* (Eccles)
      And *fain for to* flee.   *eager to*

LECHERY   Lo, Chastity, thou foul *skowte*!   *slut*
This *ilke* day here thou shalt die.   *same*
I make a fire in man's *towte*   *arse*
That *lanceth up as any leye.*   *leaps up like a flame*   2290
These cursed coals I bear about
Mankind in *tene* for to *teye.*   *suffering*   *tie*
Men and women hath no *doubt*   *fear*
With *pissing pokes* for to play.   *genitals*
      I bind them in my bonds.
I have no rest, *so I rowe,*   *in order to relax*
With men and women as I trow
Till I, Lechery, be set *on a lowe*   *on fire*
      In all Mankind's *londs.*   *loins* (conjectured)

CHASTITY   I, Chastity, have power in this place   2300
Thee, Lechery, to bind and beat.
Maiden Mary, *well* of grace,   *fountain*
Shall quench that foul heat.

Mater et Virgo, extingue carnales concupiscentias!
('Mother and Virgin, quench carnal desires!')

Our Lord God *made thee no space*   *allowed you no place (to stay)*
When his blood strayed in the street.
From this castle he did thee chase
When he was crowned with thorns great
      And green.
To dreary death when he was *dight*   *put*
And boys did him great despite,   2310
In lechery he had no delight,
      And that was right well seen.

At Our Lady I learn my lesson   *from*
To have chaste life till I be dead.
She is queen and beareth the crown,
And all was for her maidenhead.
Therefore go from this castle town,
Lechery, now I thee *rede,*   *advise*

119

For Mankind gettest thou not down,
To sully him with sinful seed:
    In *care* thou wouldst him cast.   *sorrow*
And if thou come up to me,
Truly thou shalt beaten be
With the *yard* of chastity   *stick*
    While my life may last.

2320

SLOTH   *Ware, war!* I delve with a spade.   *look out*
Men call me the Lord Sir Slow.
Ghostly grace I spill and shed;   *spiritual*
From the water of grace this ditch I *fowe*;   *clear out*
Ye shallen come right enow
By this ditch dry by banks *brede*.   *broad*
Thirty thousand that I well know
In my life lovely I lead
    That had *liefer* sitten at the ale   *rather*
Three men's songs to singen loud   *part-songs for three men*
Than toward the church for to crowd.
Thou Busyness, thou *bolned bowd,*   *swollen malt-worm*
    I brew to thee thine *bale.*   *torment*

2330

INDUSTRY   Oh good men, beware now all
Of Slug and Sloth, this foul thief!
To the soul he is bitterer than gall;
Root he is of mickle mischief.
God's service that leadeth us to heaven hall,
This *lordeyn* for to *letten* us is *lief.*   *rascal*   *stop*   *eager*
Whoso will shriven him of his sins all,
He putteth this brethel to mickle mischief,
    Mankind he that miscarried.[1]
Men might do no penance for *him this,*   *i.e. this person Sloth*
Nor shrive them when they do amiss,
But ever he would in sin iwis
    That Mankind were tarried.

2340

2350

Therefore he maketh this dyke dry
To putten Mankind to distress.
He maketh deadly sin a ready way
Into the Castle of Goodness.
But with *tene* I shall him *teye*   *pain*   *bind*
Through the help of *heaven empress.*   *i.e. the Virgin Mary*
With my *bedes* he shall *abeye,*   *prayers*   *pay the penalty*
And other occupations more and less
    I shall shape, him to *schonde*;   *shame*
For whoso will Sloth put down
With *bedes* and with orison   *prayers*
Or some honest occupation,
    As book to have in hand.

2360

Nunc lege nunc ora nunc disce nuncque labora
('Now read, now pray, now learn and now work'—i.e. always be busy)

FLESH   Ay, for Belial's bones, the King,
Whereabout stand ye all day?
Caitiffs, *let be* your cackling   *stop*
And *rap at rowtys of array.*   *strike at groups in warlike style*
Gluttony, thou foul *gadling,*   *base fellow*
Slay Abstinence, if thou may.
Lechery, with thy working
To Chastity *make a wicked array*   *treat roughly*

2370

[1] 'Whoever wishes to confess his sins causes this rascal, who misled mankind, great distress'.

> A little *throw*.   *while*
> And while we fight
> For our right
> In *bemys* bright   *trumpets*
>   Let blasts blow.

Then they shall fight for a long time

GLUTTONY
> Out Glutton, adown I drive
> Abstinence hath lost my mirth.
> Sir Flesh, I shall never thrive;   2380
> I *do* not worth the devil's *dirt*;   *am*   *excrement*
>   I may not liven long.
> I am all beaten top and tail;
> With Abstinence will I no more *dayl*;   *dally*
> I will go *cowche qwayl*   *crouch like a quail*
>   At home in your *gonge*.   *privy*

LECHERY
> Out on Chastity, by the Rood!
> She hath me *dashed* and so drenched!   *beaten*
> Yet have she the curse of God
> For all my fire the *quean* hath quenched;   *whore*   2390
>   For fear I fall and faint.
> In hard ropes may she ride!
> Here dare I not long abide.
> Somewhere mine head I would hide
>   As an urchin that were *schent*.   *disgraced*

SLOTH
> Out, I die! Lay on water!
> I swoon, I sweat, I faint, I drool!
> Yon quean with her *pitter-patter*   *bombardment of prayer-beads?*
> Hath all *to-dashed* my *skalled* skull.   *smashed*   *scabby*
>   It is as soft as wool.   2400
> Ere I have here more *scathe*   *damage*
> I shall leap away by *lurking lathe*.   *secret by-path*
> There I may my ballocks bathe
>   And *leyken* at the full.   *relax*

Probably, Sloth, Lechery and Gluttony retreat to the scaffold of Flesh

BAD ANGEL
> Yah! The Devil speed you, all the pack!
> For sorrow I mourn on the *mowle*;   *earth*
> I carp, I cry, I cower, I *kack*,   *shit*
> I fret, I fart, I *fizzle foul*.   *fart hissingly*
>   I look like an owl.

To the World

> Now, Sir World, whatso it cost,   2410
> Help now, or this we have lost;
> All our fare is not worth a *thost*;   *turd*
>   That maketh me to *mowle*.   *mess myself? grimace?*

WORLD
> How, Covetise, banner *avaunt*!   *to the front*
> Here cometh a battle noble and new;
> For since thou were a little *faunt*,   *child*
> Covetise, thou hast been true.
> Have do that damsel, *do her daunt*;   *make her tame*
> Bitter bales thou her brew.
> The *meeds*, boy, I thee grant,   *rewards*   2420
> The gallows of *Canwick* to hangen on new—   *Canwick Hill, near Lincoln*
>   That would thee well befall.
> *Have done,* Sir Covetise!   *set on*
> Work on the best wise.
> Do Mankind come and arise
>   From yon virtues all.

COVETISE   How, Mankind! I am *a-tened*   dismayed
            For thou art there so in that *hold*.   stronghold
            Come and speak with thy best friend,
            Sir Covetise, thou knowst me of old.   2430
            What devil shalt thou there longer *lende*   why the devil   stay
            With great penance in that castle cold?
            Into the World if thou wilt wend,
            Among men to bear thee bold,
                    I rede, by Saint *Gile*.   Giles
            How, Mankind! I thee say.
            Come to Covetise, I thee pray.
            We two shall together play,
                    If thou wilt, a while.

GENEROSITY Ah God help me, I am dismayed!   2440
            I curse thee, Covetise, as I can,
            For certes, traitor, thou hast betrayed
            Nearhand now each earthly man.   almost
            So much were men never affrayed
            With Covetise since the world began.   by
            God Almighty is not *paid*.   satisfied
            Since thou, fiend, bare the World's bane,
                    Full wide thou ginnest wend.   you travel far and wide
            Now are men waxen near *wood*;   mad
            They would go to hell for World's *good*.   possessions   2450
            That Lord that rested on the Rood
                    Is maker of an end.   will put a stop to it

            Maledicti sunt avariciosi hujus temporis
            ('Cursed are the covetous of this time')

            There is no *dis-ease* nor *debate*   trouble   conflict
            Through this wide world so round,
            Tide nor time, early nor late,
            But that Covetise is the ground.
            Thou nourishest pride, envy and hate,
            Thou Covetise, thou cursed hound.
            Christ *thee shield* from our gate   keep you out
            And keep us from thee safe and sound   2460
                    That thou no good here win!
            Sweet Jesu, gentle justice,
            Keep Mankind from Covetise,
            For *iwis* he is in all wise   certainly
                    Root of sorrow and sin.

COVETISE   What aileth thee, Lady *Largity*,   generosity
            Damsel *dyngne* upon thy dais?   noble
            And I spake right not to thee,
            Therefore I pray thee hold thy peace.
            How, Mankind! Come speak with me,   2470
            Come lay thy love here in my *les*.   control
            Covetise is a friend right *free*,   noble
            Thy sorrow, Man, to slake and cease;
                    Covetise hath many a gift.
            Mankind, thine hand hither thou reach.
            Covetise shall be thy *leech*.   physician
            The right way I shall thee teach
                    To *thedom* and to thrift.   prosperity

MANKIND   Covetise, whither should I wend?
            What way wouldest that I should hold?
            To what place wouldst thou me send?   2480
            I gin to waxen hoary and old
            My back ginneth to bow and bend,

I crawl and creep and wax all cold.
Age maketh man full *unthende*,   *miserable*
Body and bones and all *unwolde*;   *infirm*
    My bones are feeble and sore.
I am arrayed in a *slop*,[1]   *loose gown*
As a young man I may not hop,
My nose is cold and ginneth to drop,   2490
    Mine hair waxeth all hoar.

COVETISE   Peter! Thou hast thee more need
To have some *good* in thine *age*:   *possessions*   *i.e. old age*
Marks, pounds, lands and *lede*,   *servants*
Houses and homes, castle and *cage*.   *stronghold*
Therefore do as I thee *rede*;   *advise*
To Covetise, cast thy *parage*.   *partnership*
Come, and I shall thine *erdyn bede*;   *petition present*
The worthy World shall give thee wage,
    Certes not a *lyth*.   *little*   2500
Come on, old man, it is no *reprefe*   *reproof*
That Covetise be thee *lief*.   *dear to*
If thou die at any mischief
    It is thyself to *wyth*.   *blame*

MANKIND   Nay, nay, these ladies of goodness
Will not let me fare amiss,
And though I be a while in distress,
When I die I shall to bliss.
It is but folly, as I guess,
All this world's weal *iwis*.   *certainly*   2510
These lovely ladies more and less
In wise words they tell me this.
    Thus saith the book of *kends*.   *generations, i.e. Ecclesiasticus*
I will not do these ladies despite
To forsaken them for so *lyt*.   *little*
To dwellen here is my delight;
    Here are my best friends.

COVETISE   Yea, up and down thou take the way
Through this world to walken and wend,
And thou shalt find, sooth to say,   2520
Thy purse shall be thy best friend.
Though thou sit all day and pray,
No man shall come to thee nor send;
But if thou have a penny to pay,
Men shall to thee then listen and *lend*   *remain*
    And *kelyn* all thy care.   *assuage*
Therefore to me thou hang and *held*   *hold*
And be covetous whilst thou may thee wield.
If thou be poor and needy in *elde*   *old age*
    Thou shalt often evil fare.   2530

MANKIND   Covetise, thou sayst a good *skill*.   *argument*
So great God me advance,
All thy bidding doen I will.
I forsake the Castle of Perseverance.
In Covetise I will me *hyle*   *shelter*
For to get some sustenance.
Afore meal men meat shall till.   *man must provide himself with food before mealtime*
It is good for all chance
    Some *good owhere* to hide.   *goods somewhere*

---

[1] lines 2488–91 mention standard items in the common medieval motif, 'The Signs of Death'. So again at 2858–9.

Certes this ye well know,
It is good howso the wind blow
A man to have somewhat of his *owe*　　　*own*　　　2540
　　　What *hap* soever betide.　　　*chance*

GOOD　　Ah ladies, I pray you of grace
ANGEL　Helpeth to keep here Mankind!
He will forsake this precious place
And draw again to deadly sin.
Help, ladies, *lovely in lace*!　　*beautifully dressed*
He goeth from this worthy *wonning*.　　*dwelling*
Covetise away ye chase
And shutteth Mankind somewhere herein　　2550
　　　In your worthy *wise*.　　*way*
Oh wretched man, thou shalt be wroth!
That sin shall be thee full loath.
Ah sweet ladies, help! He goeth
　　　Away with Covetise.

Then he descends to Covetise

MEEKNESS　Good Angel, what may I do thereto?
Himself may his soul *spill*.　　*destroy*
Mankind to do what he will do
God hath given him a free will.　　2560
Though he *drench* and his soul *slo*,　　*drown*　*destroy*
Certes we may not *do there-till*.　　*interfere*
Since he came this castle to
We did to him *that us befell*　　*what befitted us*
　　　And now he hath us refused.
As long as he was within this castle wall
We kept him from sin, ye saw well all;
And now he will again to sin fall,
　　　I pray you hold us excused.

PATIENCE　Reason will excusen us all.　　2570
He held the axe by the helve.　　*i.e. he had his fate in his own hands*
Though he will to folly fall
It is to *witen but* himselve.　　*blame*　*only*
While he held him in this hall
From deadly sin we did him *shelve*.　　*protect*
He breweth himself a bitter gall;
In death's dint when he shall *delve*　　*be buried*
　　　This game he shall *begrete*.　　*lament*
He is endowed with wits five
For to rulen him in his life.　　2580
We virtues will not with him strive.
　　　Avyse him and his deed!　　*take note of him*

CHARITY　Of his deed have we nought to doen;
He will no longer with us be led.
When he asked out, we heard his boon,
And of his presence we were right glad.
But as thou seest, he hath forsaken us soon;
He will not do as Christ him bade.
Mary, thy son aboven the moon
As make Mankind *true* and *sad*,　　*make*　*loyal*　*sober*　　2590
　　　In grace for to goen.
For if he will to folly flit,
We may him not *withsit*.　　*resist*
He is of age and *can his wit*,　　*is able to think*
　　　Ye know well everyone.

ABSTINENCE　Each one ye knowen he is a fool,

124

In Covetise to *dight* his deed.   *perform*
World's weal is like a three-footed stool,
It faileth a man at his most need.

Mundus transit et concupiscencia ejus
('The world passeth away and the lust thereof—1 John 2, 17)

When he is *dight in death's dole*   *set in the valley of death*   2600
The right register I shall him read;
He shall be tore with *teneful* tool.   *painful*
When he shall burn on *gleams glede*   *bright coal*
    He shall learn a new law.
Be he never so rich of world's *wone*   *wealth*
His *seketouris* shall maken their moan;   *executors*
'Make us merry and let him gone!
    He was a good fellow.'

CHASTITY   When he is dead their sorrow is least.
The t'one sekatour saith to the t'other: 2610
'Make we merry and a rich feast
And let him lie in death's *fodyr.'*   *company*

Et sic relinquent alienis divicias suas
('And thus they will leave their wealth to others'—after Psalm 48, 10)

So his part shall be the least;
The sister serveth thus the brother.
I *let* a man no better than a beast,   *count*
For no man can *beware* by other   *be warned*
    Till he hath *all full spun.*   *done all he can*
Thou shalt see that day, man, that a *bede*   *prayer*
Shall stand thee more in stead
Than all the *good* that thou mightest get   *riches*   2620
    Certes under sun.

MEEKNESS   Mankind, of one thing have I wonder:
That thou takest not into thine *mend,*   *mind*
When body and soul shall parten asunder
No world's good shall with thee wend.

Non descendet cum illo gloria ejus
('His glory shall not descend with him'—Psalm 48, 17)

When thou art dead and in the earth laid under
Misgotten good thee shall *schend.*   *ruin*
It shall thee weighen as *peys* in *punder*   *weight*   *balance*
Thy *sely* soul to bringen in *bend*   *miserable*   *bondage*
    And make it full *unthende.*   *unprosperous*   2630
And yet Mankind, as it is seen,
With Covetise goeth on this green.
The traitor *doth* us all this *tene*   *causes*   *trouble*
    After his life's end.

GENEROSITY   Out I cry, and nothing low,
On Covetise, as I well may.
Mankind saith he hath never enow
Till his mouth be full of clay.

Avarus numquam replebitur pecunia
('The miser will never be satisfied with his wealth'—after Ecclesiastes 5, 10)

When he is closed in death's *dow*   *dough, i.e. the grave*
What helpeth riches or great array?   2640
It flieth away as any snow
Anon after thy ending day,   *immediately*
    To *wild world's* wise.   *in the manner of the unruly world*
Now, good men all that here be,

125

	Have my sisters excused and me,		
	Though Mankind from this castle flee.		
	Wyte it Covetise.	*blame*	

BAD ANGEL	Yah! Go forth and let the queans cackle!		
	There women are are many words.	*where*	
	Let them go hoppen with their *hackle*!	*feathers*	2650
	Where geese sitten are many turds.		
	With Covetise thou run *on rakle*	*in haste*	
	And hang thine heart upon his hoards.		
	Thou shalt be shaken in mine shackle.		
	Unbind thy bags on his *boards*	*table*	
	On his benches above.	*i.e. in Covetise's scaffold*	
	Par De, thou goest out of Mankind	*by God, you are different from*	
	But Covetise be in thy mind.	*unless*	
	If ever thou think to be *thende,*	*prosperous*	
	On him thou lay thy love.		2660

MANKIND	Needs my love must on him *lend*	*fix*	
	With Covetise to *welter and wave.*	*plunge and roll*	
	I know none of all my kind		
	That he ne coveteth for to have.		
	Penny-man is mickle in mind;	*i.e. the rich man is much respected*	
	My love in him I lay and *lave.*	*deposit*	
	Where that ever I walk or wend		
	In weal and woe he will me *have.*	*keep*	
	He is great of grace.		
	Whereso I walk in land or *lede*	*nation*	2670
	Penny-man best may *speed;*	*rich man* *prosper*	
	He is a duke to do a deed		
	Now in every place.		

GOOD ANGEL	Alas that ever Mankind was born!		
	In Covetise is all his *lust.*	*pleasure*	
	Night and day, midnight and morn		
	In Penny-man is all his trust.		
	Covetise shall maken him *lorn*	*lost*	
	When he is *dolven* all to dust.	*dug, i.e. buried*	
	To mickle shame he shall be *shorn,*	*fashioned*	2680
	With foul fiends to rotten and rust.		
	Alas, what shall I do?		
	Alas, alas, so may I say.		
	Man goeth with Covetise away.		
	Have me excused, for I ne may		
	Truly not do thereto.		

WORLD	Aha, this game goeth as I would!		
	Mankind will never the World forsake.		
	Till he be dead and under *mould*	*earth*	
	Wholly to me he will him take.		2690
	To Covetise he hath him *yolde;*	*yielded*	
	With my weal he will awake;		
	For a thousand pound I *nolde*	*would not*	
	But Covetise were Man's *make,*	*mate*	
	Certes on every wise.		
	All these games he shall bewail,		
	For I, the World, am of this *entail*:	*disposition*	
	In his most need I shall him fail,		
	And all for Covetise.		

COVETISE	Now, Mankind, beware of this:		2700
	Thou art *a-party well* in age.	*somewhat advanced*	
	I would not thou faredest amiss:		

Go we now know my castle *cage.*   *stronghold*
In this bower I shall thee *bliss*;   *bless*
Worldly weal shall be thy wage.
More muck than is thine iwis
Take thou in this *trost terage*—   *safe soil*
    And look that thou do wrong.
Covetise, it is no *sore,*   *wretchedness*
He will thee *feoffen* full of store,   *endow*   2710
And alway, alway say 'More and more!'
    And that shall be thy song.

MANKIND   Ah Covetise, have thou good grace!
Certes thou bearest a true tongue.
'More and more', in many a place,
Certes that song is often sung.
I *wist* never man, by banks base,   *knew*
So say in *clay till he were clung*:   *clung in clay, i.e. dead*
'Enow, enow' had never space;
That full song was never sung,   2720
    Nor will I not begin.
Good Covetise, I thee pray
That I might with thee play.
Give me *good* enow ere that I die   *possessions*
    To *wonne* in World's *wynne.*   *live   joy*

COVETISE   Have here, Mankind, a thousand mark.
I, Covetise, have thee this got.
Thou mayst purchase therewith both pound and park
And *do* thereof mickle *note.*   *make profit*
Lend no man hereof, for no *cark,*   *distress*   2730
Though he should hang by the throat,
Monk nor friar, priest nor clerk,
Ne help therewith church nor *cote*   *house*
    Till death thy body delve.
Though he should *starve* in a cave,   *die*
Let no poor man thereof have.
In green grass till thou be grave
    Keep somewhat for thyselve.

MANKIND   I vow to God, it is great husbandry.
Of thee I take these *nobles* round.   *gold coins, then worth about 50p*   2740
I shall me *rapen* and that in *hye,*   *hurry haste*
To hide this gold under the ground.
There shall it lie till that I die,
It may be kept there safe and sound.
Though my neighbour should be hangen high
Thereof getteth he neither penny nor pound.
    Yet I am not well at ease.
Now would I have castle walls
Strong steeds and *stiff* in stalls.   *sturdy*
With *high holts* and high halls,   *lofty woods*   2750
    Covetise, thou must me *seise.*   *put in possession of*

COVETISE   All shalt thou have already, lo,
At thine own disposition.
All this good take *thee to,*   *to yourself*
Cliff and coast, tower and town.
Thus hast thou gotten in *sinful slo*   *slough of evil*
Of thine neighbours by extortion.   *from*
'More and more' say yet, *have do,*   *press on*
Till thou be dead and droppen down.
    Work on with world's *wrenches.*   *tricks*   2760
'More and more' say yet, I *rede,*   *advise*

To more than enow thou hast need.
All this world both length and *brede*   *breadth*
    Thy covetise may not quench.

MANKIND   Quench never no man may;
Me thinketh never I have enow.
There ne is world's weal, night nor day,
But that methinketh it is too slow.
'More and more' yet I say
And shall ever while I may *blow*;   *speak*   2770
On Covetise is all my *lay*   *in faith*
And shall till death me overthrow.
    'More and more': this is my *steven.*   *cry*
If I might alway dwellen in prosperity,
Lord God, then well were me.
I would, *the meeds,* forsake thee   *as recompense*
    And never comen in heaven.

DEATH   Oh, now it is time high
To casten Mankind to death's dint.
In all his works he is *unsly*;   *foolish*
Mickle of his life he hath misspent.   2780
To Mankind I *ney high,*   *approach near*
With *rewly* raps he shall be rent.   *pitiful*
When I come, each man dread *forthi,*   *for that reason*
But yet is there no *gain-went,*   *road back*
    High hill, holt, *ne* heath.   *nor*
Ye shall me dread everyone;
When I come ye shall groan;
My name in land is *left alone*:   *i.e. not spoken*
    I *hatte* dreary Death.   *am called*   2790

Dreary is my death-draught.
Against me may no man stand.
I *durke* and downbring to naught   *strike*
Lords and ladies in every land.
Whomso I have a lesson taught,
Onethys sithen shall he mowe stand.   *hardly afterwards shall he be able to stand*
In my *careful clothes* he shall be caught,   *i.e. winding-sheet*
Rich, poor, free and bond.
    When I come they go no more.
Whereso I wend in any *lede*   *nation*
Every man of me hath dread.   2800
Let I will for no *mede*   *forbear reward*
    To smite sad and sore.

Dyngne dukes *arn* adread   *noble are*
When my blasts are on them blow;
Lords in land are *overled*;   *dominated*
With this lance I lay them low.
Kings *keen* and knights *kyd,*   *brave famous*
I do them *delven* in a *throw.*   *bury moment*
In *bank* I *busk* them abed,   *hillside hurry*   2810
Sad sorrow to them I sow,
    I *tene* them as I trow.   *injure*
As *keen* colts though they *kynse,*   *mettlesome wince*
Against me is no defence.
In *the great pestilence*   *i.e. Black Death, 1348*
    Then was I well know.

But now almost I am forget;
Men of Death *hold no tale.*   *do not reckon*
In covetise their good they get;

The great fishes eat the small.   2820
But when I deal my *derne debt*   *stealthy death-blow*
Those proud men I shall *avale*.   *bring low*
Them shall helpen neither meal nor meat
Till they be drawn to Death's dale.   *for when*
    My law they shall learn.
There ne is penny nor pound
That any of you shall save sound
Till ye be graven under ground:
    There may no man me *werne*.   *ward off*

To Mankind now will I reach;   2830
He hath whole his heart on Covetise.
A new lesson I will him teach
That he shall both *grucchen* and *gryse*.   *complain   shudder*
No *life* in land shall be his *leech*.   *person   doctor*
I shall him prove of mine *emprise*;   *power*
With this point I shall him breach
And *wappen* him in a woeful wise.   *hit*
    Nobody shall be his *bote*.   *cure*
I shall thee shapen a *schenful shape*.   *disgraceful appearance*
Now I kill thee with mine *knappe*!   *blow*   2840
I reach to thee, Mankind, a rap
    To thine heart root.

MANKIND   Ah Death, Death! *Dry* is thy *drift*.   *dreary   compulsion*
Dead is my destiny.
Mine head is cleaven all in a cleft;
For *clap* of *care* now I cry.   *stroke   wretchedness*
Mine eyelids may I not lift;
My brains wax all empty.
I may not once mine hood up shift;
With Death's dint now I die!   2850
    Sir World, I am *hent*.   *seized*
World, World, have me in mind!
Good Sir World, help now Mankind!
But thou me help, Death shall me *schende*.   *destroy*
    He hath *dight* to me a dint.   *given*

World, my *wit waxeth wrong*;   *mind goes astray*
I change both hide and hue;
Mine eyelids waxen all *outwrung*;   *squeezed out*
But thou me help, sore it shall me rue.
Now hold that thou hast *behete* me longe,   *promised*   2860
For all fellowships old and new
Lesse me of my pains strong.   *release*
Some *bote of bale* thou me brew   *cure of torment*
    That I may of thee *yelpe*.   *speak praise*
World, for old acquaintance
Help me from this sorry chance.
Death hath *lacched* me with his lance: *struck*
    I die but thou me help.

WORLD   Oh Mankind, hath Death with thee spoke?
Against him helpeth no *wage*.   *payment*   2870
I would thou were in the earth *beloke*   *locked*
And another had thy heritage.
Our bond of love shall soon be broke;
In cold clay shall be thy cage;
Now shall the World on thee be *wroke*   *avenged*
For thou hast done so great outrage.
    Thy *good* thou shalt forgo.   *possessions*
Worldly's good thou hast forgone

And *with tottys* thou shalt be torn.   *by devils*
Thus have I served *here-beforn*   *before now*
    A hundred thousand *mo*.   *more*   2880

MANKIND   Oh World, World, ever *worth woe*!   *be accursed*
And thou, sinful Covetise!
When that a man shall from you go
Ye work with him *on a wonder wise*.   *in a wonderful way*
The wit of this world is sorrow and woe.
Beware, good men, of this guise!
Thus hath he served many one *mo*.   *more*
In sorrow *slaketh* all his *asyse*;   *ends effort*
    He beareth a *tening* tongue.   *harmful*   2890
While I laid with him my lot
Ye seen how fair he me *behott*;   *promised*
And now he would I were a *clot*   *clod*
    In cold clay for to cling.

WORLD   How Boy! Arise! Now thou must wend
On my errand *by step and stall*.   *on foot and horseback* or *by every place*
Go brew Mankind a bitter *bend*   *captivity*
And put him out of his hall!
Let him therein no longer *lende*.   *stay*
For-bursten I trow be his *gall*,   *burst in pieces*   *gall-bladder*   2900
For thou art not of his *kende*.   *family*
All his heritage will thee well befall:
    Thus fareth mine fair *feres*.   *companions*
Often time I have you told,
Those men that ye are to least behold
Commonly shall your *wonning wold,*   *dwelling control*
    And be your next heirs.

BOY   World worthy, in *weeds* wound,   *clothes*
I thank thee for thy great gift.
I go glad upon this ground   2910
To put Mankind out of his *thrift*.   *prosperity*
I trow he *stinketh this ilke stound*[1];   *is putrefying this very moment*
Into a lake I shall him lift.
His parks, places and pennies round
With me shall *driven* in this drift   *be forced to go*
    In bags as they be bound.
For I think for to *deal,*   *give up*
I vow to God, neither corn nor meal.
If he have a sheet, he beareth him well,
    Wherein he may be wound.   2920

Then he goes to Mankind

How farest, Mankind, art thou dead?
By God's body, so I ween.
He is heavier than any lead.
I would he were *graven under green*.   *buried under ground*

MANKIND   Abide, I *breyd* up with mine head.   *rouse*
What art thou? What wouldst thou mean?
Whether comest thou for good or *qwed*?   *evil*
With pain's prick thou dost me *tene,*   *hurt*
    The sooth for to say.
Tell me now, so God me save,
From whom comest thou, good knave?   2930
What dost thou here? What wouldst thou have?
    Tell me ere I die.

[1] Or, Mankind has messed himself in fear, as the Bad Angel did at 2230 and 2407, and Envy did at 2209.

BOY	I am come to have all that thou hast,	
	Ponds, parks and every place.	
	All that thou hast gotten first and last,	
	The World hath granted it me of his grace	
	For I have been his page.	
	He *wot* well thou shalt be dead,	*knows*
	Nevermore to eat bread;	
	Therefore he hath for thee *red*	*decided*
	Who shall have thine heritage.	

2940

MANKIND   What, devil! Thou art not of my kin.
Thou didst me never no *manner* good.   *kind of*
I had liefer some *nyfte* or some cousin   *nephew*
Or some man had it of my blood.
    In some stead I would it stood.   *I wish it to be of some use*
Now shall I in a dale be delve
And have no good thereof myselve.
By God and by his apostles twelve,
    I trow the World be *wood.*   *mad*

2950

BOY   Yea, yea, thy *part* shall be the least.   *share*
Die on, for I am master here.
I shall thee maken a noble feast
And then have I *do my devere.*   *done my duty*
The World bade me this gold arrest,
Holt and halls and castle clear.
The World's joy and his *gentle jest*   *noble entertainment*
Is now thine, now mine, both far and near.
    Go hence, for this is mine.

2960

Since thou art dead and brought *of dawe,*   *out of daylight*
Of thy death, sir, I am right *fawe.*   *joyful*
Though thou know not the World's law
    He hath give me all that was thine.

MANKIND   I pray thee now, since thou this good shalt get,
Tell thy name ere that I go.

BOY   Look that thou it not forget:
My name is *I Wot Never Who.*[1]

MANKIND   I Wot Never Who! So *welaway!*   *woe*

2970

Now am I sorry of my life.
I have purchased many a day
Lands and rents with mickle strife.
I have purchased *holt and hay,*   *wood and enclosed land*
Parks and ponds and bowers *blyfe,*   *gay*
Good gardens with *gryffys* gay   *groves*
To mine children and to mine wife
    In death when I were dight.
Of my purchase I may be woe,
For *as thought, it is not so,*   *it is not as I supposed*
But a *gedelyng,* I Wot Never Who,   *rascal*
    Hath all that the World me *behight.*   *gave*

2980

Now alas, my life is *lak!*   *poverty*
Bitter *bales* I gin to brew.   *torments*
Certes a verse that David spake
In the Psalter I find it true:

Tesaurizat et ignorat cui congregabit ea
('He heaps up riches and knoweth not who will gather them'—Psalm 39, 6)

Treasure, treasure, it hath no *tak;*   *endurance*
It is other men's, old and new.

[1] Meaning that nobody knows what becomes of his possessions after his death (cp. line 105).

131

Oh oh, my *good* goeth all to wrack!   *possessions*
Sore may Mankind rue.   2990
      God keep me from despair!
All my good, without fail,
I have gathered with great travail;
The World hath ordained *of his entail*   *through his settlement*
      I Wot Never Who to be mine heir.

Now good men, taketh example *at* me.   *from*
Do for yourself while ye have *space*.   *take care of   time*
For many men thus served be
Through the world in diverse place.
I *bolne and bleyke* in bloody *ble*   *swell and blench   complexion*
And as a flower fadeth my face.   3000
To hell I shall both fare and flee
But God me grant of his grace.   *unless*
      I die certainly.
Now my life I have *lore*.   *lost*
Mine heart breaketh, I sigh sore.
A word may I speak no more.
      I put me in God's mercy.

[Mankind dies. Soul comes from bed in the Castle]

SOUL   'Mercy!' This was my last *tale*   *speech*
That ever my body was about.
But Mercy help me in this vale,   *unless*
Of damning drink sore I *me doubt*.   *fear*   3010
Body, thou didst brew a bitter bale
To thy lusts when *gannest loute*.   *you bowed down*
Thy *sely* soul shall be *akale*;   *miserable   made cold*
I *beye* thy deeds with *rewly rowte*,   *atone for   pitiful   blow*
      And *all* it is for guile.   *entirely*
Ever thou hast been covetous
Falsely to getten land and house.
To me thou hast brewn a bitter juice.
      So *welaway* the while!   *woe*   3020

Now, sweet Angel, what is thy *rede*?   *counsel*
The right rede thou me reach.   *give me the right advice*
Now my body is dressed *to dead*,   *for death*
Help now me and be my *leech*.   *doctor*
Dight thou me from devils dread: *put*
Thy worthy way thou me teach.
I hope that God will helpen and be mine *hed*,   *safeguard*
For 'mercy' was my last speech.
      Thus made my body his end.

[Page of manuscript missing. The play resumes with Bad Angel claiming Soul for Hell]

BAD ANGEL   Witness of all that be about,   3030
Sir Covetise he had him *out*.   *i.e. from the Castle*
Therefore he shall withouten doubt
      With me to hell pit.

GOOD   Yea, alas and *welawo*!   *woe*
ANGEL   Against Covetise can I not *tell*.   *argue*
Reason will I from thee go,
For wretched soul, thou must to hell.
Covetise, he was thy foe;
He hath thee shapen a shameful *shell*.   *covering*
Thus hath served many one *mo*   *more*   3040
Till they be dight to death's dell,
      To bitter bale's bower.

Thou must to pain by right reason
With Covetise, for he is *chesun*.   *the cause*
Thou art trapped full of treason
    But Mercy be thy succour.   *unless*

For right well this found I have;
Against Righteousness may I not hold.
Thou must with him to *careful cave*   *sorrowful cavern, i.e. hell*
For great *skills* that he hath told.   *reasons*   3050
From thee away I wander and *wave*;   *turn aside*
For thee I *cling* in *cares* cold.   *waste away*   *sorrows*
Alone now I thee leave
Whilst thou fallest in fiends' fold,
    In hell to hide and *hylle*.   *shelter*
Righteousness will that thou wend
Forth away with the Fiend.
But Mercy will to thee send,   *unless*
    Of thee can I no skill.   *for you I am powerless*

SOUL   Alas, Mercy, thou art too long!   3060
Of sad sorrow now may I sing.
Holy Writ it is full wrong
But Mercy *pass* all thing.   *unless*   *surpass*
I am ordained to pains strong,
In woe is *dressed* mine *wonning*,   *placed*   *dwelling*
In hell on hooks I shall hang
But Mercy from a well spring.   *unless*
    This devil will have me away.
Weleaway! I was full *wood*   *mad*
That I forsook mine Angel Good   3070
And with Covetise stood
    Till that day that I should die.

BAD ANGEL   Yah! Why shouldst thou be covetous
And draw thee again to sin?
I shall thee brew a bitter juice;
In *bolning* bonds thou shalt *brenne*.   *swelling*   *burn*
In high hell shall be thine house,
In pitch and tar to groan and grin;
Thou shalt lie *drenkled* as a mouse;   *drowned*
There may no man therefrom thee *werne*   *protect*   3080
    For that *ilke will*.   *same while*
That day the ladies thou forsook
And to my counsel thou thee took,
Thou were better an-hangen on hook
    Upon a gibbet hill.

Farter foul, thou shalt be *frayed*   *bruised*
Till thou be *fretted* and all *for-bled*.   *tortured*   *bled dry*
Foul may thou be dismayed
That thou shalt thus be *overled*.   *oppressed*
For Covetise thou hast assayed   *because you practised covetousness*   3090
In bitter bales thou shalt be bred.
All mankind may be well *paid*   *satisfied*
When Covetise maketh thee a-dread.
    With *raps* I thee wring.   *blows*
We shall to hell, both two,
And *bey* in inferno.   *pay for it*
Nulla est redemptio   *there is no redemption—(the Office of the Dead)*
    For no *kynnys* thing.   *kind of*

Now *dagge* we hence a dog trot.   *jog*
In my dungeon I shall thee *dere*.   *injure*   3100
On thee is many a sinful spot;

Therefore this shame I shall *thee* shear   *from thee*
    When thou comest to my nest.
Why wouldst thou—*shrew* shalt never *thee*—   *evil person*   *thrive*
But in thy life do after me?
And thy Good Angel taught thee
    Alway to the best.

Yea, but thou wouldest him not *leve*;   *believe*
To Covetise alway thou drew.
Therefore shalt thou evil *preve*;   *prove*   3110
That foul sin thy soul slew.
I shall *fonde* thee to grieve   *try*
And put thee in pain's plough.
Have this, and evil may thou *scheve,*   *suffer*   *attain*
For thou saidst never, 'Enow, enow'
    Thus *lacche* I thee thus low.   *drag down*
Though thou *kewe* as a cat   *mew*
For thy covetise have thou that!
I shall thee *bunche* with my bat   *beat*
    And *rouge* thee *on a row.*   *handle roughly*   *in order*   3120

Lo! Sinful tiding,
Boy, on thy back I bring.
Speedily thou *spring*!   *leap forth*
Thy *placebo* I shall sing.   *Vespers for the Dead, literally, I shall make myself*
To devils' dell   *acceptable to the Lord*
I shall thee bear to hell.
I will not dwell.
Have good day! I go to hell.

MERCY   A moan I heard of mercy *meve*   *speak*
And to me, Mercy, gan cry and call;   3130
But if it have mercy, sore it shall me grieve,
For else it shall to hell fall.
Righteousness, my sister chief,
This ye heard; so did we all.
For we were made friends *leve*   *loving*
When the Jews proffered Christ *eisel* and gall   *vinegar*
    On the Good Friday.
God granted that remission,
Mercy and absolution,
Through virtue of his passion,   3140
    To no man should be said nay.

Therefore, my sisters, Righteousness,
Peace and Truth, to you I tell
When man hath cried mercy, and will not cease,
Mercy shall be his washing-well:
    Witness of Holy Kirk.
For the least drop of blood
That God bled on the Rood
It had been satisfaction good
    For all Mankind's work.   3150

RIGHTEOUS-   Sister, ye say me a good *skill,*   *argument*
NESS   That mercy passeth man's misdeed.
But take mercy whoso will
He must it ask with love and dread;
And every man that will fulfil
The deadly sins and follow misdeed,
To grant him mercy methinketh it *no skill.*   *not according to reason*
And therefore sister, you I rede
    Let him *aby* his misdeed.   *pay for*

For though he lie in hell and stink,   3160
It shall me never *over-think*:   *make sorry*
As he hath brewen let him drink;
    The Devil shall quit him his mede.

Unusquisque suum honus portabit
('For every man shall bear his own burden'—Galatians 6, 5)

Trow ye that when a man shall die,
Then though that he mercy crave,
That *anon* he shall have mercy?   *at once*
Nay nay, so Christ me save.

Non omne qui dicit 'Domine, Domine' intrabit regnum celorum
('Not everyone that saith unto me, Lord, Lord, shall enter into the kingdom of
heaven'—after Matthew 7, 21)

For should no man do no good
All the days of his life,
But hope of mercy by the Rood   *hope of mercy by the cross alone*   3170
Should make both war and strife
    And turn to great grievance.
Whoso in hope doth any deadly sin
To his life's end and will not *blynne*   *cease*
Rightfully then shall he win
    Christ's great vengeance.

TRUTH   Righteousness, my sister *fre,*   *noble*
Your judgement is good and true.
In good faith so thinketh me;
Let him his own deeds rue.   3180
I am Veritas and true will be
In word and *work* to old and new.   *deed*
Was never man in fault of me
Damned nor saved but it were due.
    I am ever at man's end.
When body and soul parten atwin,
Then weigh I his good deeds and his sin,
And *whether of them be more or mynne*   *which of them be more or less*
    He shall it right soon find.

For I am Truth and truth will *bear,*   *support*   3190
As great God himself us bid.
There shall nothing the soul *dere*   *injure*
But sin that the body did.
Since that he died in that covetous sin,
I, Truth, will that he go to pain.
Of that sin could he not *blynne*;   *cease*
Therefore he shall his soul *tyne*   *lose*
    To the pit of hell.
Else should we, both Truth and Righteousness,
Be put to over-mickle distress   3200
And every man should be the worse
    That thereof might hear tell.

PEACE   Peace, my sister Verity!
I pray you Righteousness, be still!
Let no man by you damned be
Nor *deem* ye no man to hell.   *judge*
He is *one kin* to us three,   *akin*
Though he have now not all his will.
For his love that died on tree
Let save Mankind from all peril   3210
    And shield him from mischance.

If ye twain put him to distress
It should make great heaviness
Between us twain, Mercy and Peace,
    And that were great grievance.

Righteousness and Truth, *do by my rede,*   *take my advice*
And Mercy, go we to yon high place.
We shall inform the high Godhead
And pray him to *deem* this case.   *judge*
Ye shall tell him your intent   3220
Of Truth and Righteousness,
And we shall pray that his judgement
May *pass* by us, Mercy and Peace.   *be rendered*
    All four now go we hence
Witly to the Trinity   *quickly*
And there shall we soon see
What that his judgement shall be
    Withouten any *defence.*   *remedy i.e. appeal*

Then they ascend to the Father all together and Truth says

TRUTH   Hail, God almight!
              We come, thy daughters, in sight,   3230
              Truth, Mercy and Right,
              And Peace, peaceable in fight.

MERCY   We come to *preve*   *test*
              If Man that was *thee full leve*   *to thee much beloved*
              If he shall *cheve*   *go*
              To hell or heaven by thy leave.

RIGHTEOUS-   I, Righteousness,
NESS   Thy daughter as I guess,
              Let me nevertheless
              At thy *doom put me in press.*   *judgement*   *exert myself*   3240

PEACE   Peaceable king,
              I, Peace, thy daughter *yinge,*   *young*
              Hear my praying
              When I pray thee, Lord, of a thing.

GOD   Welcome *in fere,*   *all together*
              Brighter than blossom on briar!
              My daughters dear,
              Come forth and stand ye me near.

TRUTH   Lord, as thou art King of Kings, crowned with crown,
              As thou lovest me, Truth, thy daughter dear,   3250
              Let never me, Truth, to fall adown,
               My faithful Father *sans* peer!   *without*

Quoniam veritatem dilexisti
('Because you have loved the truth'—after Zechariah 8, 19)

For in all truth standeth thy renown,
Thy faith, thy hope and thy power;
Let it be seen, Lord, now at thy *doom,*   *judgement*
That I may have my true prayer
    To do truth to Mankind.
For if Mankind be deemed by right
And not by Mercy, most of might,
Hear my truth, Lord, I thee plight,   3260
    In prison Man shall be *pined.*   *tortured*

Lord, how should Mankind be saved
Since he died in deadly sin,
And all thy commandments he *depraved,*   *disparaged*
And of false covetise he would never *blynne?*   *cease*

Aurum sitisti, aurum bibisti
('You have thirsted for gold, you have drunk gold')

The more he had, the more he craved,
While the life left him within.
But he be damned I am *abaved*   *unless*   *amazed*
That Truth should come of righteous kin;
    And I am thy daughter Truth.   3270
Though he cried 'Mercy' *moriendo*,   *dying*
Nimis tarde penitendo,   *too late in repenting*
Talem mortem reprehendo.   *I censure such a death*
    Let him drink as he breweth!

Late repentance if Man save should,
Whether he wrought well or wickedness,
Then every man would be bold
To trespass in trust of forgiveness.
For sin in hope is damned, I hold,
Forgiven is never his trespass.   3280
He sinneth in the Holy Ghost manifold.
That sin, Lord, thou wilt not *release*   *remit*
    In this world nor in the t'other.
Quia veritas manet in eternum,   *because truth remains for ever*
Tendit homo ad infernum,   *man goes to hell*
Nunquam venit ad supernum[1];   *he never comes to heaven*
    Though he were my brother.

For Man on *molde* hath wealth and weal,   *earth*
Lust and *liking* in all his life,   *pleasure*
Teaching, preaching, *in every sele*,   *at all times*   3290
But he forgetteth the Lord *belyve*.   *quickly*
High of heart, *hap and hele*,   *fortune and health*
Gold and silver, child and wife,
Dainty drink at meat and meal,
Unnethe thee to thank he cannot *kyth*   *scarcely*   *show*
    In any manner thing.
When Man's wealth ginneth awake
Full soon, Lord, thou art forsake.
As he hath brewen and bake,
    Truth will that he drink.   3300

For if Man have mercy and grace
Than I, thy daughter *Soothfastness*,   *Truth*
At thy *doom* shall have no place   *judgement*
But he put aback by wrong duress.
Lord, let me never flee thy fair face
To make my power any less!
I pray thee, Lord, as I have space,
Let Mankind have due distress
    In hell fire to be *brent*.   *burnt*
In pain look he be still,   3310
Lord, if it be thy will,
Or else I have no skill
    By thy true judgement.

O Pater misericordiarum et Deus tocius consolacionis, qui consolatur nos in omni tribulacione nostra!
('O Father of mercies and God of all comforts, who consoles us in all our affliction'—2 Corinthians 1, 3–4)

MERCY   O thou Father, of mights most,
              Merciful God in Trinity!

[1] Psalm 117, 1.

I am thy daughter, well thou *wost,*   *knowest*
And Mercy from heaven thou broughtest *fre.*   *untrammelled*
Shew me thy grace in every coast!
In this case my comfort be!
Let me, Lord, never be lost   3320
And thy judgement, howso it be,
    Of Mankind.
Ne had Man's sin never come *in case*   *into question*
I, Mercy, should never in earth had place.
Therefore grant me, Lord, thy grace,
    That Mankind may me find.

And mercy, Lord, have on this Man
After thy mercy that mickle is,
Unto thy grace that he be *tan,*   *taken*
Of thy mercy that he not miss!   3330
As thou descendest from thy throne
And lieth in a maiden's womb iwis,
Incarnate was in blood and bone,
Let Mankind come to thy bliss
    As thou art King of Heaven!
For worldly vainglory
He hath been full sorry,
Punished in purgatory
    For all the sins seven.

Si pro peccato vetus Adam non cecidisset,
Mater pro nato nunquam gravidata fuisset[1]
('If old Adam had not fallen through sin,
Your mother would never have been heavy with child'—cf. Gregory P.L. lxxix, 222).

Ne had Adam sinned here-before   3340
And thy *hests* in paradise had *offent,*   *commands broken*
Never of thy mother thou shouldst have been bore
From heaven to earth to have been sent.
But thirty winter here and more,
Bounden and beaten and all *to-schent,*   *battered*
Scorned and scourged sad and sore,
And on the Rood *rewly* rent   *pitifully*
    Passus sub Pilato Poncio.   *suffered under Pontius Pilate*
As thou hung on the cross
On high thou madest a voice,   3350
Man's health, the gospel says,
    When thou saidest *'Scitio'.*   *I thirst—John 19, 28*

Scilicet salutem animarum
('That is, for the health of men's souls')

Then the Jews that were *unquert*   *wicked*
Dressed the drink, *eisel* and gall.   *prepared vinegar*
It to taste thou might not *styrt*   *escape*
But said *'Consummatum est'* was all.   *It is finished—John 19, 30*
A knight with a spear so *smart,*
When thou forgave thy foemen *thrall,*   *servile*
He stung thee, Lord, unto the heart.
Then water and blood gan *out-wall*   *flow*   3360
    'Aqua baptismatis et sanguis redempcionis'.
The water of *baptoum,*   *baptism*
The blood of redemption
That from thine heart ran down
    Est causa salvacionis.   *is the cause of our salvation*

[1] Source unknown, but interesting because these lines are classical hexameters, *rhymed*, and on a Christian theme.

Lord, *thou* that Man hath done more *miss* than good,   *although*   *amiss*
If he die in *very* contrition,   *true*
Lord, the least drop of thy blood
For his sin maketh satisfaction.
As thou diedest, Lord on the Rood,   3370
Grant me my petition!
Let me, Mercy, be his food,
And grant him thy salvation,
    Quia dixisti 'Misericordiam servabo'[1].
'Mercy' shall I sing and say
And *'miserere'* shall I pray   *take pity*
For Mankind ever and ay.
    Misericordias Domini in eternum cantabo[2].

RIGHTEOUS-   Righteous King, Lord God almight,
NESS   I am thy daughter Righteousness.   3380
                 Thou hast loved me ever day and night
                 As well as other, as I guess.

Justicias Dominus justicia dilexit
('The Lord who is justice loves acts of justice'—after Psalm 11, 7)

If thou Man's kind from pain acquit
Thou *dost against* thine own *process.*   *contradict*   *mandate*
Let him in prison to be *pight*   *placed*
For his sin and wickedness,
    Of a boon I thee pray,
Full often he hath thee, Lord, forsake
And to the Devil he hath him take.
Let him lien in hell lake,   3390
    Damned for ever and aye.

Quia Deum qui se genuit dereliquit
('Because he forsook the God who begat him'—after Deuteronomy 32, 15)

For when Man to the world was born
He was brought to Holy Kirk,
Faithly *followed in the fount-stone*   *baptized in the baptismal font*
And washed from original sin so dark.
Satanas he forsook as his *fone,*   *enemy*
All his pomp and all his work,
And *hight* to serve thee alone;   *promised*
To keep thy commandments he should not *irk,*   *grow weary*
    Sicut justi tui.   *as your law requires*   3400
But when he was come to man's estate
All his *behests* he then forget.   *promises*
He is worthy be damned for that,
    Quia oblitus est Domini creatoris sui.   *because he has forgotten God his creator*

For he hath forgotten thee that him wrought
And formedst him like thine own face
And with thy precious blood him bought
And in this world thou gave him space.
All thy benefits he set at nought
But took him to the Devil's *trace,*   *course*   3410
The Flesh, the World, was most in his thought
And purpose to please him in every place
    So grimly on ground.
I pray thee, Lord lovely,
Of Man have no mercy,
But, dear Lord, let him lie,
    In hell let him be bound!

[1] Because you have said, 'I shall keep my mercy'—after Psalm 89, 2.
[2] I will sing the mercies of God forever—Psalm 89, 1.

Man hath forsake the King of Heaven
And his Good Angel's governance
And sullied his soul with sins seven   3420
By his Bad Angel's *cumbrance*.   temptation
Virtues he put *full even* away   completely
When Covetise gan him advance.
He *wende* that he should have lived *ay,*   thought   for ever
Till Death tripped him on his dance;
     He lost his wits five.
Over-late he called Confession;
Over-light was his contrition;
He made never satisfaction.
     Damn him to hell *belyve*!   at once   3430

For if thou take Man's soul to thee
Against thy righteousness,
Thou dost wrong, Lord, to Truth and me
And *putteth* us from our *devness*.   withhold   rights
Lord, let us never from thee flee,
Nor strain us never in stress,
But let thy *doom* be by us three   judgement
Mankind in hell to press,
     Lord, I thee beseech.
For Righteousness dwells ever sure   3440
To *deem* Man after his *deserviture,*   judge   desserts
For to be damned it is his *ure:*   habit
     On Man I cry *wreche.*   vengeance

Letabitur justus cum viderit vindictam
('The just man will rejoice when he sees punishment'—Psalm 58, 10)

MERCY   Mercy, my sister Righteousness!
Thou shape Mankind no *schonde.*   ruin
Leve sister, let be thy *dress*!   dear   plea
To save Man let us *fonde.*   try
For if Man be damned to hell darkness,
Then might I wringen mine *honde*   hands
That ever my state should be less,
My freedom to make bond.   3450
     Mankind is of our kin.
For I, Mercy, *pass* all thing   surpass
That God made me at the beginning
And I am his daughter *yinge*;   young
     Dear sister, let be thy din!

Et misericordia ejus super omnia opera ejus
('And his tender mercy is over all his works'—Psalm 145, 9)

Of Mankind ask thou never *wreche*   vengeance
By day nor by night,
For God himself hath been his leech
Of his merciful might.
To me he gan him *beteche*   entrust   3460
Beside all his right.   against
For him will I pray and preach
To get him free respite,
     And my sister Peace.
For his mercy is without beginning
And shall be withouten ending,
As David saith, that worthy king;
     In scripture is no *les.*   falsehood

Et misericordia ejus a progenie in progenies et cetera
('And his mercy extends from generation to generation, etc'—Luke 1, 50)

140

TRUTH   Mercy is Mankind not worthy,   3470
               David though thou record and read,
               For he would never the hungry
               Neither clothe nor feed,
               Nor drink give to the thirsty,
               Nor poor men help at need.
               For if he did none of these, *forthi*   *therefore*
               In heaven he getteth no *meed,*   *reward*
                    So saith the gospel.
               For he hath been unkind
               To lame and to blind   3480
               In hell he shall be *pined*.   *tortured*
                    So is reason and skill.

PEACE   Peaceable King in majesty,
               I, Peace thy daughter, ask thee a boon
               Of Man, howso it be.
               Lord, grant me mine asking soon,
               That I may evermore dwell with thee
               As I have ever yet done,
               And let me never from thee flee,
               Specially at thy doom   3490
                    Of Man, thy creature.
               Though my sisters Right and Truth
               Of Mankind have no *ruth,*   *pity*
               Mercy and I full sore *us meweth*   *plead*
                    To catch him to our cure.   *care*

               For when thou madest earth and heaven,
               Ten orders of angels to been in bliss,
               Lucifer, lighter than the *levin*   *lightning*
               Till when he sinned, he fell iwis,
               To restore that place full even   3500
               Thou madest Mankind with this
               To fill that place that I did *nevene*.   *name*
               If thy will by reason it is
                    In peace and rest,
               Among thine angels bright
               To worship thee in sight
               Grant, Lord God Almight!
                    And so I *hold* it best.   *consider*

               For though Truth that is my sister dear
               Argueth that Man should dwell in woe,   3510
               And Righteousness with her power
               Would fain and fast that it were so,   *wishes eagerly and earnestly*
               But Mercy and I, Peace, both *in fere,*   *together*
               Shall never in faith accord thereto,
               Then should we ever discord hear,
               And stand *at bate* for friend or foe,   *in strife*
                   And ever *at distance*.   *in disagreement*
               Therefore my counsel is,
               Let us four sisters kiss
               And restore Man to bliss,   3520
                    As was God's ordinance.

Misericordia et Veritas obviaverunt sibi, Justicia et Pax osculate sunt
('Mercy and Truth have met together, Justice and Peace have kissed'—Psalm
85, 10; Douai 84, 11)

               For if ye, Right and Truth, should have your will,
               I, Peace, and Mercy should ever have *travest*.   *opposition*
               Then us between had been a great peril
               That our joys in heaven should a been *lest*.   *lessened*

Therefore, gentle sisters, consenteth me *till,*   *to*
Else between ourself should never be rest.
Where should be love and charity, let there come none ill.
Look our joys be perfect, and that I hold the best,
        In *heavenryche* bliss.   *kingdom of heaven*   3530
For there is peace withouten *were,*   *strife*
There is rest withouten fear,
There is charity withouten *dere.*   *hardship*
        Our Father's will so is.

Hic pax, hic bonitas, hic laus, hic semper honestas
('Here is peace, here goodness, here glory, here virtue for ever'—Meditations
of Bernard P. L. clxxxiv, 492)

Therefore, gentle sisters, at one word,
Truth, Right and Mercy *hende,*   *courteous*
Let us stand at one accord
At peace withouten end.
Let love and charity be at our board,
All vengeance away *wend,*   *go*   3540
To heaven that Man may be restored:
Let us be all his friend
        Before our Father's face.
We shall devoutly pray
At dreadful *doom's* day,   *judgement's*
And I shall for us say
        That Mankind shall have grace.

Et tuam, Deus, deposcimus pietatem ut ei tribuere digneris lucidas et quietas mansiones
('And we entreat your mercy, God, so that you may consider it fitting to grant him
bright and peaceful mansions')

Lord, for thy pity and that peace
Thou sufferest in thy passion,
Bounden and beaten, without *les,*   *falsehood*   3550
From the foot to the crown.
Tanquam ovis ductus es   *when you were led like a sheep*
When *gutte sanguis* ran adown,   *drops of blood*
Yet the Jews would not cease
But on thine head they thrust a crown
        And on the cross thee nailed.
As piteously as thou were pined,
Have mercy of Mankind
So that he may find
        Our prayer may him avail.   3560

Father sitting enthroned
Ego cogito cogitaciones pacis, non affliccionis
('I think thoughts of peace, not affliction'—Jeremiah 29, 11)

GOD   Fair fall thee, Peace, my daughter dear!
On thee I think and on Mercy.
Since ye accorded *beth* all *in fere,*   *be*   *together*
My judgement I will give you by,
Not after deserving to do *reddere*   *rigorous punishment*
To damn Mankind to tormentry,
But bring him to my bliss full clear
In heaven to dwell endlessly
        At your prayer *forthi.*   *therefore*
To make my bliss *perfyth*   *perfect*   3570
I *menge* with my most might   *mix*
All peace, some truth and some right
        And most of my mercy.

Misericordia Domini plena est terra. Amen!
('The earth is full of the mercy of the Lord'—Psalm 33, 5)

My daughters *hende,*   gentle
Lovely and *lusty* to *lende,*   cheerful   remain
Go to yon Fiend
And from him take Mankind.
Bring him to me.
And set him here by my knee,
In heaven to be   3580
In bliss with *gamen and glee.*   mirth and joy

TRUTH   We shall fulfil
Thine *hests* as *reason* and *skill*   commands   reasonable   proper
From yon *ghost grylle*   spirit   fierce
Mankind to bring thee *till.*   to

Then they ascend to the Bad Angel all together and say

PEACE   Ah, foul *wight,*   creature
Let go that soul so *tyght*!   quickly
In heaven light
Mankind soon shall be *pight.*   placed

RIGHTEOUS-   Go thou to hell,   3590
NESS   Thou devil bold as a bell,
Therein to dwell,
In brass and brimstone to *well*!   boil

Then they ascend to the throne, leading the Soul

MERCY   Lo here Mankind,
Lighter than leaf is on *lynde,*   lime-tree
That hath been *pined.*   tortured
Thy mercy, Lord, let him find.

The Father sitting in judgement
Sicut scintilla in media maris
('Like a spark in the midst of the sea')

GOD   My mercy, Mankind, give I thee.
Come sit at my right hand.
Full well have I loved thee,   3600
Unkind though I thee found.
As a spark of fire in the sea
My mercy is sin-*quenchand.*   quenching
Thou hast cause to love me
Aboven all thing in land,
     And keep my commandment.
If thou me love and dread
Heaven shall be they *meed*;   reward
My face thee shall feed:
     This is my judgement.   3610

Ego occidam et vivificabo, percuciam et sanabo, et nemo est qui de manu mea possit eruere
('I shall kill and I shall bring to life; I shall wound and I shall heal; neither is
there any that can deliver out of my hand'—after Deuteronomy 32, 39)

King, kaiser, knight and champion,
Pope, patriarch, priest and prelate in peace,
Duke doughtiest in deed, by dale and by down,
Little and mickle, the more and the less,
All the states of the world is at my renown;
To me shall they give *accompt* at my *dygne* dais.   account   noble
When Michael his horn bloweth at my dread doom
The count of their conscience shall putten them in *press*   crisis

And yield a reckoning
Of their *space* how they have spent,　　*space of time*
And of their true talent
At my great judgement
　　An answer shall me bring.

Ecce, requiram gregem meum de manu pastoris
('Behold! I shall require my flock from the hand of the shepherd'—after
Ezekiel 34, 10)

And I shall inquire of my flock and of their *pasture*　　*pastors*
How they have lived and led their people subject.
The good on the right side shall stand full sure;
The bad on the left side there shall I set.
The seven deeds of mercy whoso had *ure*　　*habitually*
To *fill*, the hungry for to give meat,　　*fulfil*
Or drink to thirsty, the naked vesture,
The poor or the pilgrim home for to *fette*,　　*fetch*
　　Thy neighbour that hath need;
Whoso doth mercy *to his might*　　*as much as he can*
To the sick or in prison *pight*,　　*placed*
He doth to me; I shall him *quyth*;　　*requite*
　　Heaven bliss shall be his mede.

Et qui bona egerunt ibunt in vitam eternam; qui vero mala, in ignem eternum
('And whoso does good will go to eternal life; but who evil into eternal fire'—
the Athanasian Creed, after Matthew 25, 46)

And they that well do in this world here, wealth shall awake;
In heaven they shall be *heyned* in bounty and bliss.　　*exalted*
And they that evil do, they shall to hell lake
In bitter *bales* to be burnt: my judgement it is.　　*torments*
My *virtues* in heaven then shall they *quake*:　　*powers　fear*
There is no wight in this world that may scape this.
All men example hereat may take
To maintain the good and *menden* their miss.　　*sins*
　　Thus endeth our *games*.　　*play*
To save you from sinning,
Ever at the beginning
Think on your last ending!
　　Te Deum Laudamus!　　*We praise thee, O Lord*

3620

3630

3640

3　Discussion of *The Castle of Perseverance*

17　My notes on the four tasks that I proposed (paragraph 16, p.77) will not be exhaustive, or even full on every or any point. My purpose in writing them is to establish a practical and imaginative way of looking at the play, by offering suggestions where they will most help you.

a　1705–1876: main production problems

18　You may have wondered why I started your detailed work at a stage direction—'Then they sing *Eterne rex altissime*'. The point is that, as at the Angel's appearance in the Wakefield *Second Shepherds' Pageant,* the exalted music represents a major dramatic punctuation. The initial triumph of the Virtues comes to a climax with it, and only the short sealing speech of Meekness, delivered no doubt from the top of the Castle, separates it from the furious counteraction of Belial's speech (1715). Note from the latter that World, Flesh and Devil are all *kings.*

19　The summoning of Backbiter brings in the principle of dynamic and fast-moving disorder, which contrasts with the majestic peace of the movement by which Mankind and the Virtues have just occupied the Castle. In the 110 lines or so during which he is in the play, Backbiter scours the whole arena with deadly effect, sowing distrust, discord and actual violence, all of which he delights in. He flatters Belial, Flesh and World in turn before declaring their failures in the most humiliating possible terms, and yet has time to explain himself to the audience and encourage them to be like him (1785). His appearance must contrast as much as possible both with the regal array of World, Flesh and Belial, and with the pristine appearance of the Virtues; and I think it would be wrong to present him with a modern satirical slant operating by subtle ironies—a policy which can work in the presentation of such a character as Mephostophilis in Marlowe's *Doctor Faustus*. In my production, Backbiter would be ragged and young, full-blooded and ecstatic, and his exit must be furiously and mockingly triumphant. (This occurs some time during the beating of Covetise by World in 1864–76. I disagree with Dr Southern's suggestion that he should remain to take part in Belial's marshalling of his forces for the attack on the Castle.) You will see that at two points in this section (after 1764 and 1810) a stage direction has to do duty for what ought, in any production, to be a speech: one of several pieces of evidence which suggest to me that the manuscript was not written by a man conversant with dramatic practice.

b   1878–2409: prelude to battle, and battle itself

20   Did you note all the weapons and devices used, with their wielders?
All have banners, and the 'baddies' all have lances.
Belial has gunpowder (exploded at 2194?).
Flesh rides on a horse (1940), and uses shot and sling (1944).
Gluttony has faggots to set fire to the Castle, and perhaps gunpowder (1965, 2248).
Envy slings shot (1976) and uses a crossbow (2159).
Wrath slings stones (2111), shoots a crossbow (2112) and uses wild-fire (possibly gunpowder again 2115).
Lechery *carries* her fires (2291) which are put out when Chastity drenches them (2388).
Sloth tries to shovel water (from the moat?—2329).
Your list of properties should include bagpipes and trumpets (I would add drums myself), and a huge stock of roses (and primroses?) in the Castle. I think it is necessary for the holy party on the battlements to have, as well as the roses which symbolize the Passion, at least one big cross (perhaps on a battle standard) and some communion bread.

21   The basic movement, centred on the Castle, must be circular; that is, both the prebattle vaunting by 'the sins seven' and 'the kings three', and the fighting itself, must circulate around the Castle. Since the stage directions and the dialogue both point to a long and closely contested battle, it would be appropriate to use the clear lanes from the four bad scaffolds to the Castle for advancing and retreating (see drawing, p.74), and I should certainly use the scaffolds themselves as supply centres for the attackers, complete with devil armourers and quartermasters. The main practical production problem is to make the right decision about the bombardment of roses from the Castle. Is it to be largely symbolic—more of a display than a bombardment? Or do you weight your roses so that they can at least give some semblance of missile quality as they fly through the air? Whichever you decide, you can be sure that the furious, disorderly and noisy activity of the attackers will give you your main *battle* effect; which the eventual triumph of the non-violent ladies foreshadowed in line 2022 ('Primrose playeth parlasent') caps with a precise but paradoxical point of pure doctrine.

c   Covetise

22   This is a matter of character interpretation. The first point is one I might have made already about the six other deadly sins: the essence of the abstraction must be manifest in every single thing about such a character. Covetise cannot think, talk or move in response to any prompting except that of his essential nature, which is covetousness. A dramatist creating an abstract quality has to follow such a prescription as Ben Jonson devised for a Humour:

As when some one peculiar quality
Doth so possesse a man, that it doth draw
All his affects, his spirits, and his powers,
In their confluctions, all to runne one way,
This may be truly said to be a Humour.
(*Everyman Out of his Humour*, from *Collected Works of Ben Jonson*, Vol. III, pp.431–2.)

23   After the furious activity of the battle, the scene in which Covetise and Mankind come to agreement must be slow, sparing of action, and absolutely concentrated on meaning. For it is here that the main message of the play is conveyed; the dramatist's opinion that although people at various stages of their lives may yield to, or resist, other vices, when they become old they fall a prey to covetousness. For this to be demonstrated forcibly, there must be between Covetise and Mankind, from the outset, a concord or harmony. The quietness and slow deliberation of Covetise go with the pathos of ageing Mankind (2479–91)—a speech, as I have already pointed out, on the common medieval theme of the Signs of Death, which finds expression in many lyrics. You will have to decide what use to make of the original instructions about the cupboard of Covetise: I should incline to use it as a kind of cornucopia, from which an appropriate valuable object could be produced whenever it fitted the dialogue. It might enhance the mesmeric effect of the riches on Mankind if every new article or purse were brought to Covetise by a servant.

24   The second exchange between them, beginning at 2700, takes Mankind fully into Covetise's power as a preparation for the arrival of Death. I see Mankind, ill and old, haggard like the proverbial miser, up on the scaffold of Covetise, surrounded and hampered by mounds of riches; Covetise detached and sardonic (he has seen and done it all before, and being a deadly sin, he cannot even delight in his achievement). All the references to him and his works during the subsequent death of Mankind press home the lesson; you might want Covetise to be present during the terrible scene between Mankind and Boy, but if you want the action to be concentrated on those two, you had better keep Covetise upon his scaffold, and draw the curtains on him at the moment of Mankind's death.

25   The importance of Covetise is to fix the audience's attention on one of the main practical and spiritual problems of life, from both the religious and the social point of view. Then as now, humankind understood and occasionally experienced the full potentialities of rich being in an environment mostly hostile to such a state. But man's stage of social and technological development and his capacity to attune nature and the organization of society to the real needs of men and women left each person with little choice but to live a life mostly concerned with acquisition, in the furious pursuit of self-preservation. Hence covetousness dominates, and the Church fulminates against it in this play with good biblical precedent but rather little sense of how to make the acquisitive urge redundant.

d   i   Death

26   There is a single point to be made about Death. His long speech is a complete poem on one of the main poetic themes of the Middle Ages. Except for the references to Covetise, this fine poem, with its strong alliteration and slow malevolent pomp, could be lifted out of the play. Try reading it aloud.

ii   Boy

27   Throughout the play, World, Flesh and Belial have sought to operate through subordinate powers, a process that comes to a climax with the hideous function of Boy at the death of Mankind. The same character appears in the York Butchers' play, *The Death and Burial*, in which he offers Christ on the cross eisel and gall. Boy represents a strain in human thinking that makes, for example, Lightborn[1], the murderer of Edward II in Marlowe's play of that name, appear lovingly solicitous to his victim before revealing and carrying out his purpose: the same strain produced, in the concentration camp literature following the Second World War, a common phenomenon of torturer and victim having an insidiously close relationship. There is a nice paradox here in that Boy, though a creature and an instrument of World who gains by becoming the beneficiary at Mankind's death, is the bringer of Mankind's orthodox retribution and its attached moral. And there is something ghoulish about his observation concerning Mankind's body (2923–4). The dramatic character of Boy, like that of Backbiter, shows the author of this play at his best; fully creative in his representation of a dark side of human experience.

[1] Lucifer, the devil's name, means 'light bearer'.

4   Conclusion

28   In a partial study such as this, I cannot ask you to make a concluding focus on the play as a whole; **all I can do is to suggest a last,** *but strictly optional,* **reflection or two on the conclusion of the play.**
Either read from line 3129 to the end, making notes on the religious meaning and dramatic action after the death of Mankind and then reading my following comments,
or simply read my following comments without reading or rereading the end of the play,
or stop reading at once, and proceed to my short summary of this study of medieval drama (paragraphs 1–13, pp.147–9).

29   The ending of the play is a debate among the four daughters of God about the destiny of Mankind. Shall he have God's mercy or not? Mercy and Peace believe that he should, and Righteousness and Truth that he should not. In the daughters' appeal to God there is further debate, involving close consideration of the way divine justice works. Then God delivers his judgement that the soul must be taken away from the Devil. Dramatically speaking, it is important that the audience have a visual point of reference for Mankind. Shall he remain in full view on Belial's scaffold during the debate?

30   There is a marvellous change of tone at the moment when the debate begins. The Bad Angel, you remember, jubilantly carries Mankind's soul off to hell, with blasphemous jokes and threats to batter Mankind in hell. The spirit of hell spills out into the 'place', and Mankind is hauled suffering to Belial's scaffold. Then the four daughters of God enter (from underneath God's scaffold?— the curtains of whose upper level are closed as they have been throughout the play, waiting to open for the majestic appearance at 3229). The first quiet line, spoken by Mercy, picks up Mankind's dying plea for Mercy from some seventy lines back:

A moan I heard of mercy meve.

After the Bad Angel's fleering 'Have good day! I go to hell', and the noisy triumph of Belial's party, this melodious and regular line, with its unusual word order, slows the pace and raises the tone of the drama to one of feeling meditation. What strikes Mercy with compassion is the 'moan' —a word which then carried an even stronger meaning of lamentation than it does today. So, not 'A moan of mercy I heard meve' nor 'I heard meve a moan of mercy', but 'A moan I heard of mercy meve', in which the lamentation is emphasized standing out alone, and then a separate focus is made on the subject, mercy, all within eight syllables. This is alliterative dramatic verse at its best.

31   The next thing to note is the way this change of tone is followed up. The debate of the holy sisters, unfolding in its first stage of a hundred lines the arguments for and against allowing Mankind to go to damnation, is conducted with beautiful manners and decorum. And their harmoniously unanimous decision is to submit the case to the judgement of the Trinity.

32   Accordingly, the four daughters of God process to the scaffold of 'the high Godhead', and the appearance there of God is the dramatic moment which lifts the play doctrinally and emotionally to the plane of divine judgement. Here, without the verbal intercession of God, who is silent after his welcoming speech, the four sisters resolve the problem. As they do so, they describe and explain the crucifixion and its meaning for Mankind. The divine presence ensures their success and although Mercy is naturally the most successful pleader, in this second stage of the debate, it is Peace who again senses and expresses their harmonious agreement. All that is left for God to do is to commend their judgement, and instruct them to free Mankind from the Devil. (A dignified two-part tableau of frustrated devils and gravely rejoicing angel-kind?) When Mankind returns, God renews his promise of judgement to all Mankind, and gives the standard advice to the audience of the medieval Expositor (3643–4):

All men *example* hereat may take
To maintain the good and menden their miss.

The play then ends, as many medieval religious plays did, with the singing of the *Te Deum*.

MEDIEVAL AND MODERN DRAMA

1   Forward-looking revision on medieval drama

1   Think about the characteristics of medieval drama under three general headings of content, staging and action, and make any comparisons with modern practice, as far as you know. Then read my notes.

Content

2   *Social relevance.* Medieval playrights seem rarely to forget their particular audience and its problems in life. Drama being a public art, we should expect good playwrights over the centuries to follow their example. Since the sensibility and morality of European humanity seem to shift within a fairly narrow range over the years, it would not be surprising if you were to think that a play which had social relevance for its own age would probably be socially relevant to succeeding ages, as (to take two examples of plays you have studied so far) *The Bacchae* and the Wakefield *Second Shepherds' Pageant* are to our age.

3   *History as source for drama.* Plays based on the Bible are public enactments and interpretations of the stuff of actual life, in both its public and private manifestations. In most ages of the theatre, you will find good new plays (so far as state censorship permits) fired by contemporary or otherwise relevant public events being written and performed.

4 *Mixing the serious and the comic.* This was on the whole shunned in classical times, and forbidden in Europe's neoclassical age; and it has been mostly avoided in conventional plays written in modern times. But with the decline of pure tragedy as a relevant form for the supposedly unheroic age in which we live, more and more dramatists are writing plays which cannot be strictly defined as comedies or tragedies; mostly serious plays in which funny things may be enacted, and funny plays in which serious things may be enacted. Medieval dramatists teach us not to get trapped in rigid notions of genre.

5 *Characters—human, superhuman, abstract.* In this kind of drama, playwrights have complete freedom in the conception and development of stage character, and every kind of character can behave in a different, typical way. Renaissance playwrights learnt especially from two main medieval practices in this field: one concerned historical characters (whether divine, biblical or saintly) who were presented realistically, and the other concerned morality characters, who began as abstractions but had, from the very first, realistic contemporary human qualities. The structure of the morality play, which has one central character who is the focus of all actions, ideas and emotions, as Mankind is in *The Castle of Perseverance,* and as Everyman is in the play of that name, is important in itself for two aspects of heroic drama. One is the concentration on the hero, and the other is the idea of the hero as representative of a type of humanity at large. In *Doctor Faustus,* which you will know if you studied A201[1], and *Peer Gynt* which you will study later on this course (Study 7), the individuality of the heroes gains universal significance partly from the structural elements which are directly or indirectly derived from the medieval Morality. There are many other plays of which this might be said.

6 *Dialogue simple, performance complex.* The dialogue of most medieval plays is simple in the sense that it is *open,* carrying a plain meaning. This quality is essential to public performance before a big audience composed of all sorts of people. This makes the play texts easy *reading.* The complexities, when they exist, are developed through time in the action and in the combined realism and symbolism inherent in the play's content, structure and performance. On the question of verse, and especially stanzaic dialogue, you must judge its effectiveness from the television programme rather than from the printed page. Formal verse drama is now out of fashion among contemporary dramatists, but in Pinter's *Silence*

you have already met one kind of dramatic speech which is akin to poetry.

Staging

7 *Acting area.* The various types of arena presentation found in medieval drama with or without ancillary acting areas on the same level or raised, indicate a freedom of approach to the problem of accommodating action, spectacle and audience in suitable relation. Not being tied to purpose-built theatres, the presenters of drama, even if they wished to draw on a standard ideal of a central 'place' with perimeter 'scaffolds', were free except that they always had to take account of the local facilities and location. Their standard ideal, which as we have seen brought play company and audience into unusually close relation when fulfilled, is one which has had a marked effect on modern drama, whenever directors have been able to escape the limitations of the proscenium theatre. There should be no limits to the scenic imagination.

8 *Presentation conventions.* These were much freer in conception and operation than modern ones, because through them realism was approached pragmatically rather than dogmatically. Though pride was clearly taken in achieving illusion and spectacular effects, there was no ruling principle of illusion-making which had to be followed. The art of the possible was the only guide and limitation. So Noah's Ark was built in 'the place', model doves rose in mock flight on cords, and God appeared enthroned on a 'scaffold' which might on another occasion have served to raise a juggler above the level of the audience. A rich assortment of devices were available. The governing attitude allowed anything that worked; thus it encouraged a variety of conventions and so fostered flexibility of imagination in audiences. A comparable spirit is at work among our best directors and in our less conventional theatres today.

Action

9 *The range of performance activity.* Performing could include fights, games and dances, which might be real or symbolic or both, and the spirit of these activities pervaded dramatic work. Dance was of two kinds, the one religiously stately and suited to the Church, the other secular, deriving from popular culture and folk dance.

10 *Movement and gesture.* These were derived from several different conventions, such as those of the dance, the pulpit and law court, and the repertory of the professional mime; and were

[1]The Open University (1972) A201 *Arts: Renaissance and Reformation,* Units 31–32, *English Renaissance Drama,* The Open University Press.

incorporated in the plays in various ways according to requirement.

11 *Music and musical activities.* These were essential components of the drama. You will find that music is essential in Shakespeare, if less pervasive than in medieval drama, and that only a few modern playwrights, among whom Brecht is preeminent, conceive some of their work in partly musical terms.

12 *Style.* It seems that speech and action were vigorous—something like what we see in debased form in the circus arena today. The need to project speech in the open air, and to be clearly seen performing familiar real and symbolic actions, went hand in hand with a desire to achieve literal realism. **Turn yet again to the Fouquet miniature on the cover, and look for the different kinds of action represented in it.** Such vigour is found in today's theatre mainly in farce and horror plays; in our age in general, a more inward kind of dramatic style is preferred in serious drama.

13 *Addressing the audience.* Most often it is the Expositor or Doctor who mediates in this way between audience and stage action, but note that God does so at the end of *The Castle of Perseverance,* and that Jesus in his last speech in the York *Crucifixion* appears to address both the other characters in the play and the watching audience. Think what differences there are between such techniques and those, respectively, of the Greek chorus, and the chorus or prologue in such Shakespeare plays as *Henry V* and *Romeo and Juliet.* Such techniques survive in modern drama and have been developed in various forms, though not by dramatists writing conventional 'realistic' plays. The effect can be to distance the action emotionally, usually with didactic purpose, or, in such a play as Anouilh's *Antigone,* to bring the audience into close community with the stage action. Either way, audience participation of some kind is implicit in the use of the technique.

POSTSCRIPT ON MUSIC

Here are three suggestions to follow up if you are interested in modern musical works based on your set medieval plays. They are *optional* activities.

a   Benjamin Britten uses the Chester Play as the basis for his *Noye's Fludde* (Record—Decca ZNF 1). What cuts and additions does he make to the text? How effective is this version in performance? Is it only for children? How does the music, in particular the hymn-singing, involve the audience?

b   Listen to *Captain Noah and His Floating Zoo* by Michael Flanders and Joseph Horovitz (Argo ZDA 149). This music has been used as background to mimed action on television, and also for a ballet. Make a comparison between this version of the Noah story and the Chester Play, using similar headings to those suggested in *a* above.

c   The first of *Three Canticles* by Benjamin Britten (Decca ZRG 5277) is a concert version of the Chester *Abraham and Isaac.* (I recommend this and the other musical recreation because the musical setting enforces the stylised delivery of the words which modern conversational delivery can only enfeeble.)

FURTHER READING FOR STUDY 4 (UNITS 5–6)

Happé, P. (ed.) (1975) *English Mystery Plays,* Penguin. Contains thirty-eight plays, including the four cycle plays studied here, in a good text with glossary and notes and a useful general introduction. This is the book to read to give this study its proper dimension.

Taylor, J. and Nelson, A.H. (eds.) (1972) *Medieval English Drama: Essays Critical and Contextual,* University of Chicago Press. Probably the best collection of critical essays in a single volume.

Wickham, Glynne (1974) *The Medieval Theatre,* Weidenfeld & Nicolson. The best succinct account of the beginnings, development and varieties of drama, explained in their social and religious contexts.

Rossiter, A.P. (1950) *English Drama from Earliest Times to the Elizabethans,* Hutchinson. An erudite, racily written and often idiosyncratic book, the first hundred or so pages of which deal fascinatingly with the long period between the decline of classical civilization and the late Middle Ages, with vivid evocation of many aspects of the changing drama.

Nicoll, Allardyce, (1929, 5th edition 1966) *The Development of the Theatre*, Chapter 3, Harrap. A good short account of medieval staging and performance methods.

Southern, Richard (1975) (2nd edition) *The Medieval Theatre in the Round*, Faber. A full assessment of the evidence concerning medieval practice in mounting performances in the round with localized raised acting areas on the perimeter.

Davies, R.T. (ed.) (1972) *The Corpus Christi Play of the English Middle Ages*, Faber. Contains, in slightly modernized spelling, all the surviving Abraham and Isaac plays, and the whole of the *Ludus Coventriae*, and useful brief criticism.

Cawley, A.C. (ed.) (1956) *Everyman and Medieval Miracle Plays*, Dent. A useful little book containing sixteen varied plays.

REFERENCES FOR STUDY 4 (UNITS 5–6)

Anderson, M.D. (1963) *Drama and Imagery in English Medieval Churches*, Cambridge University Press.

Augustine, Saint *De Civitate Dei*, trans. Watts, G.G. and Monahan, Grace (1952) *The Works of Saint Augustine*, Washington.

Carpenter, N.C. (1951) 'Music in the *Secunda Pastorum*', *Speculum*, XXVI, pp. 696–700.

Cawley, A. C. (1956) (ed.) *Everyman and Medieval Miracle Plays*, Dent.

Cawley, A.C (ed.) (1958) *The Wakefield Pageants in the Towneley Cycle*, Manchester University Press.

Crohn Schmitt, Natalie (1972) 'Was there a medieval theatre in the round? a reexamination of the evidence' in Taylor, J. and Nelson, A.H. (eds.) (1972) *Medieval English Drama*, University of Chicago Press.

Davies, R.T. (ed.) (1972) *The Corpus Christi Play of the English Middle Ages*, Faber.

Eccles, Mark (ed.) (1969) *The Macro Moralities*, Early English Text Society, Oxford.

Huizinga, J. (1972) *The Waning of the Middle Ages*, Penguin.

Johnston, A. and Dorrell, M. (1971) 'The Doomsday pageant of the York mercers', *Leeds Studies in English* (New Series) V.

Jonson, Ben *Everyman out of his Humour* in Herford, C.H. (ed.) *Collected Works*, Vol. 3, Oxford.

Lumiansky, R.M. and Mills, D. (eds.) (1974) *Chester Cycle Plays*, Early English Text Society, Supplementary series, no. 3.

Mayer Brown, H. (1963) *Music in the French Secular Theater, 1400–1500*, Harvard University Press.

Nagler, A.M. (1959) *A Source Book in Theatrical History*, Dover Publications.

Nelson, A.H. (1974) *The Medieval English Stage*, Chicago University Press.

Nicoll Allardyce (1927 5th edition 1966) *The Development of the Theatre*, Harrap.

Pollard, A.W. (ed.) (1972) *English Miracle Plays, Moralities and Interludes*, Oxford University Press.

Purvis, John Stanley (1969) *From Minster to Market Place: York Mystery Plays*, St Anthony's Press.

Rose, Martial (ed.) (1961) *The Wakefield Mystery Plays*, Evans.

Southern, Richard (1975) (2nd edition) *The Medieval Theatre in the Round*, Faber.

The Open University (1977) *Theatres and Staging*, The Open University Press.

Wickham, Glynne (1974) *The Medieval Theatre*, Weidenfeld & Nicolson.

Wickham, Glynne (1959) *Early English Stages*, Vol. 1, Routledge & Kegan Paul.

Woolf, Rosemary (1972) *The English Mystery Plays*, Routledge & Kegan Paul.

ACKNOWLEDGEMENTS

Brian Stone and John Purkis particularly wish to thank N. R. Havely for advice on medieval language text, translation and glossing, and for his help with critical interpretation; Francis Clark for checking all the work on religious matters and medieval Latin translation; and Keith Whitlock for his careful critical comments on matters of drama and medieval English.

Grateful acknowledgement is made to the following sources for material used in this Study:

Text

Canon J. S. Purvis, *From Minster to Market Place,* 1969, St Anthony's Press by permission of Herald Printers, York; A. W. Pollard, *English Miracle Plays, Moralities and Interludes,* 8th edn 1927 by permission of Oxford University Press.

Illustrations

Grateful acknowledgement is made to the following for material used: Mansell Collection 59, 62; Oxford University Press (from C. W. Hodges, 1964, *Shakespeare's Theatre*) 30; Royal Commission on Historical Monuments (England) 38; Staatliche Kunsthalle Karlsruhe 51; York Minster Library 65.

DRAMA